WomanSoul

WomanSoul

The Inner Life of Women's Spirituality

**Edited by Carole A. Rayburn
and Lillian Comas-Díaz**

Women's Psychology
Michele A. Paludi, Series Editor

Westport, Connecticut
London

Library of Congress Cataloging-in-Publication Data

WomanSoul : the inner life of women's spirituality / edited by Carole A. Rayburn
and Lillian Comas-Díaz.

    p. cm. — (Women's psychology, ISSN 1931-0021)
  Includes bibliographical references and index.
  ISBN-13: 978-0-313-35109-9 (alk. paper)
  1. Women—Religious life. 2. Spirituality. I. Rayburn, Carole A. II. Comas-Díaz,
Lillian.
  BL625.7.W625 2008
  204'.4082—dc22   2008004570

British Library Cataloguing in Publication Data is available.

Library of Congress Catalog Card Number: 2008004570
ISBN: 978-0-313-35109-9
ISSN: 1931-0021

First published in 2008

Praeger Publishers, 88 Post Road West, Westport, CT 06881
An imprint of Greenwood Publishing Group, Inc.
www.praeger.com

Printed in the United States of America

∞™

The paper used in this book complies with the
Permanent Paper Standard issued by the National
Information Standards Organization (Z39.48-1984).

10 9 8 7 6 5 4 3 2 1

We dedicate this book to our mothers, Mary Helen Milkie Miller and Maria Emperatriz Díaz Comas, and to our grandmothers, Jennie Hannah David Milkie and Louise Schnabel Mueller, and Antonia Morales Diaz and Petra Ramirez Comas. We bless their memories, compassion, wisdom, and inspiration for helping us to become the spiritual women and seekers of illumination and goodness that we are today.

Contents

Series Foreword

WomanSoul draws attention to the inequities and injustices suffered by women because of the inherent sexist treatment of them by established patriarchal religions. It teaches us to question the portrayal of women and femininity in religions, for example, how women are defined in terms of their husbands and thus portraying an unmarried woman or widow as not having an identity.

WomanSoul provides women's accounts of how they defined for themselves how to be a mother, partner, and professional. It teaches us to not look upon women as the "other" or as second-class participants in religious rituals. It also teaches us to value ourselves and stop comparing ourselves to other women and men. We learn about ancient goddesses and we celebrate the nature of the divine.

WomanSoul reminds us of the way some religions (for example, Presbyterian and Episcopal churches as well as the United Church of Christ) have celebrated God as mother.

It is an honor for me to have *WomanSoul* included in the Women's Psychology Series. Western psychology has typically avoided spirituality. I congratulate and thank all the contributors to this book for making us aware of the importance of spirituality in our lives. It is valuable reading for therapists since many of the contributors to this book discuss how they integrate spirituality into their own lives, including their therapeutic approaches. I recommend sharing this book with girls so they may place more value on themselves and not be defined by external definitions of who they are.

—Michele A. Paludi, Women's Psychology Series Editor

Acknowledgments

We wholeheartedly thank John A. Prestbo, editor and executive director of Dow Jones Indexes, for his invaluable knowledge, skills, patience, and dedication to doing a task exceptionally well, and in the spirit of graciousness, kindness, and accuracy.

—Carole A. Rayburn and Lillian Comas-Díaz

Introduction

Throughout the ages, women have shown a strong interest in and fascination with spirituality. Indeed, they have associated the spirit with a freeing force that allowed them to express themselves most fully, to be more productive and creative, and to be less restricted by rules and regulations often held by specific groups of seekers. With spirituality, women could be more individualistic, assertive, and affirmative. They were not seen primarily as part of the crowd of lesser lights, of the horde of faceless followers of the patriarchal establishment, of unknowing and impotent forces with which to be reckoned in the really important, vital matters of living.

Choosing whenever possible to break away from the stifling walls that boxed them into a male-dominated religiousness that took their concerns and needs too seldom into account, women often chose spirituality alone or in conjunction with their own kind of religiosity. Women, in their spirituality, were more focused on caring for others, seeking goodness and truth, recognizing transcendence in the sense of realizing and attending to external influence (God, nature, trusted guide, etc.), and viewing cooperation, peacefulness, and forgiveness as beneficial and worthwhile goals of life. In caring for others, they reached out to protect other people, animals, nature, the world, and the universe—in short, life itself. Women have viewed creativity and giving birth to something new—children, ideas, the life force, and peace itself—as essential to their interactions with all that surrounds them.

While religion has also been a force in the lives of some women, unless spirituality plays a big part in the tenets and rituals of religion, such a belief system is shallow, hollow, lukewarm, and certainly not affirming of the inner caring, strength, and ultimate potential for seeking the good and true values in life. Spirituality is the core, the heart, the vital being of all religious belief systems. It is the appeal to the one-to-one outreach to others and to life at its most meaningful and caring. Spirituality gives authenticity to the true experience of personhood. The nurturing aspects of spirituality, for both oneself and others, set it aside from what would otherwise be a cold, formal set of rules and rituals.

In their journeys to discover who they are and to evolve into their finest and most goddess-like selves, women often wander many paths and travel many rocky terrains to seek the good and true. They are more likely to allow themselves to be open to new experiences and to be curious about connections between what they knew from the outset and what looks new but may have a familiar ring after more earnest and intense examinations. Women are apt to make efforts to integrate their old and new precepts into what evolves as their spiritual anchors. To be most satisfying, woman's spirituality must be tailored to fit the particular woman and groups of women and not just be second-hand suits passed down from a male patriarchy to women, on whom these garments may be quite ill fitting.

We call women's spirituality *WomanSoul*. By this we mean the way women experience spirituality. WomanSoul is affirming, nurturing, creative, and compassionate. We characterize WomanSoul as compassionate illuminate. The operational term reflects the sine qua non of women's spirituality: compassionate caring for others, and wisdom and the search for goodness and truth. We hold that out of spirituality grows creativity and the sort of openness from which intuition is born, fostered, nourished, and celebrated. "When the spirit moves us," we sense the impetus to bring forth new, often-mysterious ideas and connections. Women seem to be more trusting than men of such intuition and have less fear in expressing themselves with such knowledge and insightful information.

While women's comfort with their spirituality—and at times their defiance of men's religion—has sometimes placed them in the ranks of saints, they have at other times been condemned as witches and sorcerers. Being "different" in their searching for what constitutes their innermost and most authentic selves has placed women in danger of being anathema to male society and in a defiant outside group. In this book, then, women write about what they think spirituality is and how it impacts women as an affirming force that is more gender-fair, culturally less biased, and less restrictive than many religious denominations in general. Our contributors represent many diverse cultures and religious/spiritual orientations. One looks at the Divine Spirit from pre- to postmodern times and the need for unifying relationships among people and universal and transformational harmony. Another examines the saving grace of spirituality, bringing about hope, vitality, and creativity. In working with older women, who must learn spiritually to "play the hand that they are dealt," another contributor looks at the eclectic forces in her life that bring together her ties with Greek Orthodoxy and Reform Judaism. "Friendship" with women saints as role models and as sources of spirituality is vitally important to another contributor. The Black Madonna, representing the hidden feminine qualities of healing, ancient wisdom, and intuition, has also been held to be a source of justice, empowerment, and reconciliation. The mysteries of the living Kabbalah are approached by another contributor in a way that focuses on the receiving of truth, God's way, and openness to all. Spirituality and Tibetan Buddhism are analyzed for applications to women's spirituality and the integration of the male-female identities of some Buddhist deities.

Other contributors examine the following topics: women's spirituality and the resilience of Filipinos; Sufi healing; American Indian women healers; women and their careers; female young adults; science; a unique goddess group; agnosticism and a questioning, open mind; the diversity of perspectives in African American women's experiences; spirituality as a stepping stone to a fuller life; Hindu spirituality and female identity; women's spirituality and psychology; strange attractors in the search for the meaning of spirituality; and the spiritual awareness in children from the perspective of mothers and therapists. We thought from the outset that the inclusion of a Muslim woman and her spirituality was highly important. We asked a Muslim psychology professor who was teaching and residing in the United States to write her thoughts and feelings about being a Muslim and being a spiritual woman. She even presented at our professional association on this topic, saying that she truly appreciated her Muslim background and its teachings and that she felt free and unrestricted in expressing her spirituality through Islam. Sadly and unfortunately, she returned to her country at the very last stages of the book's preparation, and though numerous contacts were made by the editors in an effort to obtain her chapter for publication, she was unable to complete it due to her new academic duties. So, regrettably, we could not include a chapter on Muslim women and spirituality. Although different, we include a chapter on Sufism, which is the mystical part of Islam.

All of the contributors to *WomanSoul* share with you, our readers, their experiences, feelings, thinking, hopes, and longing that could not have been so fully and continually realized without their being in touch with spirituality, most especially with women's spirituality. They share and write in hopes of inspiring you to claim women's spirituality—WomanSoul—for yourself and so to rediscover your inner strength, hope, joy, intuition, and creativity. Through this, you will enjoy a fuller, more meaningful, and productive life. Celebrate the joy of WomanSoul!

—Carole A. Rayburn and Lillian Comas-Díaz

PART I

History of Women and a Spiritual Life

Chapter 1

Worldviews and Women's Spirituality

Eileen Eppig

As a teacher of religious studies at a women's college, I have noticed two phenomena in the past few years: first, a student's worldview impacts her spirituality; and second, feminist claims about women's spirituality seem to resonate with students. Even though this spirituality has been articulated only since the 1970s, there may be a timeless element to it. A brief review of history reveals that some aspects of what today is called "women's spirituality" are found in the writings and actions of various "mothers" and "sisters" who have gone before us. Did their worldviews affect the spirituality of these women? This is an important question.

A worldview is a system of meaning that initially arises at a particular time in history.[1] People are born into a community that has a particular worldview, and they unconsciously internalize this view through socialization in family, school, and religion. A coherent worldview interprets the purpose, value, and truth of events and verbal claims. The worldview existing in one's culture exerts a powerful influence upon its members through its underlying system of meaning. It is possible for individuals to transcend the prevailing worldview by accessing higher levels of consciousness,[2] though this is difficult and somewhat rare. Some persons, nonetheless, are able to achieve this feat. A high level of consciousness enables one to develop the kind of spirituality that perceives the divine presence in oneself and in all things.

Sandra Schneiders holds that spirituality is "the experience of striving to integrate one's life in terms of self-transcendence toward the ultimate value one perceives."[3] Perhaps I like this definition because it speaks to what I have been striving to do for most of my life. My deepest longing is to transcend the part of myself that is overly concerned about my own security, self-esteem, and control, so that my work and relationships are integrated around my desire to build a better world. This is my spirituality.

What then is "women's" spirituality? It can be defined as the journey of self-integration toward the divine with concern for certain principles: a foundation in experience; the connection between body and spirit; mutuality and equality in relationships; a sense of oneness with other people and all creation; a concern for wholeness and healing love; power *with* and *for* rather than *over* and *against*; and social transformation.[4] These spiritual elements appeal to me and, to some extent, each inhabits my spirituality. So what about my worldview and that of my students? Do people have just one worldview? Can it ever change?

Today, worldviews are often classified into three categories: premodern, modern, and postmodern. While each of these designations corresponds to a particular time span in history, as personal perspectives all three exist in today's twenty-first-century world. My experience with college students attests to this truth. Some students are fundamentalists or premodern when it comes to religion and life's questions. They know the answers that have been handed down for generations and they cling to them tenaciously. Others demonstrate a modern worldview by formulating their own belief systems, sometimes outside of any organized religion. A dramatic example of this is a student named Pam, who described her religion as "Pam-ism." Still others are at ease with the plurality and ambiguity of a postmodern religious worldview. These students can accept the fact that people hold different beliefs about God and reality; they are not threatened by this diversity, but may in fact delight in it.

At times I see more than one worldview operating within myself. I was born in the 1940s and grew up in the Roman Catholic Church with a premodern worldview in which all questions and answers about life and reality were known and memorized. While I have transcended that worldview, there are times when I catch a glimpse of a conservative (premodern) strain within myself. In terms of modernity, when the Catholic Church cautiously embraced the modern world at the Second Vatican Council in the 1960s, I welcomed it wholeheartedly, learning to think and reason for myself. That independence in thinking is still strong within me, but I am also more aware now of the need to listen to the wisdom of others and to make some decisions communally. Forty years after the Second Vatican Council, postmodernity is one of the worldviews in the Catholic Church and it is my view of life and reality insofar as it indicates an awareness that all of creation is interrelated; there can be unity in diversity. I believe this is my strongest worldview. As my worldview has evolved, so has my spirituality.

This chapter will explore the connection between worldviews and women's spirituality. How do some women change the worldview they inherited at birth? Is there something about women's spirituality that enables them to transcend the prevailing worldview? In this chapter, I will call upon the example of one woman's life experience in each era—premodern, modern, and postmodern—to demonstrate that 1) women's spirituality has ancient roots and 2) women's spirituality makes it possible to transcend the prevailing worldview.

PREMODERN WORLDVIEW

The premodern or classical period spans a very long time from antiquity to the beginning of the seventeenth century. This was a religious and patriarchal period.[5] All power, including religious power, was in the hands of men. The earth was seen as an ordered place: "God's in his heaven; all's right with the world." World religions and sacred writings, such as the Torah, the Bible, and the Qur'an, gave meaning to the whole of life. Since the spiritual world was considered to be more valuable and real than the material one, religious authorities were not questioned. Certain ideas, values, and norms were considered to be universal and eternal. The answer to "Who am I?" was determined largely by one's place in society and, unfortunately, both women and nature were devalued due to the Greek dualistic thinking of man over woman and heaven over earth.[6]

While the general spirituality of this long period was not monolithic, all religious authority figures were male and, for the most part, the divine was imaged in male terms. An exception to this occurred in gardening societies, which arose about 10,000 BCE. In these societies, in which women produced roughly 80 percent of the village food with the use of a hoe, about one-third of the local deities were female, such as "Earth Mother." With the development of farming societies and consequently the invention of the plow about 4,000 BCE, the food producers became male, and so did the gods.[7] It is interesting that the deity seemed to resemble whoever put food on the table.

During the premodern period, the beliefs and rituals of the great world religions—Confucianism, Buddhism, Taoism, Hinduism, Judaism, Christianity, and Islam—were designed by men with specialized roles. Rabbi Michael Lerner claims that these religions "were shaped to meet the needs of the ruling elites of the society."[8] Male perspectives fashioned sacred texts and religious traditions. Certainly, the divine spirit of these religions was present in women as well as in men, yet due to the prevailing worldview, which held that men were superior to women, the wisdom of women often went unrecorded, or was written down by men. Women's experiences were largely ignored in this period and their voices were not heard.

I lived with a premodern mentality until at least the age of twenty-six. While I was intellectually rebellious in some areas of my life, I was unfazed by the fact that most religious authority was in the hands of men. I believed that God was a male. I was sure that everything I had learned about God and the Bible were literally true. At age twenty-four, as a member of the Catholic Charismatic Renewal,[9] I experienced the "baptism in the spirit"[10] spoken about in the New Testament. Afterward, I was quite sure that everyone was meant to have this experience and eventually would. I was certain that God intended everyone to have a personal relationship with Jesus. Although the Charismatic Renewal had a very positive effect on my life, my spirituality at that point was far from what is called "women's" spirituality. It was narrow in both focus and expanse. I was totally unaware of other world religions, the environment, and social justice issues. I was even a little suspect about feminists, and did not want to be identified as one. I was in a very comfortable "box" and felt a certain self-righteousness about it.

Perhaps that is why today, having morphed several times in my spiritual life, I am an admirer of Hildegard of Bingen. Hildegard was a German woman who lived from 1098 to 1179. She is intriguing and admirable to me not just because she was a nun, theologian, preacher, and writer (roles with which I can somewhat identify). She was also a homeopathic physician and a composer of music for worship that can be found in music stores today. In her own era, Hildegard was respected by popes and nobility alike for her deep spiritual contact with the Divine.[11] Hildegard, a holy woman, was anything but narrow in her life and spirituality.

Twelfth-century Europe in which Hildegard of Bingen lived was filled with social upheaval and religious division. In the hierarchical (premodern) worldview of this society, the male nobility and clergy were considered "highest" and closest to God, and could therefore mediate wisdom to those in the "lower" groups. Everyone knew his or her place and believed it to be divinely ordained by God.[12]

In many ways Hildegard was a product of her own time and culture when it came to gender issues. At times Hildegard spoke of herself as a "poor little female" and called her time period "effeminate" because men had become weak and "womanish." But she also spent thirty years (from age seven to thirty-seven) in solitude, prayer, and scripture study with a hermitess named Jutta. This experience of growth and expansion enabled Hildegard to transcend the premodern view of male and female roles. In her later life, she intimated that the sexes are equal, stating, for instance, that "woman may be made from man, but no man can be made without woman."[13] How did Hildegard make this transition? I suggest that three decades of quiet and meditation, utilizing the sacred text of the Bible, opened her mind and spirit to a truth inherent in the world of human beings. She intuited that men were not her superiors, but her equals.

As a product of her time, Hildegard deemed the human being to be the center of creation. Yet, she also perceived the obligation that humanity has for creation, stating that humans are responsible for the well-being of the entire cosmos. In one of Hildegard's visions, she saw the earth's elements crying out to the "cosmic man" to rescue them. Upon reading her description, one might think this commentary was written in the twenty-first century.

> Now all the winds are filled with the decay of leaves, and the air spits out pollution so that people can hardly open their mouths anymore. The greening life force has weakened because of the ungodly erring of deluded human souls.[14]

There were times when Hildegard was fearful of sharing her visions or speaking assertively. On other occasions, such as the following, she showed herself to be quite indomitable. In 1178, the bishop of her diocese confronted Hildegard with the fact that an excommunicated man was buried on the monastery property; he insisted that the body be removed. Hildegard stood up to the bishop, claiming that the man had been reinstated to the church before his death. In the midst of a long-running argument, Hildegard decided to camouflage the grave. In response, the bishop then deprived the nuns of the sacraments. Still, Hildegard was not deterred. She called upon her friend, the bishop of Cologne, who finally resolved the matter in her favor.[15] Such courage on the part of a woman certainly was not "par for the course" in her day.

Hildegard was ahead of her times in many ways. The fact that she came to believe in the equality of the sexes, that she had a vision of suffering Earth calling out for humanity's care, and that she prevailed in her clashes with male religious authority can be attributed, I believe, to her spirituality. As her spirituality grew and changed, so did her worldview. Hildegard was able to rise above the limitations of her era.

This is why I love doing my own inner work, raising my consciousness level, working on my evolving spirituality, and helping young college women do the same. Earth and its peoples, along with their cultures, religions, and spiritual paths to God, enrich my own small world, our own small world, beyond measure. We become so much more than we thought possible. This becoming enables a person in turn to have a transformative effect on the world.

MODERN WORLDVIEW

Moving into the modern period, which occurred from the second half of the seventeenth century to the middle of the twentieth, we find that truth which had been absolute for so many centuries, was not relativized, eliminating the need for God and religious authority altogether. Truth was seen to be rational, scientific, and historically conditioned. In 1858, the theory of evolution came into being, testing sacrosanct religious beliefs. Individualism and self-determination became paramount values. The modern worldview was a challenge to both religious and secular institutions and authorities. God and religion were driven out of the public square, forced into the margins of life and society, alongside women, who were undervalued and still seen but not heard.[16] The spirituality of the modern age had its assets and its limitations. To human advantage, open-mindedness, tolerance, and acceptance became the attitudes of the day. These ideals, however, applied only to men, while women were thought to be naturally inferior and incapable of rational thought. Those spiritual persons who did not conform to the "science-is-god" or "reason-is-god" mentality, those who had intense spiritual experiences, were labeled "mystics" in a derogatory manner.[17]

Today my own spirituality has some modern elements in it, but there was a time when the modern worldview was especially active in my life. In my late twenties and into my early thirties I rebelled against the idea of the pope and bishops, or any authority figure for that matter, telling me what to believe or do. I became self-determined, opinionated, and individualistic (fitting in well with American culture). I came to support women's liberation, and spoke out in favor of women's ordination in the Catholic Church. After several years, I hung up my rebel hat, but I will always be grateful for this time of growth in my life. My internalization of modernity in the 1960s and '70s encouraged me to become my own person. I began walking a path on which I knew it was important to think my own thoughts, know my own mind, and decide for myself.

What I never embraced of modernity was the thought that reason was king. I was greatly interested in spiritual experience and intuition. I was, and continue to be, very drawn to mysticism and experiential knowledge of God. In addition, in some ways I was always searching for a guru, whether it be Dorothy Day, the Catholic Worker servant of the poor, or Thomas Merton, the humanistic monk, or Richard Rohr, a modern-day contemplative in action. I somehow knew, having given myself to God, that I could not succeed in life based on my own small wisdom. I needed the help of others who had walked the spiritual path before me.

This time in my life corresponds with the Enlightenment, the age when women became publicly active, first as abolitionists and later as feminists. One such woman whom I admire is Maria W. Stewart, a Black woman born free in Hartford, Connecticut, in 1803. She was orphaned at the age of five and became a servant for a White clergyman's family until she was fifteen.[18] At the age of twenty-six, after three years of marriage, Maria was widowed, and then swindled out of her inheritance by some White businessmen. That same year Maria experienced a religious conversion that convinced her that she should give her life to serve her Black sisters and brothers. Like all women in antebellum America, she was combating the evil of sexism; with her Black sisters she also was fighting the iniquity of slavery and racism.

While an immense disparity existed between the social positions of Black and White women, there were also some similarities. Both Black and White women were subject to the White male; in effect, neither woman belonged to herself. Both were looked upon as objects to meet the needs, wishes, or demands of White men. Both women were subject to abuse—physical and psychological. Neither woman was allowed to own property or to participate in the public affairs of business or politics.

Yet the differences between Black and White women at that time are striking. The aspiration of the White woman was to gain a husband, please him, and become a model of virtue. She was expected to dem-onstrate the virtues of piety, purity, submissiveness, and domesticity, according to the "cult of true womanhood," a dominating ideology in the American South from the 1820s to the 1860s. All overt signs of sex-uality needed to be repressed.[19] The Black woman, on the other hand, was prized for her sensuality, and for having the physical strength and endurance to work hard. Thus, White society determined that a Black woman could never become a "true woman."

Considering the status assigned to her as Black and female, Maria Stewart's accomplishments are more than remarkable. With little or no schooling, she recognized and utilized her best resource—her ability to speak. And speak she did, especially to Black women, whom she believed had a special obligation and the inner resources needed to strengthen the Black community in their trials. Stewart not only entered an arena from which she had been doubly excluded, but she proceeded to challenge Black women to work for justice. She accomplished this task by becoming a speaker, writer, and teacher.

The spirituality of Maria Stewart—a truly modern woman— embodies the best of the modern age. She knew she could not trust po-litical or social authorities to encourage Black people to hold fast to their values and achieve their dreams. Instead, she counted on the wis-dom and courage of Black women to accomplish this daunting task. Stewart rose above her surrounding sociohistorical worldview by preaching cooperation instead of individualism, and by advocating de-pendence on God and the Black communal wisdom, especially the wis-dom of Black women. From these sources, she believed, would come a new social order for Black people.[20]

Maria knew the Bible and the U.S. Constitution well, and considered both to be sources of liberation and equality. Maria Stewart spoke pas-sionately about Black women: "How long shall the fair daughters of Africa be compelled to bury their minds and talents beneath a load of iron pots and kettles?"[21] Of herself as a person of worth, who had the right to speak out, she wrote:

> What if I am a woman; is not the God of ancient times the God of these modern days? Did he not raise up Deborah, to be a mother and a judge in Israel? Did not Queen Esther save the lives of the Jews? And Mary Magdalene first declare the resurrection of Christ from the dead?[22]

I conclude that it was her connection with the divine spirit that enabled Stewart to respond to her double oppression not with despair, fear, or anger, but with the true power of courage. She managed to rise to a higher level of consciousness.[23] Combining raw courage with faith in God, Stewart was able to transcend the worldview into which she had been born and to use her gifts to radically alter her social situation. She knew her life was in danger, but took the risks necessary to become a political activist and America's first Black female political writer. Her spirituality took her into the fray of politics, instead of merely comforting her with a "Jesus and me" mentality. Stewart acted as a mentor and model to other Black women.

My own spirituality has not led me to become a political activist. However, I do believe that the test of my commitment, morality, and integrity rests not just in what I believe but in how I act. In my ministry, I am privileged to be able to teach religious studies and theology. I also have occasions to offer presentations at my college, in churches, and at other venues. However, very little of what I say and do puts my life at risk. Perhaps it is enough for me to emulate Maria Stewart by being a mentor and model. My students may not remember what I said, but they will remember how I treated them. My hope is that how I say what I say and do what I do will help others, especially women, to develop a true sense of self-worth; to cultivate their own gifts and spirituality; and to deepen their own level of consciousness that takes them to the point of acting courageously to change our world.

POSTMODERN WORLDVIEW

As worldviews and humanity evolve, each progression of human consciousness includes what is valuable from the previous stage and moves beyond it, adding its own insights and perceptions.[24] What is valuable from modernity, especially the ideals of personal freedom and equality for all, is included in a postmodern worldview.

Postmodernity, which began forming in the second half of the twentieth century, is keenly aware of the limits of human rationality in the face of massive global suffering, including two world wars and the Shoah, or Holocaust.[25] Secondly, a postmodern worldview rectifies the error of excluding the divine spirit from the human realm. Lastly, there is an acknowledgment and appreciation of the differences in people, views, cultures, and religions.

This respect for diversity, in turn, can also lead to ambiguity in terms of truth, values, and religious beliefs. There is no one center in postmodernity, but rather a web of centers. Truth is known relatively rather than absolutely; all knowledge is considered partial and contextual. This is very unsettling for some.

With a twenty-first century awareness of both human possibilities and human limitations, there is, in a postmodern worldview, a turn toward compassion, reconciliation, and interdependence.[26] This happens especially when people have achieved a high level of consciousness. At higher levels, people view life as hopeful, harmonious, and meaningful, rather than disappointing, antagonistic, and demanding.[27] In this atmosphere, space is allowed for the "other" and for difference. The rights of the disenfranchised—including women and Earth—are acknowledged and given consideration.

A postmodern spirituality is not threatened by a multiplicity of views and beliefs, but rather is energized and encouraged by the interconnectedness of all persons and the whole of creation. One's thinking becomes more inclusive, even cosmic. There is a growing appreciation for the presence of the divine in all creation. The turn to the divine spirit in postmodernism coincides with the inclusion in history of those who are oppressed and marginalized. There is a call inherent in this worldview to pay attention to these voices, and to advocate for the "new poor," the Earth.

My own slow move to a postmodern worldview began in the 1970s (thus overlapping with my modern period) when I was studying theology at Fordham University in New York. I learned that contemporary Catholic and mainline Protestant scripture scholars do not read the Bible literally, but rather interpret it in light of literary form and historical context. This was a shocking eye-opener for me at the time. Then, in the late 1980s and early 1990s, I studied Black theology at Xavier University in New Orleans, further expanding my horizons. I found it easy to identify with African American theology because of its openly affective involvement with the Divine. This corresponded well with both my experience in the Charismatic Renewal and my work among Hispanic farmworkers in Florida from 1980 to 1986.

In the Black, Hispanic, and Charismatic spiritualities it is considered natural to move the body in prayer, in sync with the movement of the divine spirit within. Each of these spiritualities sees God present and engaged everywhere in human life. All three have an emphasis on healing. Black and Latin American liberation theologies emphasize social transformation as well. In retrospect, I see that my worldview and spirituality were being changed by my experience with others, especially those who are disenfranchised by society.

At the same time, I began practicing centering prayer[28] in the late 1980s, which has the effect of expanding one's consciousness. To my delight I found that I was growing into a greater acceptance and appreciation of myself, of others with their distinctiveness, and of creation, which has always spoken to me of God. My compassion for myself, other people, and other creatures was expanding with my worldview. My desire to understand more about world religions, especially Judaism and Islam, was taking me into new and rewarding adventures, relationships, learning, and teaching.

One part of the postmodern worldview is an increased awareness of Earth and its threatened condition. The postmodern age is witnessing the desire and attempt—especially on the part of women—to integrate ecological concerns and practices with theology and spirituality. There seems to be an initial yet global movement of the Spirit in every major world religion toward this end.[29]

Ecofeminism is a feminist theological movement that has been born in this atmosphere. It is part of the postmodern landscape. Ecofeminists perceive a connection between the domination of women and the domination of Earth, since both have been devalued by patriarchal systems and societies. This Earth-woman movement stretches across religious boundaries. While feminists believe in the equality of the sexes and work to overcome the oppression of women wherever it is found, ecofeminists work for the liberation of both women and Earth.

Lynn Gottlieb, who has been a rabbi for the last thirty years, does not describe herself as an ecofeminist, yet there are signs in her writing of an ecofeminst spirituality. Gottlieb is a Jewish feminist who would like to create an eleventh commandment: Thou shalt be ecological.[30] As a woman who does not feel bound by religious tradition, Gottlieb was one of the first Jewish women ordained a rabbi. A true postmodernist—seeking unity in diversity—she attempts to unite feminism, mysticism, storytelling, and social action with the traditional teachings of Judaism.

Gottlieb calls her ecological practice "eco-krashalt, or keeping kosher from an ecological perspective."[31] "Keeping kosher" refers to using only what is permissible in Jewish ethical practice. The primary Jewish ethic, she claims, is to act with compassion toward all living beings.

Gottlieb's proposed eco-krashalt is instructive for women's spirituality and for the care of Earth. It includes seven admonitions: honor the Mother; offer hospitality; save life; do not be wasteful; be kind to living creatures; do not oppress others economically; and keep the Sabbath.[32] I would like to present Gottlieb's thinking on the first and last of these principles: honor the mother and keep the Sabbath. These seem to resonate in a special way with women's spirituality.

Eco-krashalt begins with a love of physical matter, the body—which is often separated from spirit in a patriarchal mindset and judged as being less valuable. Eco-krashalt encourages human beings to love the body of Mother Earth and to erase the notion that Earth and women's bodies are somehow inferior to other facets of creation. Using the Hebrew language, Gottlieb explains that the words "womb" (*rechem*) and "compassion" (*rachamim*) share the same root.[33] Then she explains that Earth is our common mother, the womb that bestows on creatures the gift of life and the compassion that nurtures and nourishes them, as long as they treat her well. The fate of the mother is in the hands of the children; the fate of our global sisters and brothers also depends on the way we collectively care for, or do not care for, our common mother.

Keeping Sabbath is another practice that fits with women's spirituality. The Hebrew word for Sabbath—*Shabbat*—signifies "returning to one's resting place." Sabbath is a time of return to one's spiritual center in order to be renewed. This period of stillness enables one to receive new energy and creative insights from a divine source. In addition, on the Sabbath, no person, animal, or the Earth performs any utilitarian purpose; the intrinsic value of all beings is honored. All social hierarchies from the world of industry and commerce are disregarded on this day; the equality and mutuality of all is respected.[34] In the words of Lynn Gottlieb:

> Shabbat can become the perfect vessel for the creation of an eco-krashalt world, a world free of gender, class, and race oppression, a world that is hospitable to animals and children, a world that values the pursuits of the imagination, a world that honors creation.[35]

Gottlieb's eco-krashalt is one example of how women around the globe—women from Latin America, India, North America, and Africa—are developing a postmodern women's spirituality.[36] Seizing what is wholesome and healing in postmodernity, these women are developing a worldview that is neither pessimistic nor despairing about the negative realities of our time. Rather, they embrace the beauty and potential of Earth and its peoples in all their diversity. Relatedness, they realize, is our human condition, the way we were fashioned; we all share a common mother.

Lynn Gottlieb's eco-krashalt speaks to me and my spirituality because I have recently become aware of the moral necessity to care for and preserve Earth for present and future generations. Each species carries a vestige or trace of God; each is an unrepeatable expression of the divine. Caring for Earth sometimes means doing what is uncomfortable (turning off the air conditioning) or inconvenient (recycling all recyclable items) for the sake of the common good. Secondly, the idea of taking time for the Sabbath is very significant in my spirituality. I easily fall into the workaholic mode of our American culture. This way of living is harmful to myself and precludes my being available to others, mentally or physically. Keeping the Sabbath enables me to do this more easily.

The Sabbath is also helpful in another area of postmodern spirituality—the movement to an intuitive level of consciousness. This level of consciousness is characterized by "harmony, cooperation, forgiveness, negotiation to resolve differences, mutuality rather than competitiveness; a sense of oneness with others and of belonging to the universe."[37] The key to achieving intuitive consciousness is taking the time to renew oneself (Sabbath) and to allow the personal transformation offered by the inner divine spirit to take place. Then women have real power to make a difference in the world.

CONCLUSION

From this brief and selective historical excursion, one can see examples of women's spirituality in each period of human history. Hildegard of Bingen saw the need to move beyond the bounds of tradition and authority for the sake of the common good. Maria Stewart saw the need to rise above apathy, fear, and anger in the face of injustice, calling others to risk with her in building a moral society wherein all are valued. Lynn Gottlieb used (and uses) the raw materials of her own religious tradition to stretch her arms around the entire planet Earth for its flourishing. Perhaps there is something about women's spirituality that speaks to women across ages, cultures, and religions. As an educator—a shaper of minds and hearts—I know the responsibility to develop this type of spirituality in myself and offer it to others. So I try to create space within myself (through prayer and simplicity of life) and space outside myself (through silence and solitude) to experience the divine presence that imparts in me the desire to live life for the good of the whole.

In our fast-moving, twenty-first-century world, a world filled with noise, busyness, and material possessions, both younger and older women need guidance and companionship on the road to wholeness, so they, in turn, can be healers and guides. Just as Maria Stewart believed that Black women of the nineteenth century had the resources and obligation to strengthen the Black community, so I believe that women of the twenty-first century have the inner resources and social responsibility to strive for personal integration, to share our spiritual vision with others, and to mend our hurting world with the beauty, truth, and goodness of women's spirituality.

NOTES

1. Wilbur, 294–96; Luckmann, Chapter IV.
2. David Hawkins speaks of levels of human consciousness moving progressively upward from shame to guilt to apathy, grief, fear, desire, anger,

pride, to courage, neutrality, willingness, acceptance, reason, love, joy, peace, and, finally, enlightenment. These attitudes or emotions act as energy fields, organizing one's behavior. Hawkins claims that those who have reached the level of courage or higher consciousness have real power in the world. See Hawkins, 68–69 and 100–101.

3. Schneiders, 395.

4. Schneiders, 1996, 30–32, 56; Fiorenza, 137.

5. Maher, 1999 (videotape).

6. Burke, 30–31.

7. Ruether, 144–55; Wilbur, 46–47.

8. Lerner, 50–51.

9. The Charismatic Renewal in the Catholic Church, which began in 1969, is similar to the Pentecostal Movement that began in the Protestant Church in the early 1900s. Its focus is a lived experience of the spirit of God acting in one's life and prayer.

10. The baptism in the spirit is mentioned in Acts 1:5. Jesus tells the disciples not to leave Jerusalem, explaining, "John baptized with water, but you will be baptized with the Holy Spirit not many days from now." The experience as it exists today in the Catholic Charismatic Renewal consists of a person praying in unison with others, to give the control of his or her life to the Holy Spirit. Often the gift of tongues mentioned in 1 Corinthians 12 is received amidst great rejoicing. From that day forward, the person experiences the spirit of God leading them daily in surprising ways. Some Protestant fundamentalist denominations require the gift of tongues as an authentication of one's commitment to Jesus.

11. Craine, 94–95.

12. Craine, 23; Madigan, 91–93.

13. Madigan, 96.

14. Craine, 66–67.

15. Madigan, 94–95.

16. Maher.

17. Tracy, 40.

18. Sterling, 153.

19. Carby, 23–26; Welter, 21–41.

20. Madigan, 307.

21. Richardson, 21.

22. Ibid., 22.

23. Hawkins, 68–69; Wilbur, 125–28.

24. Wilbur, 60–61.

25. Many Jewish people today prefer the term *Shoah* meaning "the devastation."

26. Maher.

27. Hawkins, 68–69.

28. Centering prayer is a form of contemplative prayer in which the practitioner sits quietly for twenty to thirty minutes, focusing one's consciousness on God and letting go of each thought as it comes.

29. Ruether, Chapter 2, Introduction, 1996, 1–8.

30. Gottlieb, 173.

31. Ibid.

32. Gottlieb, 175.
33. Ibid.
34. Gottlieb, 190.
35. Ibid., 191.
36. Ruether, ed., 1996, Gabriele Dietrich, "The World as the Body of God: Feminist Perspectives on Ecology and Social Justice." Chapter 3. 82–98.
37. Keating, 146.

BIBLIOGRAPHY

Burke, Christine. "Globalization and Ecology." In Denis Edwards, ed. *Earth Revealing, Earth Healing*. Collegeville, MN: Liturgical Press, 2001, 21–42.

Carby, Hazel V. *Reconstructing Womanhood: The Emergence of the Afro-American Woman Novelist*. New York: Oxford University Press, 1987.

Craine, Renate. *Hildegard: Prophet of the Cosmic Christ*. New York: Crossroad, 1997.

Fiorenza, Elisabeth Schussler. "Feminist Spirituality, Christian Identity, and Catholic Vision." In Christ, Carol P., and Plaskow, Judith, eds. *Woman-Spirit Rising: A Feminist Reader in Religion*. San Francisco, CA: HarperCollins, 1979/1992, 136–148.

Gottlieb, Lynn. *She Who Dwells Within: A Feminist Vision of a Renewed Judaism*. San Francisco: HarperSanFrancisco, 1995.

Hawkins, David M. *Power vs. Force: The Hidden Determinants of Human Behavior*. Sedona, CO: Veritas, 1995.

Keating, Thomas. *Invitation to Love*. New York: Continuum, 1992.

Lerner, Michael. *Spirit Matters*. Charlottesville, VA: Hampton Roads Publishing Company, Inc., 2000.

Loewenberg, Bert, and Bogin, Ruth, eds. *Black Women in Nineteenth-Century American Life*. University Park, PA: Pennsylvania State University Press, 1976.

Luckmann, Thomas. *The Invisible Religion*. New York: MacMillan, 1967.

Madigan, Shawn, CSJ, ed. *Mystics, Visionaries, and Prophets*. Minneapolis: Fortress Press, 1998.

Maher, Mary V., SSND. *Women Religious Living in Many Worlds*. Videotape produced by School Sisters of Notre Dame. St. Louis, MO, 1999.

Richardson, Marilyn, ed. *Maria W. Stewart: America's First Black Woman Political Writer: Essays and Speeches*. Bloomington, IN: University Press, 1987.

Ruether, Rosemary Radford. *Gaia and God: An Ecofeminist Theology of Earth Healing*. San Francisco: HarperCollins, 1992.

———. *Integrating Ecofeminism, Globalization and World Religions*. New York: Rowman & Littlefield Publishers, Inc., 2005.

Schneiders, Sandra M., IHM. "Feminist Spirituality." In Joann Wolski Conn, ed. *Women's Spirituality: Resources for Human Development*. New York: Paulist Press, 1986, 1996, 30–67.

———. "Feminist Spirituality." In Michael Downey, ed. *The New Dictionary of Catholic Spirituality*. Collegeville, MN: Liturgical Press, 1993, 394–406.

Stanton, Elizabeth Cady, Anthony, Susan B., and Gage, Matilda Joslyn, eds. *History of Woman's Suffrage*. Rochester, NY: Susan B. Anthony, 1881, 1970.

Sterling, Dorothy. *We Are Your Sisters: Black Women in the Nineteenth Century.* New York: W. W. Norton & Co., 1984.

Tracy, David. *On Naming the Present.* New York: Orbis Books, 1994.

Welter, Barbara. *Dimity Convictions: The American Woman in the Nineteenth Century.* Athens, OH: Ohio University Press, 1976.

Wilbur, Ken. *A Brief History of Everything.* 2nd ed. Boston, MA: Shambhala, 2000.

Chapter 2

The Goddess Has Returned!

Darlene Prestbo
Hazel Staats-Westover

"Mama," our first utterance, is a word familiar in a myriad of the world's languages, evoking the nurturing, steadfast bond of all that is mothering in our existence. The first Neolithic carvings were of the Great Mother, the creatrix. Early cultures, from the cities of Crete to Celtic villages, were matriarchal. Religious writings from 2,000 BCE by the Sumerians depict the courageous saga of the beloved goddess Inanna (Ishtar). Women of the Old Testament caught the ire of temple priests for bringing sweet cakes to the "Queen of Heaven" (Jeremiah 7:18). Sophia, or Wisdom, was once the honored name for the Holy Spirit, reflecting the feminine aspect of the Christian trinity. The power of divine mothering energy is a thread woven into the tapestry of most religious traditions, sometimes brightly visible and sometimes faded to an obscure gray. Trace memories of the Great Mother remain in the veneration of the Black Madonna, especially in Europe and Latin America, and in the devotion to the Virgin Mary. But essentially the Goddess was ignored for more than 2,000 years.

With the flowering of the women's movement in the 1970s came a yearning for a spirituality that celebrated the nurturing feminine creative energy. A counterpoint was needed to balance the vast power of the patriarchal system. In response to that need, women scholars in anthropology, sociology, and religious studies produced brilliant works recounting the history and vitality of the divine feminine. By fascinating coincidence, Margot Adler, a commentator for National Public Radio, published *Drawing Down the Moon*[1] on the same day in 1979 as Starhawk's book *The Spiral Dance*.[2] Both books describe the resurgence of the Goddess energy in America and act as guides for creating women's spirituality ritual. The basic credo of the movement resonated deeply, "The energy you put into the world comes back." In 1982, Marion Zimmer Bradley published *The Mists of Avalon*, a retelling of the Arthurian legend from the vantage point of women and the honoring of the Great Mother.[3] Respected scholar Riane Eisler, in 1987, presented her study of the power of benevolence and peace through the divine feminine in *The Chalice and the Blade*.[4] The Goddess had truly returned.

Women's spirituality honors the Goddess, as both outward positive energy and as inner illumination. In its modern form, the rituals are based on historical traditions from a variety of cultures, including ancient Greek, Roman, Celtic, Native American, and Hebrew. There are many variations in the way the Goddess is honored, from Wicca gatherings in a Wisconsin garden to "Cakes for the Queen of Heaven" groups within the Unitarian Church to sharing the power of the divine feminine in a New Jersey home.

The underlying focus is recognition of the feminine principle within both women and men. The emphasis is directed toward the bond between people, the land, and the seasonal cycles. There is great respect for the individual, for diversity, and for living in harmony with the earth. The rituals are a celebration and honoring of the essence and precious quality of all life, as well as the energy of creativity.

The great mystery in women's spirituality holds the image of the circle. As Starhawk describes this, "every ending is but a new beginning." Past the barren winter darkness awaits the spring. The traditional *charge*, or ritual poetry in the voice of the Goddess, reflects this concept. The Great Mother announces that she was the creatrix before time began, the one who gave birth to all creation. Life withers and dies, returning to the soil to be refreshed and regenerated in a continuous cycle. Life begins anew with the greening of nature and the wondrous emergence of all living forms.

It is the unwavering belief in the sacredness of creation that gives rich and lasting power to the vitality of the divine feminine. The abiding principle is the oneness of all people and things of the Earth. Core values include loving-kindness as the pathway to healing, empowerment, sensuality, maternal nurture, tolerance, and inspired creativity. This is reflected in the rituals, using the "powerful role of imagination in weaving myth, symbol and ordinary life into poetry, art, story and song," as noted by Marjorie Thompson in an essay on feminine spirituality published in *The Princeton* [New Jersey] *Seminary Bulletin*.[5]

In her essay "Why Women Need the Goddess," Carol Christ states, "The most basic meaning of the symbol of Goddess is the acknowledgement of the legitimacy of female power as a beneficent and independent power."[6] Rituals are reminders and conduits for the integration of this truth within a woman. There is an awakening and flourishing of intuition, wisdom, and self-esteem. The ritual dramatizes the cycle of life, death, and rebirth in nature and culture in all its beauty and vitality.

The honoring of the divine feminine leads to the affirmation and appreciation of the shape and cycles of a woman's body through all the phases of life from childhood to maturity to old age. In ritual this is symbolized by the triple image of the Goddess as maiden/mother/crone. Women are led to the realization that all phases of their lives are to be valued, whether it is the zest of youth, the creativity of adulthood, or the vast wisdom of aging. As the spirit finds regeneration, a woman's body is cherished for its unique and natural form.

REV. HAZEL'S STORY

My path toward establishing a women's spirituality group was a lifelong journey nurtured even before birth by parents who came from traditional church backgrounds. They were loving, happy, nurturing, altruistic people. I was a cheerful child, born and raised in Griggstown, New Jersey, and cradled by their love. Endowed with a gift for music, by the age of nine I was the pianist for our Sunday school, where my father served as superintendent.

I cherished and admired my father. My teenage world was shattered when he was killed in an automobile accident at the age of thirty-eight. Mother was left alone to raise me, age fourteen, and my brother, age twelve. Experiencing her strength in taking charge of life after tragedy certainly influenced me without my conscious realization.

While I was a high school student, I became the organist at our church. But it wasn't until I was in college that I realized my religious nature. The responsibility of helping to create a spiritual space for worship through my music greatly influenced the development of my spirituality.

During my sophomore year at the University of Southern California, I was sent to a student leadership conference as a representative of the chapel youth group. Each day began with a class on faith taught by the Reverend Allan Hunter, followed by a class given by the Reverend Dr. John Muhlenberg, a noted Old Testament authority. Both ministers inspired me profoundly. When the conference ended, I realized that religion was my true path of study. But to drop using all the skills I had developed in music left me feeling uneasy.

I decided to change schools while I figured out what to do. I transferred to the University of Redlands, California, which has a religious focus. A meeting with the dean of woman was providential. She had been a missionary in China and suggested that I combine my music with theology and teach music in the mission field. My future was clear! Transferring schools once again, I finished my degree in music education at Northwestern University in Illinois. My focus then turned to religion and I entered Chicago Theological Seminary. Along with my maturation in spirituality came the blossoming of love and then marriage to a theologian.

In 1944, while a student at seminary, I worked with the Chicago Council of Churches helping to find safe housing for the Japanese Americans released from national internment camps. I accepted a summer internship in 1945 to work with a minister in Los Angeles who had been an inspiration to me while I was an undergrad. Prejudice was still very strong against Japanese Americans and they were often the focus of hostility.

In general, Japanese Americans did not try to return to their homes in California. However, one insurance salesman went back, believing he had many friends there because of his success in the insurance business. He was shunned by his former associates and tried to commit suicide twice. His wife was able to stop him until his third attempt, when she was unable to get the knife away from him.

When the phone call came in to the church parsonage, I was the only minister available to respond to this emergency. As I entered the foyer of their home, I saw the walls splattered with blood where the wife had struggled unsuccessfully to get the knife away. I found her on her bed, lying in a fetal position, crying out in Japanese. I didn't know the language and wondered how I could help her. I stayed with her for several hours, holding her in silent communication. When I left the house, I felt so inadequate, wondering if I had been any help at all.

Twenty years later in Germany, while I was assisting in building the International Peace Center Freundshaftsheim, the daughter of the widowed Japanese woman came to visit the center. Recognizing my name, she said, "You will never know how much you meant to my mother that terrible day." My understanding of spirituality soared from that chance meeting. It defined ministry for me. One doesn't need to say a word to give comfort and support, just be truly present in the moment. That is the help the heart can supply.

In 1947, I accompanied my husband as he began his first ministry at the Fellowship Church of All Peoples in San Francisco, California, with the Reverend Dr. Howard Thurman. This was another big jump spiritually for me. The church was one of two interracial, interfaith congregations in the nation. (The other was in Philadelphia, Pennsylvania.) The two years we spent with Rev. Thurman were full of growth and learning. It was my first experience being part of a congregation made up of one-third African Americans, one-third Asians, and one-third Caucasians, as well as a mixture of Christians, Jews, agnostics, and other spiritual people. Immersed in this amazing culture, I learned that we are all of the same spirit, needing to recognize our shared sisterhood and brotherhood. Our beautiful daughter was born while my husband and I were in that sacred environment.

In 1948, there was a announcement that the United States was soon to have its first peacetime draft. Peacemaking had become another important dimension of my spirituality. For a year, my husband and I met in a cell group discussing what the correct perspectives should be for world peace. Two men in the group, as ministers of peace, decided they needed to oppose the draft and refuse to register. One of these men was my husband. He and his colleague were given a three-month jail sentence.

This was another experience of spiritual growth as we sought insight and direction for our lives. My husband and I had become members of the International Fellowship of Reconciliation. I was employed to fill his position at the Fellowship Church while he was ministering to his fellow prisoners. At the completion of his sentence, he was invited by Bayard Rustin, a prominent peace leader, to make an international trip speaking at peace centers in France and the Netherlands. At the end he would go to Cambridge, England, where he had been awarded a scholarship to study.

Our daughter was eighteen months old as we began traveling for a year throughout Europe and England, sharing the message of peace in Dresden and Petzen, Germany, as well as Belgium and Flanders. I developed and deepened my firm belief that each of us has been created to live together in harmony, helping one another attain the spirit of inclusion for all humanity.

Returning to the United States, we lived for the next three years in Hinsdale, Illinois, where my husband served on the ministerial staff of the Congregational Church. Heeding the call to further study, he enrolled in Union Theological Seminary in New York City. Our daughter and I accompanied him to the East Coast where our family was blessed with a new spirit in the birth of a son. Finally we returned to California, where we built a home in Claremont. Here we stayed for ten years, nurturing our children and working in the religious community. I was minister of education at the Congregational Union Church for eight years and then taught in the Claremont Unified schools.

A dramatic expansion of my life's work occurred when we accepted a call to become part of the faculty and staff of Chicago Theological Seminary. Following my involvements in parenting, peacemaking, and interracial equality, I responded to the challenge by female students at the seminary to create a course for women in religion. The National Organization for Women had inspired the students to petition me, seeking to find a way to use this new excitement about feminism in their ministry. I co-led a course entitled Human Liberation that was the first course specifically targeted for women in any seminary in the United States. The students and I founded the Ecumenical Women's

Center in Chicago to support equality of women in the field of religion.

In 1968, our family joined forty-four Methodist ministers for a United Nations Church Center peace tour, spending three weeks behind the Iron Curtain. I was asked to preach during a Sunday service in Moscow at the Baptist Church, which was the only church allowed to hold a Christian service. There were more than 2,000 congregants, a transforming experience. In 1971, I was the American speaker at the May Day Vietnam Protest parade in Paris, where more than 110,000 people gathered to condemn the war. Spiritually, these moments were profoundly moving. However, it was a challenge to convey a meaningful interpretation of love and friendship for different cultures.

My greatest spiritual challenge came in 1972 when my husband said he needed to explore personal liberation. He asked to leave our marriage. I loved him but knew I had to let him go. Lost and adrift, I registered for the women's studies program developed by the Boston Theological Institute. My two-year study at Harvard Divinity School, working with Mary Daly, PhD[7] and Rosemary Radford Ruether, PhD,[8] helped strengthen my own feminist spirituality, nurtured originally by my strong and intelligent mother.

Moving to Princeton, New Jersey, I set up a women's center at Princeton University after its revolutionary change into a coed institution. Eventually I became a chaplain at the university, ministering to the female students, a post I held for more than thirty years. I found love once more, marrying a man who has been my spiritual partner and anchor for the past twenty-nine years. I believe that faith and love have provided me with the energy to be adventuresome, to trust as I venture into the unknown, to be in touch with my inner spirit, and to find the strength and wisdom to respond to crises. This is my spirituality, a blessing we all can achieve when given nurturing and support.

DARLENE'S MEMOIR

If my Sunday school teacher had asked me to paint a picture of God and my idea of spirituality when I was a little girl in Fort Wayne, Indiana, back in the 1940s, the painting would have been swirls and broad slashes of Black with blobs of angry red. I was tutored about the divine as a member of the Disciples of Christ, a fire-and-brimstone church that my family faithfully attended. Fear of God's wrath guaranteed that I was well behaved and quiet. An only child and deeply sensitive, I amused myself by playing with my imaginary friends and by exploring the musty ancient volumes in my grandparents' home where we lived. I was drawn almost hypnotically to the 1895 edition of Dante's *Inferno*, with its large and vivid etchings of the gruesome tortures of hell.

No matter how hard I tried to create a gossamer shield of goodness over our family to protect us from pain, my naiveté was shattered again and again. My beloved Grandma Mattie died from cancer when I was five years old. Grandpa Walter, whom I cherished beyond measure, despaired about the ravages of aging and took his life when I was twelve. Both my uncles, who lived next to our elegant Victorian home, suffered through long illnesses and died in spite of my prayers, uttered as I pierced my slender arms with a needle in frail imitation of the sufferings of Jesus. Before I entered high school, I vowed to dedicate my life to the easing of suffering, somehow.

During my teen years I became absorbed in the excitement of scholarship and the joys of breaking through my shyness into the dazzle of theater. I was gifted in the art of entertainment, both musical comedy and drama. Immersed in the persona of a character, I transcended my entanglement in the world of pain and suffering.

After high school I attended Northwestern University, famed for the dramatic arts. I had a double major in theatre and literature, thrilling to the expansion of my personal universe. The burden of my religious upbringing became lighter. Upon college graduation and a marriage that continues to enrich my life, I pursued a career in professional theater in Chicago. Fully disillusioned by the dysfunctional behavior of fellow performers and floundering with uncertainty about my future direction and purpose, I was shaken into remembrance of my childhood vow to serve and heal.

Guided by synchronicity, I entered the theater of the real by becoming a caseworker for the city of Chicago, ministering to the elderly living in project housing for the poorest of the poor. Years later, I learned that Hazel was in Chicago at the same time, promoting social justice through her work in the church. As I held trembling, wrinkled hands, wiped tear-drenched cheeks, and fought fiercely for more funding and a reinstatement of dignity and respect for the elders who languished in despair, I felt myself unable to ignore the call to service. With the blessing of my husband, I entered graduate school and trained intensely in clinical social work. In a useful recycling of talent, I was able to use my dramatic skills to portray the emotionally ill patient during our sessions of educational role-play.

After earning a master's degree in social work and giving birth to our son, I left all that was familiar and grounding to me when my husband was transferred to New Jersey. The transition to a totally different culture and milieu of the New York metropolitan area, with its fast pace, sparkling excitement, and radical ideas left me dazed and adrift. Within the harbor of a small private practice in psychotherapy, I was able to explore my new surroundings. Simultaneously, I discovered a Presbyterian church community that revealed a compassionate and forgiving God and a social center whose focus was the newly immerging feminist movement of the 1970s. From Isaiah, I heard the message of a nurturing God: "The Lord will have mercy upon his afflicted. Can a woman forget her sucking child? I will not forget thee. Behold, I have graven thee upon the palms of my hands" (Isaiah: 14–16). From the women's center I heard the message of feminine empowerment, expansion of spirit, and individual courage to explore the edges of possibility. I was beginning the painful, challenging, exhilarating metamorphosis of becoming the person of wholeness who I was truly meant to be.

A few months after our daughter was born, my husband was transferred to Cleveland, Ohio. This move to a new home was for me both a chance to start over and a return to my Midwestern roots. I established a therapy practice under the auspices of our local Presbyterian church and submerged my radical feminism enough to blend into a more traditional community. I was thrust into a totally new awareness of the interface of spirituality and healing when my husband and I were invited to become members of a church-sponsored intensive study group, striving to experience and apply the mystery of healing through prayer and the "laying on of hands." The power of compassion and loving-kindness proved to be dynamic. I found a new level in which to practice the expansion of possibilities.

Once again, my husband's company awarded him with a transfer back to New Jersey, this time to the Princeton area. I had to establish myself anew as a social worker in private practice. Using my training in the dramatic arts and my experience in theology, I also became a lecturer and workshop leader as well as a deacon at the local Presbyterian church. A chance meeting of Hazel at a workshop we both attended led to an enduring friendship in which we shared humanitarian, spiritual, and environmental ideals.

Open to learning more about the various paths to emotional and physical healing, I began a four-year training in Therapeutic Touch. This system of healing both body and spirit was developed by Dolores Krieger, PhD, RN, a professor of nursing at New York University. Thoroughly tested in clinical settings, Therapeutic Touch is a form of "laying on of hands." Initially taught to nurses, the program had recently been made available to therapists. My instructor mentor, Peggy Fuhs, PhD, RN, was a protégé of Dr. Krieger. Throughout the training, Peggy patiently guided me toward my own emotional healing and the expansion of trust in the vibrant reality of the unseen and the union of holiness and wholeness. She taught the necessity of honoring, respecting, and protecting all that is alive in nature as well as humanity.

During this time, I also attended other intensive workshops in mythology, drama, transcendent spirituality, and psychology. My understanding of the divine was further transformed by the teachings of Father Matthew Fox, a Dominican scholar who lectured and wrote about his radical understanding of the original foundation message of

Christianity. His courageous message encompassed women's spirituality, inclusiveness and honoring of all humanity, respect for nature and the healing of the earth, and a godhead (divine higher power) which embodied the nurturing feminine. Through him I came to know the revelations of Julian of Norwich, an English anchoress and teacher from the 1300s who electrified people with her teachings about Jesus as mother/healer. "The deep wisdom of the Trinity is our Mother, in whom we are enclosed."[9] She also celebrated physical sensuality and taught that the human body in all aspects, sexual and functional, is both holy and beautiful. If someone asked me during this period of my mid-forties to paint a picture of the God/Goddess, I would use the colors of the rainbow in all the vibrant hues imaginable, sparkling with luminescence and alive with joy.

Several times over the years, Hazel had encouraged me to join a local women's spirituality group she was coleading. I finally accepted her invitation. I also continued to expand my inner awareness and heightened consciousness as a student in a year-long intensive course in holistic healing for therapists, led by artist and psychotherapist Ute Arnold. Using psychodrama, poetry, painting, movement, ritual, group dynamics, and times of solitude in nature, Ute challenged each of us to transform our own crippling emotions and behaviors. As healers, we began to heal ourselves. I embraced the mystical aspects of myself that had been a part of my childhood. As a result of this catalyst of creativity, my writings, photographs, and poetry appeared in publications such as *Fellowship in Prayer* and *Testament* (produced by Princeton Theological Seminary).[10]

An avid gardener, I started to sense the shimmering energy of flowers and trees, the devic (one of an order of good spirit, the Shining One) dance in all its ancient glory. I developed an avocation as a landscape photographer, quietly revealing the essence of nurturing beauty within the myriad variations of nature. In the garden, I had met the Goddess.

My work as a therapist evolved as I allowed myself to open into radical trust. I was guided in this transformation by a multifaceted mentor and role model, Linda Fitch, MA. Linda described my emotional and spiritual journey as being "shattered into wholeness." Using music, art, dance, improvisation, and compassionate acceptance, she created the template that allowed me to be both grounded and luminous.

Using traditional therapy as the basis of my work with clients, I added meditation and, when requested, Therapeutic Touch. Betsy had been in counseling with me about personal growth issues when she was diagnosed with a cancerous facial tumor. Extensive surgery and radiation saved her life but left her physically changed and emotionally shaken. During her long period of recovery, she and I partnered in the experience of meditation and Therapeutic Touch, both enriched by the

respectful nurturing and spiritual comforting. Betsy experienced healing in both body and soul. In the office, I had met the Great Mother,
the creatrix.

WOMEN'S SPIRITUALITY IN PRINCETON

The Princeton, New Jersey, women's spirituality group was started
in 1979 by two women who were active in the local chapter of the
National Organization for Women. One of the founders, Hazel, had
recently completed her studies for ordination in the United Church of
Christ. She believed that it was important for women to analyze what
theology and spirituality are in personal terms. Francesca, the
cofounder and former Roman Catholic, had long dreamed of the possibility of women designing their own rituals and celebrating their spirituality together. As she shared with Hazel, "I admire women who stay
in traditional religions and work for change. However, I need a new
and meaningful way to express my deepest self. With women's spirituality I can celebrate my connection to the sacred in an atmosphere that
in turn celebrates the sacred in me as I am."

Their discussions led to a decision to run an ad in the local papers.
At one newspaper office, the lady who took the ad looked skeptical and
queried, "What is this? It sounds strange." But at another news office
the woman on staff responded, "This sounds terrific! I'd like to come!"
The ad, groundbreaking for this area of New Jersey in 1979, stated:

> A group of women is being formed locally to explore and share women's
> personal experiences of spirituality. The group is open to any woman
> who wishes to examine a variety of spiritual experiences, particularly
> from a feminist, nontraditional point of view. The group will meet on a
> regular basis and will concern itself with the way in which women
> undertake a spiritual quest. For further information . . .

Hazel and Francesca received several phone calls from women in
the area, some antagonistic, some enthusiastic. Eight women and one
man attended the first meeting. Some felt unsure about the Goddess-
oriented, shared leadership model that was suggested, so they formed
a separate group. However, four women who were willing to break
with tradition agreed to explore feminist spirituality. They were uncer-
tain about how to proceed until it was decided to plan an evening of
women-designed ritual.

Francesca remembered her trepidation as she helped create a ritual
so different from what she had experienced as part of the Catholic tradition. "I was deciding for myself how I wanted to celebrate my womanhood and my participation in the sacred. The words *sinner* and
heretic rose up before me. Yet I knew I had to act on my belief that it

was my right to decide how to give expression to my spirituality. After we had lit the candles in the darkened room and turned on music to dance in a circle, I felt a moment of such ecstasy—I will never forget it."

The act of creating their own rituals seemed to energize the members of the group. Meetings were held monthly, new members joined through friendship or word of mouth, and confidence increased. Hazel recalled how essential the combination of hard work and spiritual conviction was to provide impetus for the group to learn and grow.

The greatest challenge for the group was finding their way through the thicket of disagreements and differences of opinion, especially as the number of participants greatly increased. Looking back, Francesca wished this issue had been handled differently. "It would have made sense to set up regular times to discuss where we were going and what we were doing, to see differences as healthy and as issues to negotiate," she said. "We had one painful meeting in which unresolved differences spilled over and resulted in unnecessary hurt for some members. At that point, the group split in two."

THE DAUGHTERS OF GAIA

Thus, in early 1987, several members, in consideration of the well-being of all, made the decision to form a separate group, The Daughters of Gaia. Hazel and Darlene are charter members of this vibrant gathering. The group has met monthly in the Princeton area for twenty years, the remaining original core members enriched by the vitality of women entering the group as others have moved away. Our community includes social workers, counselors, writers, poets, educators, activists, humanitarians, and a pastor. We represent many walks of faith: Presbyterian, United Church of Christ, Quaker, Buddhist, Jewish, agnostic, and a student of the Course in Miracles.

The Daughters of Gaia is a blend of the best aspects of women's spirituality. We follow the guidelines for philosophy and ritual as set down by Starhawk in *The Spiral Dance* and Diane Stein in *The Women's Spirituality Book*.[11] Wending around the Wheel of the Year, observing ancient traditional festivals and celebrations, we also creatively incorporate the personal religious or ethical heritages of each of our members. Creativity grounded in matriarchal tradition plus mindfulness of the present moment keep the group experience meaningful and vitally alive. This is reflected in our personal credo, as created by Darlene:

We are dedicated to the celebration and renewal of the Earth and each other. We pledge a commitment to strive for the empowering of feminine energy for regeneration, peace, love, healing and joy; and we pledge to take that vibrant feminine energy out into a world which is so greatly in need.

Each monthly gathering has the same ritual framework, to which the coleaders for the evening can bring creative elements. We always begin with The Casting of the Circle, a setting aside of sacred space and an invocation for the blessing of the spiritual guardians. Susan, a founding sister of the Daughters of Gaia, wrote an invocation so rich in imagery that it is often used to begin our meetings:

> We call on the spirits of the East, creatures of Air.
> Sweet scent of violets on the breeze.
> Butterflies among the primrose and pansies,
> Eagle soaring in the aspen-covered mountains.
> Cleansing winds, clear away the mists.
> Luminescent dawn sky,
> Open space for imagination.
>
> We call on the spirits of the South, creatures of Fire.
> Scorpion and lizard enlivened by the sun.
> Red cactus flower,
> Bristlecone pine offering your seed
> Only to the flame.
> Sap rising in the tree, blood in the veins.
> Keep us strong in your spirit.
>
> We call on the spirits of the West, creatures of Water.
> Willow, lotus, reed and dulse.
> Porpoise, whale, frog and fish,
> Opalescent mountain stream,
> Salt-tangy sea.
> Rain returning home again and again.
> Keep us mindful of your balance.
>
> We call on the spirits of the North, creatures of the Earth.
> Worm and grub, bison, bear.
> Groves of oak, fields of grasses,
> Place of root and seed.
> Web of life,
> Hold us fast
> To the greater body.
>
> —Susan

At the conclusion of the invocation, we recite a ritual litany that bonds us with the grandmothers and wise women through the ages who created space within the circle they had formed. We Cast the Circle, closing ourselves within it, detaching from the swirl and clanking of ordinary life. In the weaving of words, all fragments and divisions of daily living meld and blend so that darkness and light, grief and delight, beginnings and endings all meet at the still point in the center of being.

With the room in a soft darkness, illumined by candles on a table decorated with flowers and symbolic objects, the group enters into a period of meditation. The cares and stress of everyday life are put aside as the mind and body relax into a place of peace. Each month a different woman volunteers to lead this exercise. A typical example is the Moon Meditation, adapted by Darlene:

"Breathe deeply while you gaze at the candles. As you inhale, receive energy and light. As you exhale, release tension and limitations. Close your eyes. Remember a time when you stood by the ocean or at the edge of a lake and gazed at the moon, round, full, shimmering with beauty and gentle light. Visualize the water with the full moon suspended above it. See the path of moonlight on the water, a pathway wide and magnificent to behold. Let yourself be drawn to that path of moonlight. Allow the light to soften and soothe you. Imagine the patterned waves of moonlight flowing into you. There is a wise woman in the moon. You can see her face. She smiles as she greets the wise woman within you. A surge of power flows between these wise women. You feel an igniting of energy within you. You are moonstruck, filled with awe, peace, and joy. The wise woman in the moon whispers words of guidance and comfort to you. Listen to her. Let yourself become playful. If you wish, you can dance along the moonlit path in the water. Soon it will be time to bid the moon farewell for this night. Before you leave, thank the moon for her presence in your life. You are restored to quiet and clarity, deepened, renewed and empowered. When you are ready, slowly open your eyes."

Another member now leads the group in a chant, focusing energy for the evening. The chant, which is voiced in unison, can come from any spiritual or cultural tradition. Sometimes it is a song. A favorite chant comes from Theravada Buddhism, calling forth loving-kindness.

May I be happy
May I be peaceful
May I be free.
May my friends be happy
May my friends be peaceful
May my friends be free.
May my enemies be happy
May my enemies be peaceful
May my enemies be free.
May all beings be happy
May all beings be peaceful
May all beings be free.

All this is preparation for the centerpiece of the gathering, the Ritual, conducted each month by two members who act as copriestesses. The Daughters of Gaia follow the sabbats and festivals around the Wheel of the Year. We begin with the ancient New Year celebration of Samhain at Halloween, then winter solstice in December, followed by a January blessing, Candlemas in February, the spring equinox, an April honoring of Earth Day, Beltane with the Maypole dance, the summer solstice, a respite for the summer, and a joyous return with a potluck supper and ritual for the fall equinox.

At the conclusion of the ritual, with its interweave of familiar patterns and creative color, we dance to music which evokes the rhythms of nature, either pensive or passionate. It is joyful to behold our elder sisters discover within themselves a lively verve and grace as they dance, aspects of aging melting away. Coming back to the circle, we quietly begin the Sharing, offering thoughts and feelings in an atmosphere of caring and trust, reflecting upon a topic suggested by one of the group. With great anticipation of the feasting to come, we then Open the Circle. This ritual honors the paradox that with leave-taking there is still connection. We invoke the peace of the Goddess as we go our separate ways, holding the joyful knowledge in our hearts that some day we shall meet again.

Always close to consciousness in our meetings is the awareness of the triple aspect of the Goddess as maiden/mother/crone. At different intervals in the lifespan of our spirituality group, a particular aspect has presented itself to us in a dramatic way. In the fall of 1988, Darlene's daughter Laura began menstruating. By this time, the feminist movement had led to a more open acknowledgment of this passage in a young woman's life. However, the topic was still a delicate one in our area of New Jersey. In a moment of inspired innovation, the Daughters of Gaia invited Laura and a close friend of the same age to attend a meeting dedicated to the celebration of their elevation to womanhood, evoking the maiden. We chose elements of Native American and Celtic traditions to honor and cherish this life passage. After a respectful ritual and the bestowing of roses, the elder women of the group spoke about their bewilderment as very young women in an era of shame about the body. The women shared stories of pain, secrecy, and embarrassment at the time of their first menstruation. In the evening's celebration of the two young maidens, the older women found healing and a belated sense of celebration for themselves, an unexpected blessing that had a profound impact upon all of us.

The opportunity to invoke the aspect of the Mother as nurturer and healer presents itself to us whenever a member becomes injured, ill, or broken with grief. Holding a sister within a circle of tender caring invariably leads to a healing of the heart and body. Several years ago, one of our members received a call about a woman newly arrived from

Eastern Europe who was in physical pain from stress. In her native land, women healers were held in high esteem. Could she come to our meeting for just a few minutes, to receive healing? We agreed, trusting the guidance of the Mother and our own intuition, to serve the highest good of the person in our care. The warmth of our encircling arms touched our visitor's heart and she departed with a smile and words of gratitude. Years later, a friend of hers called on her behalf to ask if once again she could come for healing and blessing. Her life was askew and she needed the lifting of the dark cloud that seemed to follow her. Honoring her trust in us, she was welcomed into our arms. Once again, the energy of the Mother enfolded her and she was uplifted and restored. We have not heard from her again but we remember how we, too, were uplifted and blessed by this nurturing bond.

Whenever a member reaches the age of fifty-six, she is eligible to participate in the ceremony of the Crowning of the Crone. This is a joyous mini-ritual that delights in the wisdom, vitality, and importance of the woman as elder. It is an elevation of aging to a position of esteem, restoring the concept of crone as a holder of power rather than a fragile and impotent being. The ceremony is led by those who have already achieved this honored status.

Facing the initiate, the reigning crones reveal the truth that in ancient times crones held more power than younger women. In formal meetings they always had an honored place to sit. Sadly, modern society tends to demean or neglect elderly women. It is vitally important that we remember our history, restore respect to the name of "crone," and celebrate the wisdom that the years have carved upon our faces and bodies. The elder ones are especially beloved of the Goddess.

The newly initiated crone honors the long and challenging path from birth to elderhood. Gratitude is given to the Goddess for all the seasons that have been traversed, and thanksgiving is expressed for all the days that lie ahead.

Violet and Hazel, both venerated crones within our circle, are grateful that the ceremony "honored the process of aging and allowed the graceful acceptance of growing older." Linda cherishes the memory of her crowning, "with its recognition of wisdom and status that comes with age."

Women's spirituality groups tend to be diametrically opposed to traditional organized religion with fixed regulations and hierarchical leadership. The Daughters of Gaia group is typical with its shared leadership, acceptance of diversity, and fluid creativity within a matriarchal framework. A bond of friendship and trust, developed through months of meeting and sharing and reenacting ritual, holds the group together whatever challenges arise.

Donna reflects on this aspect of our group experience: "Relationships keep me coming to the group. This is my spiritual voyage through life that cannot be done alone. It is in relationship with others that I eventually see myself reflected. In having a safe place to share personal stories, we avoid the fatal flaw of trying to fix each other or solve another's problems. While we elevate all that unifies us, we also celebrate all that makes us unique." Diane agrees, adding that the group has helped her to embrace spontaneity and joy. "I experienced the permission, given by example, of simply enjoying good things and pleasures such as laughing, eating, dancing in a garden with the full moon shining, rather than being anxious."

Each meeting is a microcosm of the Wheel of the Year, with a deepening awareness of the changing seasons within the earth and within ourselves, an honoring of the ebb and flow of creation with its dance of light and dark, birth and death, and withering and renewal. Each gathering of the circle produces moments both light-hearted and profound. Bineke describes a Samhain celebration in her home that was transformative for her: "My intent was to lead the women into darkness first, followed by guiding them into the light, physically experiencing the contrast. From the dark cellar we entered a room upstairs, where I lit candles encircling my husband's sculpture of a female model adorned with jewelry and golden cloth. As the women took their seats around the circle of candles, each face shone as radiant as the goddess herself as I imagined her. It was a moment when I understood that underneath all the struggles of life, we are goddesses incarnate."

Joyce joined the Daughters of Gaia during the time when her husband Gary was diagnosed with bladder cancer. She felt the need for spiritual support and "the network of wise, kind women" during this period of crisis. The sisterhood sustained her through Gary's long illness and death and sustains her still. "What I enjoy most about the group is the sense of continuity, which translates for me into spiritual continuity. Whether Gary is healthy, ill, alive, or dead, the group continues. This is a focus of women's spirituality: the continuance and cycle of seasons, the fact that the shortest day of the year is also the beginning of our stride towards the longest. My favorite ritual is the summer solstice. As I throw rose petals into the pond of Darlene's garden and make my wishes, I recall the years of wishes I have made ... some granted, some not ... and realize at the same time how little my personal wishes matter and yet how lucky I am to be able to make them."

Karen, one of the newer members of the group, is enchanted with the ceremonies that have allowed her to expand into deeper dimensions. She has been transported by "the ritual tales of ancient goddesses, intertwined with flowers, candles, and artifacts." However, for her the greatest gift the sisterhood has given her has been during our moments of sharing. She remembers a cold winter Monday, driving back from Washington, DC, in tears after consoling her daughter and son-in-law in the very recent deaths of his father and the couple's baby boy, who died five and one-half months *in utero*.

"I didn't think I would have the energy to attend the Daughters of Gaia meeting that evening, but I drove myself to the group," she said. "In the sharing, I told the story of my heartache for my daughter and her precious family. Somehow the warmth and compassion of my Gaia sisters lifted me up as if I were being supported by a labyrinth of love and filled me with hope about living beyond those losses."

Involvement in a women's spirituality group requires a high level of participation and commitment, a willingness to respect the greater good of the community, and respecting and honoring the self. The gifts received are numerous. Violet, a member of Daughters of Gaia for many years, acknowledges that her life has been enriched. "This group is very supportive, warm, and accepting. As a woman of Jewish background, I have learned so much through our group meetings about the values of women from other religions. I am grateful for the opportunity we have to exchange and accept nonjudgmental ideas from each other." Karen agrees, adding that, "The wide age range and unique attributes of each member have deepened my perspective on life's journey."

Linda has experienced an emotional and spiritual transformation in the years she has been involved in women's spirituality within our group. "I tend to get depressed and anxious, particularly worrying about the state of the world. These sisters share my concerns. But each one is doing something to help impact society, and together we can feel empowered and hopeful. The regular seasonal rituals have enriched my life, made me feel part of a long tradition and a greater whole. The process is also a lot of fun. We play and laugh in ways that are a wonderful contrast to my serious professional lifestyle. It has opened me to be more creative and spontaneous, and to enjoy life more."

Jeanne speaks with an eloquence inspired by the depth of feeling evoked within the feminine energy of the group process. "As an ex-Methodist, starved for ritual, I have savored the joy and peace of the group's rituals. I sit there watching candles flicker and let the words of the ritual pour over me like purifying water. I don't struggle to catch the meaning as much as I simply let the sounds lull me into a sense of peace and belonging. I feel the presence of the circle of women, a gentle energy that connects us each to the other. I feel the pull of sky lifting me upwards, inviting my spirit to soar, and the energy of Earth, holding me fast, keeping me grounded and centered."

Reflecting a moment, Jeanne continues. "One of the major themes within the group is movement, the coming and going, the endless change within unchanging patterns, the leaving behind and embracing the new. I love this. It speaks of hope ever renewed as well as acceptance of what has gone before. The process has helped me bring into conscious awareness my fears or concerns and then to let them go while then asking for what I want in their place. I believe that conscious awareness leads to the kind of change I want in myself and in the world."

Rev. Hazel, who has shared oversight of the Daughters of Gaia with Darlene since its beginning twenty years ago, cherishes her involvement. "The group provides a time set aside for quiet contemplation and a reordering of one's life. It is empowering to be with women having similar life experiences. It helps us to know we are not alone and it spurs our creativity to keep persevering in the quest for positive change. I believe that every human being has been created with a sacred center. In our group, we attempt to touch each other at that center in a spiritual way. If all people tried to do this, I believe our world would be a better place."

Involvement in women's spirituality has had a profound positive impact upon the professional lives of our members. Several of the Daughters of Gaia are trained in the healing arts. As Jeanne relates, "Women's spirituality has affected my work as a body-centered psychotherapist in many ways, particularly my work with women. The concept of a circle of women working collaboratively and peacefully together over a period of years has given me a model for helping my clients. I am able to open them to the idea of new hope and new possibilities for how they might want to be in the world. I give them an alternative to the hierarchical, competitive system in which they have been struggling."

Sue has been a clinical social worker and peace activist for many years. "Our rituals, which are based on the cycle of seasons in the natural world, help to ground me. This is one reason why I haven't burned out already." Darlene, a social worker in private practice, agrees. "The nurturing and healing energy of our group nourishes and enlivens me. I am also reminded that I am not alone. A community of spirit surrounds and supports me in the daily challenges I face with clients." Karen, a nurse practitioner in psychiatry and family therapist, is grateful for the vibrant creativity within women's spirituality. "My own creativity is enhanced, allowing me to think about doing things in different ways. As I think outside the box, I find innovative ways to help my patients."

Joyce, a retired high school English teacher, shares her appreciation of women's spirituality. "I received encouragement in my teaching from the Daughters of Gaia. When my work became routine or I didn't think I was accomplishing more than simply doing my job, I would tell a little story about an interaction at my school during the group sharing. The positive response on the women's faces then and their words later at the feasting always encouraged me to continue on." Violet, a retired clinical psychologist and author, recalls working with a broad spectrum of women in her practice. "Through my experience with women's spirituality, I was a more effective therapist. I gained a deeper level of acceptance, a wider openness, a letting go of value judgments. If there were more spirituality groups like ours that welcome women of different backgrounds and religions, the world could be transformed."

Throughout her career in ministry, Hazel has upheld her focus on women's spirituality. "I believe this is the foundation for building women's self-esteem. We populate over fifty percent of the earth, but in many countries women hold only a second-rate position of value. My work, after teaching the first women's spirituality-based courses in two seminaries and after founding three women's centers, has demonstrated that women are able to achieve more of their created potential when we are in touch with our feminine spirituality. We change how we feel about ourselves, as well as how we develop our space within the world."

Linda is the director of a professional agency as well as a political activist. "In the past few years I have been devoting much of my spare time and energy to activism, since I have a sense of responsibility for *tikkun olam*, or healing the world. This has been difficult and often frustrating. My spirituality group shares my values. The constant support and appreciation have done a great deal to keep me going. A number of our members are doing extraordinary things for the benefit of humanity in the United States, South America, Africa, and Central Asia. I am greatly inspired by these examples and feel their spiritual power. I see the group as a safe place to play, deepen, be ourselves, and nurture each other, knowing that we share this basis of ideals and commitment."

Donna, a retired professional in secondary education, gives an eloquent summation of the contrast between the workplace and our spiritual community. "My experience of the workplace was one of competition, judgmental attitudes, and the possibility of betrayal. The group has gifted me with a contrast, allowing me to question the ethos of the corporate system. Within the group I have found a haven, a womb, a circle of safety in which to grow, as opposed to the hammer and anvil of the everyday work world. I know now that there is a different model to promote within the workplace, a model of acceptance, encouragement, appreciation, and respect."

Women's spirituality is a nourishing dimension of life. We as women can make this spiritual contribution by nourishing ourselves. By being in touch with our sacred center, we are able to reach out and nourish those around us, our families, our communities, our country, and, hopefully, our world. The vibrant celebration of the gift of life moves like electrical energy throughout the universe in a unifying communication. More than fifty percent of the human population is women. If we as women develop our potential and our spiritual strength, we could be part of the healing of the hurts that cause such violence and destruction in our world. May it blessed be!

Women hold the key to remembering.
Let us recall the sacred teachings.
Nurture, heal and strengthen.
Return balance to Self and Earth.
From the writings of Diane and Shuli
We return thanks to our Mother, the Earth,
Who sustains us.

—Iroquois prayer

NOTES

1. Adler, Margot, *Drawing Down the Moon*, 1979, 1986.
2. Starhawk, *The Spiral Dance*, 1979, 1989.
3. Bradley, Marion Zimmer, *The Mists of Avalon*, 1982.
4. Eisler, Riane, *The Chalice and the Blade*, 1995.
5. Thompson, Marjorie, "Celtic Spirituality and the Divine Feminine," 2005.
6. Christ, Carol, "Why Women Need the Goddess," 1978.
7. Daly, Mary, *Beyond God the Father*, 1973; *The Church and the Second Sex*, 1975.
8. Ruether, Rosemary Radford, *New Woman New Earth*, 1975; *Womanguides*, 1985.
9. Doyle, Brendan, *Meditations with Julian of Norwich*, 1983.
10. Prestbo, Darlene, *Where Love Is Needed*, 1991. Prestbo, Darlene, *Sanctum, Transcendence* (poems), 1994; Prestbo, Darlene, photographs, 1997.
11. Stein, Diane, *The Women's Spirituality Book*, 1986.

BIBLIOGRAPHY

Adler, Margot. *Drawing Down the Moon*. Boston: Beacon Press, 1979, 1986.
Bradley, Marion Zimmer. *The Mists of Avalon*. New York: Ballantine Books, 1982.
Christ, Carol. "Why Women Need the Goddess." *Heresies* (1978): 273–287.
Daly, Mary. *Beyond God the Father*. Boston: Boston Press, 1973.
———. *The Church and the Second Sex: With a New Feminist Postchristian Introduction by the Author*. New York: Harper & Row, 1975.
Doyle, Brendan. *Meditations with Julian of Norwich*. Santa Fe, NM: Bear & Company, 1983.
Eisler, Riane. *The Chalice and the Blade*. New York: HarperCollins, 1995.
Prestbo, Darlene. *Where Love Is Needed*, Princeton: Prestbo Press, 1991.
———. Sanctum, Transcendence (poems). *Testament*, Princeton Theological Seminary, Spring 1994, 16–17.
———. Photographs, Fellowship in Prayer, February 1997, 27, 39.
Ruether, Rosemary Radford. *New Woman New Earth*. New York: The Seabury Press, 1975.
———. *Womanguides*. Boston: Beacon Press, 1985.
Starhawk. *The Spiral Dance*. San Francisco: Harper & Row, 1979, 1989.
Stein, Diane. *The Women's Spirituality Book*. St. Paul, MN: Llewellyn, 1986.
Thompson, Marjorie. "Celtic Spirituality and the Divine Feminine." *The Princeton Seminary Bulletin* 26 (2005), 277–293.

Chapter 3

The Saving Grace of Spirituality: Restoring Hope, Vitality, and Creative Joy

Carole A. Rayburn

A clinical, consulting, and research psychologist, I have always regarded myself to be both religious and spiritual. On my maternal parentage, my family was from the Holy Land and from the lineage of the House of David. In that part of the world, all Christians were historically first Hebrews before they converted to Christianity. My maternal ancestors all converted to Christianity 100 years after the crucifixion of Christ. My grandmother, a deeply religious and spiritual woman, was always listening to religious programs, attending church services, and living a truly spiritual life of loving-kindness and caring for others. During my adolescence, my mother considered crossing over her Christian Orthodox denomination and becoming a Roman Catholic nun. Before he became an internal medicine physician and then a psychiatrist, my uncle was a Roman Catholic priest. He later married his operating room nurse, who was the sister of a nun. My father was a German American Lutheran who distanced himself from his church in late childhood, when a close friend was killed while riding his bicycle to church. My father's burning question was, why would God allow such a devout person to be killed? He also thought that the congregation was too replete with hypocrites to please God. Nonetheless, he identified himself all his life as a Lutheran. Perhaps because my grandmother had passed onto her children—my mother being the only one who thought the matter important—that they were descended from the Judges of the House of David in the Bible (my

 name was Sheikh Daod (literally, "Judge of the
d my grandfather's family name was Malik (liter-
ther without exception rented the upstairs of our
e in Washington, DC, to Jewish people. They
.... of our family of four, and one elderly Russian
Jewish couple were like grandparents to my brother and me. In fact,
my mother gave me the middle name of the Jewish woman who was
renting from my parents when I was born. Jewish holidays and customs, as well as the strong and loving Jewish sense of family, were
parts of my background from a very early age, thanks to the warmth
of the Jewish people living in our house.

My mother had a beautiful voice and sang solos in many churches
when I was a child, taking me along to services and acquainting me
with many different denominational settings. Nor were Roman Catholic influences lacking in my life: From age seven to nine, I played with
a Catholic child several days a week. Her parents were very impressed
that I loved to draw pictures of children at prayer. When I was eleven,
I moved to a new neighborhood and started an Upper Room group in
which I and three or four other children would read from the Bible
and study lessons from my Sunday school Upper Room booklets. Naturally, I took the role of the Sunday school teacher! When I was fourteen, I was very serious in my attendance at Sunday school, church,
and choir, being quite shocked to learn years later that some of my
peers had sneaked out of the classes to run to the nearby drugstore for
ice cream sodas. To me, the fun was at the church and not at the soda
shop.

Nonetheless, after high school graduation I planned to major in
music (voice) and fashion design in college, since I had reluctantly, in
the back of my mind, conceded that the ministry was only for men
and that religion was largely patriarchal in a man's world. Later, I
developed a serious interest in psychology and decided to major in
that field, minoring in music and sociology.

My father was a male chauvinist, though he verbalized to others
how proud he was of my accomplishments. My mother and her
mother were feminists throughout their lives, and I modeled my life after them and their philosophical stances. I tended to measure what
was good and true in life by what equal opportunities were provided
for both males *and* females. When I became a United Methodist, the
church's greater gender equality had been one of the shibboleths by
which I decided that that denomination was my home.

During my graduate college years, I met the man who was to
become my husband. Though both of us were Methodists, we met at a
Presbyterian young-adults group. He was a very religious and spiritual
person and a feminist man. Ronnie had a very high functioning mother
and an open-minded father, both of his parents being religious and

spiritual people. In fact, his father was a Methodist church elder, his mother taught Sunday school, and his uncle was a circuit-riding Baptist minister. It was Ronnie who urged me to continue my education to get a doctorate in psychology.

Before he finished his doctorate in electrical-electronic engineering and before I graduated with my psychology doctorate, Ronnie contracted cancer and died in less than two years. Had he lived, he wanted to become a minister. His endearing and unforgettable words to me were, "I guess, after all, you are my major accomplishment."

Though deeply saddened by my loss of Ronnie, I somehow managed to survive and to function in private practice, as well as on a District of Columbia children's center staff, working with adjudicated juvenile delinquents and as a consultant to three Montessori schools. In several instances, my patients wanted to discuss theological/psychological issues pertaining to their problems. Though I always referred them to the staff pastoral counselor, they also wanted to talk to me about these issues. This touched off my earlier interest in religious and spiritual work with others. I mentioned this to a colleague, and she said that if I still sensed a calling to ministry, I should consider answering it. After much prayer about this, I enrolled in a local Methodist seminary to take a few classes. After Ronnie's death, I had joined the Seventh-day Adventist Church, seeing many of the beliefs in that setting as closer to scripture. The problem was that, with the more orthodox tenets, there were serious gender discrimination biases that I had not encountered in the Methodist Church. This was to become a terrible stumbling block for me and for other religious egalitarian women and men. As a feminist and as a spiritual person whose core belief was that being loving and caring to all living creatures—females as well as males, young and old, all ethnicities—and to the environment as a whole, equal opportunities for self-expression and participation at all levels of ecclesia would be vital to optimal functioning in God's world.

When I entered seminary, having left high-status employment and professional organizational supports, I was shocked to learn, as only one of four women in seminary, just what secondary citizenship in a man's world meant. I had not joined the National Organization for Women before leaving Maryland for the seminary in Michigan, but becoming a NOW member and calling feminist friends in Maryland frequently were the only means of retaining a balanced gender stance, as well as overall sanity. In classes in which at least twice a day I and the few other women were collectively addressed as "men" and "brothers," I was criticized for making top grades on tests and graduating magna cum laude. This was regarded as taking such kudos away from some better-deserving male seminarian. In my much-fought-for field-evangelism practicum (at that time, I think I was the only woman who was finally allowed to participate with male seminarians in this way), one of the male seminarians compared me to Judas, explaining that I was "the different one." What he actually meant was that I lacked the necessary male appendages that lent the reasoning to connecting "testimony" and "testament" to "testicle" and "seminary" and "seminal" to "semen" or "seed bed."

I gave sermons in the Talk To God chapel presentations, largely an African American activity, and I became active in the Black Students Association of Seminary and its treasurer. I was interviewed by church recruiters only once after I had asked why I previously had not been given interview opportunities. The answer was simple: Photos of seminarians in a booklet revealed that I was a woman and not a man, cause to pass over me for any church position. The only African American minister on the huge campus church personally came to see me with the information that he had recommended me for a campus ministry position, saying "she is certainly the most qualified person we could ever have, being a PhD in psychology and in her last year of seminary." The three other ministers replied, "Are you crazy? She is a woman!" That apparently closed any further discussion. He wanted me to know how bad the situation was for women. This minister was not only religious but spiritual, a caring and inclusive leader and guide. Unfortunately, such a combination did not extend to the other leaders of that church community.

As though my religious support system from the seminary staff was not slipping badly enough, I found that I was not being offered a position on a church staff, as I had been told would be available when I graduated. SDAs, Seventh-Day Adventists, concerning women in clerical positions, have what Latter-day Saints (Mormons) would term "double-speak": Women on church staffs are called "associates in pastoral care" rather than "ministers" and do not have the same opportunities for advancement or the same remuneration as do their male peers. A high church official, ironically one who spoke in favor of my going to seminary, later said that he thought that I was going to seminary to become a better psychologist (though I was already a PhD in psychology long before I arrived at seminary, and from the outset of being at seminary, I was invited to guest lecture in pastoral counseling classes). It was later found out that he had written a letter to seminary staff saying that I was "a crusader who would only bring the poor, Black, and 'needy' into the large and affluent White church in Maryland." It was also held against me that I was part of the Black Students Association of Seminary (BSAS), presumably less than acceptable for Caucasians—particularly Caucasian women. In contrast, during Black History Week when a distinguished African American SDA minister had been invited to guest-speak at the university and a bomb threat had been made to ward off his message, I urged the BSAS to send letters of protest far and wide. One member suggested that I write the letter, but another member said that such a letter should come from a Black member. The first member, earnestly looking at me, said, "Carole, aren't you Black?" This filled my heart with sheer joy, at the thought of such total color-blindness and acceptance of one human being by another, transcending racial and ethnic boundaries. Truly, this was spirituality at its finest and working at its zenith, the ultimate in caring for others spiritually!

Applying for a pastoral position in the SDA church that I had been led to believe would hire me when I finished seminary, I was flatly denied such employment. No reason was given, but digging by sympathetic high church officials (African American men) and a seminary professor (a Caucasian man) found that the letter warning that "she is a crusader who would only bring the poor, Black, and needy into the church," and also noting that I was even a member of the BSAS, hurled the most damaging blow at me.

Sensing a tremendous need to question ethnic minority and gender discrimination, particularly in a setting that is supposedly a caring, loving, kind, and Godly one, I sought redress from the internal channels of the church hierarchy. When none was forthcoming, and after long, prayerful, and painful deliberation, I sought legal redress on behalf of women and ethnic minorities. Unfortunately, Title VII of the Annotated Legal Code concerning church relationships and discrimination forbade such complaints "between a church and its minister." While women were not actually "ministers" within that denomination, the U.S. Supreme Court declared me a minister and thus got out of deciding a case pitting gender and racial discrimination on one side and the freedom of religion on the other. Those in clerical positions may be freely discriminated against by the religious establishment and have no recourse to make a complaint.

Picking myself up and dusting myself off from the pain of rejection and abandonment, I never laid such bad behavior at the feet of God but aimed it squarely on the doorstep of the church. Reconnecting with psychological organizations, I was elected president of my state psychological association and several area ones. I became very active in my state NOW chapter. I was a consultant for churches, ministers, priests, and was even invited to preach and participate in the laying on of hands in a healing and blessing service at the predominantly African American SDA churches of a seminary friend of mine.

Nonetheless, the experience that I had suffered while in seminary and the aftermath left scars on my psyche. I found it compelling to write about my experiences, both as a therapeutic healing for me and for any others who would enter seminary or be most likely to suffer from discrimination within ecclesia. It simply had to be documented. Perhaps because I had such an egalitarian, religious, and spiritual

ecclesia.
spirituality
the heart of
religion.

...dmother, I looked for and actually expected to find a ...ng, egalitarian atmosphere in any religious and spirit- ... As long as I associated the spiritual as being limited ...ious, however, I was to be disappointed and disen- ...that it was not only unwise but inaccurate to equate ...ny church leaders and officials with the sanctified, the ...l, or the all-inclusive side of loving-kindness or caring for others.

Addressing my strong frustration with my church's response to women in ministerial roles, I formulated with Lee Richmond the *Religion and Stress Questionnaire* (RSQ).[1] Then I developed the *Religious Occupations and Stress* (ROS)[2, 3] inventory with psychology co-researchers Lee Richmond and Janice Birk (a former Roman Catholic nun).

The ROS was designed to study the stress in seminarians, nuns, brothers, and clergy, and it took into account for the first time the stress from gender discrimination.[4] The answers that I received from the ROS studies enhanced my feelings of the spiritual and gave me a very freeing and affirmative sense of being: Sometimes ecclesiastical settings or traditions (if not the tenets or doctrines) fail to be truly inclusive of girls, women, and ethnic minorities. Since I had a strong and open-minded model of womankind and personhood from my mother and grandmother, and since I was born and raised in Washington, DC, with Jewish as well as Christian and African American and American Indian as well as Euro American neighbors, such exclusionary behavior at seminary and within my religious denomination did not sit well. I had been drawn to my denomination by the close adherence of the doctrine to biblical scripture. Only later was I truly to awaken to the traditions that disenfranchised women and minorities in some significant ways. All in all, it did not seem right and it certainly did not seem spiritual or seemly for any God-fearing Christian establishment. Much corrective soul work would need to be done before true spirituality formed the core and the heart of the religious establishment.

In any remedial steps to bring ecclesia back to its finest and truest purpose, it had to be recognized that spirituality is the heart and the very essence of the teachings of religion, the seeking of truth and goodness, the transcendence, the caring for others, and the valuing of cooperation, peacefulness, and forgiveness (of self and others for imperfections and faults) put into action. Words without the accompanying loving-kindness and caring behavior are hollow and meaningless. In I Corinthians 13:1, Paul spoke of the emptiness of words when they were not accompanied by loving actions: "If I speak in the tongues of men and of angels but I have not love, I am only a resounding gong or a clanging cymbal." I fervently hold onto my Christian faith, but I want to put substance into the words. Otherwise our faith is really like the dry bones spoken of in Ezekiel 37:1–4, desperately needing the blood of life to move to action and shout with joy and caring for others as well as for oneself.

Two very important role models for spirituality, particularly women's spirituality, were Sojourner Truth (Isabella Van Wagenen) and Alice Paul. Sojourner Truth, the vibrant African American woman, was a devoutly spiritual preacher, abolitionist, and freedom fighter who stood up to even Frederick Douglass in demanding equality for women and recognition of the vital roles and positions of women.[5–7] Alice Paul, the Quaker woman who saw resistance to tyranny as obedience to God, had a fierce tenacity that brought her through physical and psychological suffering, starvation, and imprisonment to win for women the right to vote (through the passage of the Nineteenth Amendment of the Constitution of the United States. Further, Paul wrote, introduced, and fought for the passage of the Equal Rights Amendment (ERA), which stated that "equality of rights under the law shall not be denied or abridged by the United States or by any State on account of sex." She added equal gender rights to Title VII of the Civil Rights Act of 1964 that protected the rights of all Americans, without regard to race or color.[8, 9] Both of these women were aflame with spirituality, seeking goodness and truth, caring for others, being led by the transcendent spirit that influences advocacy on behalf of others, and valuing an end result of cooperation and peace with the forgiving attitude that comes after conciliation. They represent the epitome of women's spirituality, and what Lillian Comas-Díaz and I have termed "compassionate illuminate," reflecting fervent caring for the best for others and radiating with spiritual enlightenment.[10]

While still in seminary, I was invited to Washington, DC, to march with the Roman Catholic Quixote Center and to picket the visit of Pope John Paul II on behalf of inclusion of women to officiate in the Lord's Supper and at the Last Rites. I was the only non-Catholic protesting, with my picket sign of Galatians 3:28, "... in Christ there is no male or female, all are one in Christ Jesus." Later I learned that one of my psychology colleagues from New York, a staunch Roman Catholic and an officer of the American Psychological Association's (APA) Division of the Psychology of Religion, announced that I was "a dangerous subversive." I laughed and thought to myself, "I and Che Guevara!" In the early 1980s, when the Equal Rights Amendment (ERA) was failing to achieve the vote in the remaining three states for passage throughout the country, I was part of a group of women going in teams of two, like Mormon missionaries, to Utah, one of the hold-out states, to bring the ERA to the forefront of the mostly Mormon population. Unfortunately, the ERA did not get the required number of states to ratify it. Also while I was in seminary, a fifth-generation Mormon, Sonia Johnson, who had strongly spoken out in her church in favor of the ERA and who picketed my SDA church when my court case was proceeding, spoke before the APA in 1979 in a symposium about women's rights. She presented a paper, "Patriarchal Panic." Although fewer than fifty people attended that session, the fact that she was seen as "taking the ERA to the world" in defiance of her church's position on equal rights was cause to excommunicate her from the Mormon Church.[11]

Using my spirituality, intuition, and creativity, I set about designing several new inventories that would connect to spirituality and concern for others.

With Drs. Birk and Richmond, I developed the *State-Trait Morality Inventory* (STMI),[12–14] convinced that much of the world needed serious shoring up of more honest approaches to decision-making in matters of right versus wrong. When Dr. Richmond, then president of the 60,000-member American Counseling Association (ACA), suggested that the APA's Division on the Psychology of Religion look at the differences between religiousness and spirituality (something about which the ACA had long been aware[15]), hesitant and doubting members reluctantly agreed to put together a symposium on the issue. I was the only one who spoke for the possibility that spirituality could exist outside religion as well as within it.[16] Some male psychologists of religion quite reluctantly conceded that, though religion and spirituality in rare instances might be different, they strongly questioned whether *mature* spirituality could exist outside religion. From such discussions and ponderings came the development of the *Inventory on Religiousness* (IR)[17, 18] and the *Inventory on Spirituality* (IS).[19, 20] Now I was feeling even more female-freeing affirmation of spirituality. The studies affirmed that women in particular saw themselves as more spiritual than religious, though many women saw themselves as both (men often identified first with being religious and only secondly with being spiritual). The interest in these findings on gender, spirituality, and religiousness and in women's spirituality had been growing.[21–25]

One of the men, an African American who attended seminary with me, had been a strong supporter of my ministerial outreach. He invited me several times to his African American churches in Texas and Louisiana to serve as a psychotherapist, consultant, and even preacher. He was very open-minded about women in ministry, though the church as a denomination was not. He and I witnessed the look of joy on the faces of especially the women in the congregation when their needs and concerns were addressed with love and understanding. This was spirituality at work, and I felt the caring going between the women and the African American congregants and me. The experience was joyful, nurturing, healing, and a fervent thing of beauty, delight, and love. This was without question what I had sensed was lacking in the words without action and the doctrines without sufficient loving-kindness for all. When spirituality is an essential part of relationships, there is a desire to share good experiences and a modeling of passing on that fervor to others and to see them, in turn, pass that onto others. This is the love and caring that can go around the world, the freedom for dancing in the streets, the singing for joy and gladness, and the passing on of all the good and true that we can find in life. It is looking at possibilities and seeing the best potentialities in others and doing the most to enhance their traversing from the beginnings to the highest levels of self-actualizing they can attain. It is about wanting the best, the good, and the most beautifully delightful joy and truth of existence, not only for oneself but for others.

Looking at spirituality and its impact on everyday life, I and my co-researchers developed the *Organizational Relationships Survey* (ORS)[26]; *Inventory on the Supreme and Work* (ISAW)[27]; *Sports, Exercise, Leadership, Friendship* (SELF)[28]; the *Life Choices Inventory* (LCI)[29]; *Body Awareness and Sensitivity to Intimacy Comfort Scale* (BASICS)[30]; *Inventory on Well-Being* (IWB)[31]; the *Peace Inventory* (PI)[32, 33]; the *Children's and Adolescents' Peace Inventory* (CAPI)[34]; *Traumatic Experiences and Children's and Adolescents' Health* (TEACH)[35]; and *Health and Traumatic Experiences in Adults* (HTEA).[36]

Being a lover of nature and a person curious about how things came into being and continued to interact, I (with Lee Richmond) proposed a new field and discipline: theobiology, the interfacing of theology, religion, and spirituality with biology and all the other sciences.[37–39] This was an effort to find mutually beneficial and insightful information from science about the religious and spiritual and vice versa. In a spiritual sense of the world, to exclude science or the spiritual from the perceptions of life, environment, and being seemed unnecessarily lopsided. As a psychologist and also a human being, I saw interest in the scientific as an outgrowth of caring for others (not just an ingrown and self-satisfying answer to important questions concerning life and its evolving processes).

To me, caring for others (people, animals, plants, the environment, and indeed the universe itself) is an intrinsic and germane part of spirituality. So is transcendence of some kind, seeing an influence on oneself as coming from something outside the self. Certainly, seeking goodness and truth—an essential part of spirituality—is also a part of scientific quest. In addition, valuing peace, cooperation, and forgiveness are vital parts of spirituality.[40] These make us more human.

As one who holds spiritual fervor in high regard, I have also maintained a strong respect for creativity and intuition. In my view, being spiritual helps to open people to the possibility of tapping into our unconscious, immediate, and undeliberated thoughts and to trust more in placing confidence in these mystical intrusions into more planned and rational cognition. Intuition, a phenomenon about which I know

sthand because I am highly intuitive, involves urgent ideas ursting forth, fully formed and meaningfully connected, like e or Neptune's daughter emerging in complete adult form ; through growing pains of slow, piece-by-piece develop- ituition not as a "feeling" in the sense of an emotion but n-delayed bringing together in a sheer rapid manner related factors in a rather mystical, mysterious fashion. When we ue spirit moves us," I think that we are expressing being moved by our intuition.

I see spirituality as highly connected to creativity, with the openness to the new, different, and original playing an important part. Spirituality awakens our heightened sensing of awareness of ourselves, others, and our world, and of social responsibility. Involving all of our being, spirituality touches our emotions, intellect, intuition, hopes, dreams, visions, needs, desires, and physical senses. It enables us to deconstruct or take apart what we see to better understand it, and then to reconstruct it to more fully comprehend the entire picture.

I was so curious about the creative personality and intuition, in fact, that I developed the *Creative Personality Inventory* (CPI)[41] and the *Intuition Inventory* (II).[42] For me, the freeing and affirmative force of spirituality has led me to seek answers to puzzling questions, and I am always joyous in the process of the detective work involved in tracking down answers to queries. Exploring creativity and spirituality is like unwrapping a beautiful package at a birthday party or holiday event; part of the joy of discovery is in peeling away the many layers of life's unfolding petals and inhaling the wondrous scents of the vibrant and challenging underpinnings that await us.

From early childhood, I grew up around neighborhood dogs and cats. At times I was fortunate enough to have an animal companion of my own. Often both my brother and I had our own cats, one the happy owner of the mother cat and the other of her kitten. I fully agree with Susan Chernak McElroy[43] in her book, *Animals As Teachers and Healers*, that the lessons in spirituality and becoming better humans that we learn from animals are invaluable. Those who deny such priceless teaching from animals and who choose to regard animals as objects, particularly unfeeling and senseless objects rather than as subjects in their own right, are divesting themselves of some of the world's greatest and most selfless teachers. People would do well imitating the ways of many animals and learning to be more human by doing so.

In *Animal Grace: Entering a Spiritual Relationship with Our Fellow Creatures*, Mary Lou Randour reminds us how very important it is to reconnect with the spiritual, overcoming barriers to connectedness and dissolving boundaries to gain better togetherness. Such awareness happens in the context of relationships with other creatures and aligns us with the "sacredness of creation." There is a continuity of creation, of life in its many and diverse forms—people, animals, plants, and environments. Recognizing such unity and continuity of life lessens the feelings of aloneness or anomie that we might otherwise experience. Many studies have been done that raise questions about the ability of animals to think and/or reason,[44-46] feel, and even have extrasensory perception and perhaps to transcend the language barriers between humans and other creatures in communicating needs, desires, pleasures, mutual cooperation, and caring for others.

There is no doubt in my mind that animals have brought me closer to better appreciating and understanding nature, myself, and others. Though we do not fully understand what animals are capable of, I think that the true essence of spirituality lies within animals as well as humans. Studies of visiting animals in nursing homes and in children's hospitals have proven the comforting results of merely stroking a cat or dog. This is not merely a sensual tactual act but some sort of mutual interaction and satisfaction between the animal and the human that translates to caring for others. Otherwise, we could just as well be stroking a block of wood with fur on it. Perhaps refusing to consider the sentience of animals and the possibility that many animals are similar to humans in intellect and feelings makes it easier for us to treat them as laboratory experiments. Such attitudes, though, may drastically damage our humanity and our view of the unity and continuity of life and creation.

The rather recent recognition (1998) of dark energy on physical cosmology presents a puzzling element in not only scientific but also religious and spiritual circles. Originally seen as a form of energy permeating all space and tending to increase the rate of expansion of the universe, dark energy is now taken quite seriously and soberly by astrophysicists and other scientists and observers of nature. It is a mysterious force not fully understood, but which causes the universe to fly apart or to be accelerated. Chaikin[47] noted that astronomers are still clueless about galaxies being pulled apart by some mysterious force. When supernova studies suggested that some mysterious force was acting against the pull of gravity and causing galaxies to fly away from each other at great speeds, many scientists had to admit that perhaps two-thirds of all scientific knowledge had joined the ranks of the unknown. Thinking had to be modified in light of the discovery of dark energy. Is this the intrusion of the spiritual, including the transcendent, on the creation and meaning of life? Is this theobiology at its most relevant? Is this the harbinger of a call to acknowledge a life and meaning beyond that which we have dealt with confidently and perhaps in too knowing all ways in which we have staked our total "faith"? Is there indeed something beyond what we know or at least *think* we know? The openness that allows us to be more spiritual also opens us to the possibilities to envision and deal with the concept and reality of a dark energy, defining this however we may.

I think that all humans have a built-in potential for spirituality, intuition, and creativity. How we choose to use these innate resources is an individual matter. In my work as a psychotherapist, I use the knowledge I have attained from researching spiritual issues involved in personality and gender differences to better recognize, appreciate, and understand people with whom I work. My study of spirituality, religiousness, clergy stress, state-trait morality, creative personality, and intuition, which have flowed from my own spirituality, has led me to see the need for therapists and others to listen intuitively, recognize gender differences in all of these matters, and learn how to develop the means to appreciate these distinctions while empowering both female and male clients to transcend these differences in order to realize their best potential in self-actualization.[48, 49]

As a psychotherapist, I must be more open to what enables others to be more comfortable with me and more willing to forgive myself and others for being imperfect. While confrontation of clients may be necessary to challenge flawed thinking and dysfunctional feelings, an overall reaching for cooperation and an attitude of peacefulness would be the optimal goal in the therapeutic relationship and for interpersonal exchanges in general.

SPIRITUALITY BROUGHT INTO CLINICAL WORK

Julie is an intellectually superior fifteen-year-old Caucasian European American. She is attractive but quite thin. She was rather defiantly proud of her atheistic stance and denounced religion at every opportunity while attending an Anglican parochial school. The only child after her parents had lost a child two years before her birth, she was the center of her parents' lives, especially that of her mother. An introvert, Julie preferred to relate only occasionally to a schoolmate. Most of the time, she chose to isolate herself in her room and write poetry and play her flute. Mostly she wrote about dying and death, only some of which was for shock value. A perfectionist and anxious and depressed, Julie had been medicated by her psychiatrist with antipsychotic drugs to the point that she was quite sleepy much of the time. When she felt most angry, anxious, and depressed, Julie pulled her hair and cut herself, mainly on her arms. Her parents, a highly perfectionist and anxious mother and a somewhat more easygoing father, were understandably worried about her self-destructive tendencies. Julie enjoyed both the attention she received due to her behavior and the control she had over others because of it. At the same time, she rebelled against being monitored by her parents and the school staff whenever they discussed her cutting and avoidance of others. Her academic performance began to suffer, and she became worried about failing. An idealistic young woman, she was deeply concerned with protecting the environment. This strongest conviction overrode her pre-occupation with thoughts of destruction, dying, and death.

Convinced that she really did not matter to others and could make no true, meaningful, and lasting contributions to life, Julie doubted the existence of any higher power and any transcendent influence on her life. Because she was so bright, idealistic, and environmentally concerned, I was able to get a foothold into her reasoning by focusing on her search for goodness and truth (Whether relative or absolute, there were certainly truths and good realities in the world of all individuals that were awaiting discovery, and possibly creative and intuitive thinking.) If she chose to maintain her self-destructive, highly defensive behavior and themes of dying and death, she could possibly cut herself off from realizing her potential and being a voice for environmental protection. Illness and death would guarantee an opting out of viable interactions with others and the world to make a difference. In essence, her exerting such negative control on her own life would do to her what her worst enemies could not do—to destroy her desires and actions to bring about some amelioration in the world. She would be tying her hands—and arms—quite literally—from being a caring person toward herself and others. Failing to get enough rest and sleep and to eat more healthfully would not be caring for herself either. She valued being peaceful already, but emotionally punished herself for not being perfect. The need to forgive both herself and others for being imperfect was stressed. Adamantly holding onto her atheism and her rejection of God or any other transcendent higher power, she did manage to accept being spiritual but not religious. She was all right with seeing nature itself as the transcendent influence in her life. It was in this way that she was able to connect to a spiritual psychotherapist, one who cared for others, valued cooperation, forgiveness, and peacefulness, sought goodness and truth, and was influenced by transcendent connections outside herself (whether this was God, a creator, nature, a guru, a trusted guide, or some other valued outside influence). She was comfortable and accepting of my being spiritual, as long as she knew that I would respect her right to be an atheist and not attempt to criticize her or to proselytize. She could even identify herself as being spiritual, in the way that I defined spirituality for her (independent of religion). The fact that I as her therapist gave her very positive messages about herself but did not demand of her any perfect performances eventually helped bring about changes in her behavior and thinking. She started eating better and getting more much-needed rest and being less angered by her mother's smothering behavior. Sessions with the mother and recommendations that her mother be in therapy herself also brought about much better interrelationships between mother and daughter. Julie was able to get her grades back on course and establish a few more positive relationships with her peers, both female and male. The hair pulling and cutting stopped once she truly forgave herself for both her real and imagined flaws and once she saw herself as being a force for positive actions in life, the world, and its inhabitants. She was able to identify with being a spiritual person and to derive joy in this newly recognized persona.

Spirituality is the vibrant force at the core of most people's being. It is the female—as well as the male—freeing affirmative force. Contrasted with religiousness with its doctrinal tenets and tests of obedience, spirituality is the governor or heart that runs the structure of the religious leaning or the general teaching that controls one's life. Even in the absence of religiousness, spirituality is the source of passion and enlightenment that causes the glow, the joy, the loving-kindness to permeate from us to others and to flow from that which has transcended our being and passes to other beings. It is the spirit and our spiritual nature that gives us life and joy in being alive!

NOTES

1. Rayburn and Richmond, *Religion and Stress Questionnaire*, 1982.
2. Rayburn and Richmond, *Religious Occupations and Stress*, 1986.
3. Rayburn, and Birk, *Religious Occupations and Stress*, 1993, 1996.
4. Rayburn, *Religious Occupations and Stress Questionnaire: Stress in Clergy*, 1996.
5. Butler, 2003.
6. Mabee and Newhouse, 1995.
7. McKissack and McKissack, 1995.
8. Fry, 1976.
9. Rayburn, "Alice Paul," 2007.
10. Rayburn, "Compassionate Illuminate," 2008.
11. Johnson, Sonia, 1981.
12. Rayburn, Birk, and Richmond, *State-Trait Morality Inventory*, 1987.
13. Rayburn, Birk, and Richmond, *Development of the State-Trait Morality Inventory*, 1991.
14. Birk, Rayburn, and Richmond, *Religious Occupations and Stress (ROS); Instrument Development*, 2001.
15. Richmond, 2004.
16. Rayburn, "Religion and spirituality: Can one exist independently of the other?" 1996.
17. Rayburn, *Inventory on Religiousness*, 1997.
18. Rayburn and Richmond, *Inventory on Religiousness*, 2004.
19. Rayburn and Richmond, *Inventory on Spirituality*, 1996.
20. Goetz, 1998.
21. Bochini, 1992.
22. Gorman, 1994.
23. Osman and Rayburn, 2000.
24. Randour, "Changing of the Gods," 2000.
25. Randour, *Animal Grace*, 2000.
26. Rayburn and Richmond, *Organizational Relationships Survey*, 1987.

27. Rayburn and Richmond, *Inventory on the Supreme and Work*, 1999.

28. Rayburn and Richmond, *Sports, Exercise, Leadership, Friendship*, 1997.

29. Rayburn, Hansen, Siderits, Burson, and Richmond, 1999, 2004.

30. Rayburn and Richmond, *Body Awareness and Sensitivity to Intimacy Comfort Scale*, 1993, 1996, 1999, 2003.

31. Rayburn and Richmond, *Inventory on Well-Being*, 2004, 2006.

32. Rayburn, Handwerker, and Richmond, *Peace Inventory*, 1999.

33. Rayburn and Osman, "Women, Peace, and Spirituality," 1999.

34. Rayburn, Handwerker, and Richmond, *Children's and Adolescents' Peace Inventory*, 1999.

35. Rayburn and Richmond, *Traumatic Experiences in Children's and Adolescents' Health (TEACH)*.

36. Rayburn and Richmond, *Health and Traumatic Experiences in Adults (HTEA)*.

37. Rayburn and Richmond, "Theobiology: Attempting to Understand God and Ourselves," 2005.

38. Rayburn, "Theobiology, Spirituality, Religiousness, and the Wizard of Oz," 2000.

39. Rayburn, "Theobiology, Spirituality, Religiousness, and the Wizard of Oz," 2001.

40. Rayburn and Richmond, "Woman, whither goest thou?," 2002.

41. Rayburn, *The Creative Personality Inventory*, 2005, 2006.

42. Rayburn, *Intuition Inventory*, 2005, 2006.

43. McElroy, 1998.

44. Carey, 2007.

45. Johnson, George, 2007.

46. Pennisi, 2007.

47. Chaikin, 2002.

48. Rayburn, "Morality, Spirituality, Religion, Gender, and Stress," 1992.

49. Rayburn, "Religion, Spirituality, and Health," 2004.

BIBLIOGRAPHY

Birk, Janice M., Carole A. Rayburn, and Lee Richmond. "Religious Occupations and Stress Questionnaire (ROS): Instrument Development." *Counseling and Values* 45 (2) (2001): 136–144.

Bochini, Mary Trinitas. "Conflicts between psyche and spirit." Symposium, Discovering and Hearing Women in the Psychology of Religion Dialogue. Carole A. Rayburn, chair. American Psychological Association, Washington, DC (8/15/92).

Butler, Mary G. *Sojourner Truth: From Slave to Activist for Freedom*. New York: Rosen Publishing Group, 2003.

Carey, Benedict. "Brainy Parrot Dies, Emotive to the End." *New York Times*, 9/11/07, A21.

Chaikin, Andrew. "Dark Energy: Astronomers Still 'Clueless' about Mystery Force Pushing Galaxies Apart." *Science Tuesday* (1/16/2002).

Fry, Amelia R. "The Interviewer's Impression of Alice Paul." Online Archive of California, Conversations with Alice Paul: Woman Suffrage and the

Equal Rights Amendment, 1976: Woman Suffrage and the Equal Rights Amendment, 1976. http://texts.cdlib.org/dynaxml/servlet/dynaXML?do cId=kt6f59n89c&doc.view=entirtee.text (accessed August 13, 2004).

Goetz, Donna J. "Gender and the Inventory on Religiousness and the Inventory on Spirituality." Symposium, Women and the Psychology of Religion—Healing through Change." Carole A. Rayburn, chair. American Psychological Association, San Francisco (8/16/98).

Gorman, Mary Margaret. "Psychology of Religion and Feminist Spirituality." Symposium, Women Making a Difference in the Psychology of Religion. Carole A. Rayburn, chair. American Psychological Association, Los Angeles, CA (8/12/94).

Johnson, George. "Alex wanted a cracker, but did he *want* one?" *New York Times*, 9/16/2007, WK1, 4.

Johnson, Sonia. *From Housewife to Heretic: One Woman's Struggle for Equal Right and Her Excommunication from the Mormon Church*. Garden City, NY: Doubleday, 1981.

Mabee, Carleton., and Susan Mabee Newhouse. *Sojourner Truth: Slave, Prophet, Legend*. New York: New York University Press, 1995.

McElroy, Susan Chernak. *Animals as Teachers and Healers*. New York: Ballentine Books, 1998.

McKissack, Pat, and Frederick McLissack Jr. *Sojourner Truth: Ain't I a Woman?* New York: New York Scholastic Press, 1992.

Osman, Suzanne, and Carole A. Rayburn. "Life Choices, Religiousness, and Spirituality in Third-Millennium Women." Symposium, Third-Millennium Women and Spirituality—Addressing the Wounds of Traditionalism. Carole A. Rayburn, chair. American Psychological Association, Washington, DC (8/5/2000).

Pennisi, Elizabeth. "Primates Demonstrate Humanlike Reasoning." *Science* 317, no. 5843 (September 2007): 1308.

Randour, Mary Lou. "Changing of the Gods: Emergence of the Women's Spirituality Movement." Symposium, Third-Millennium Women and Spirituality—Addressing the Wounds of Traditionalism. Carole A. Rayburn, chair. American Psychological Association, Washington, DC (8/5/2000).

———. *Animal Grace: Entering a Spiritual Relationship with Our Fellow Creatures*. Novato, CA: New World Library, 2000.

Rayburn, Carole A. "Morality, Spirituality, Religion, Gender, and Stress: Unraveling the Puzzles." New Fellows Address, Div. 36. Invited Address. American Psychological Association, Washington, DC, 1992.

———. "Religion and Spirituality: Can One Exist Independently of the Other?" Symposium, What Is the Difference between Religion and Spirituality? Kenneth I. Pargament, chair. American Psychological Association, Toronto, Canada (8/11/96).

———. "Religious Occupations and Stress Questionnaire: Stress in Clergy." Symposium, Measuring Intimacy, Leadership, Morality, Faith, and Stress, Carole A. Rayburn, chair. American Psychological Association, Toronto, Canada (8/12/96).

———. *Inventory on Religiousness*. Washington, DC: U.S. Copyright Office, 1997.

———. "Theobiology, Spirituality, Religiousness, and the Wizard of Oz." Invited Address: Wm. C. Bier Award, Div. 36. American Psychological Association, Washington, DC (8/5/2000).

———. "Theobiology, Spirituality, Religiousness, and the Wizard of Oz." *Psychology of Religion Newsletter* Div. 36 26 (1) (2001): 1–11.

———. "Religion, Spirituality, and Health." *American Psychologist* 59 (1) (2004): 52–53.

———. *The Creative Personality Inventory (CPI)*. Washington, DC: U.S. Copyright Office, 2005, 2006.

———. *Intuition Inventory (II)*. Washington, DC: U.S. Copyright Office, 2005, 2006.

———. "Alice Paul: Constitutional Amendment Mover and ERA Author." In Eileen A. Gavin, Aphrodite Clamar, and Mary Anne Siderits, eds. *Women of Vision: Their Psychology, Circumstances, and Success*. New York: Springer Publishing, 2007, 61–78.

———. "Compassionate Illuminate: Spirituality's Caring for Others, Seeking Goodness and Truth, Peacefulness, and That 'T' Word—Transcendence." *Child and Family Behavior Therapy* 30 (2008).

Rayburn, Carole A., Janice M. Birk, and Lee J. Richmond. *State-Trait Morality Inventory*. Washington, DC: U.S. Copyright Office, 1987.

———. "Development of the State-Trait Morality Inventory." Poster Session. American Psychological Association, San Francisco (8/18/91).

Rayburn, Carole A., L. Sunny Hansen, Mary Anne Siderits, Phyllis Burson, and Lee J. Richmond. *Life Choices Inventory (LCI)*. Washington, DC: U.S. Copyright Office, 1999, 2004.

Rayburn, Carole A., and Lee J. Richmond. *Body Awareness and Sensitivity to Intimacy Comfort Scale (BASICS)*. Washington, DC: U.S. Copyright Office, 1993, 1996, 1999, 2003.

———. *Religion and Stress Questionnaire*. Washington, DC: U.S. Copyright Office, 1982.

———. *Religious Occupations and Stress Questionnaire*. Washington, DC: U.S. Copyright Office, 1986.

———. *Organizational Relationships Survey*. Washington, DC: U.S. Copyright Office, 1987.

———. *Inventory on Religiousness*. Washington DC: U.S. Copyright Office, 2004.

———. *Inventory on Spirituality*. Washington, DC: U.S. Copyright Office, 1996.

———. *Sports, Exercise, Leadership, Friendship*. Washington, DC: U.S. Copyright Office, 1997.

———. "Theobiology: Attempting to Understand God and Ourselves." *Journal of Religion and Health* 37 (4) (1998): 345–356.

———. *Inventory on the Supreme and Work*. Washington, DC: U.S. Copyright Office, 1999.

———. "Women, Whither Goest Thou? To Chart New Courses in Religiousness and Spirituality and to Define Ourselves!" In Lynn. H. Collins, Michelle R. Dunlap, and Joan C. Chrisler, eds. *Charting a New Course for Feminist Psychology*. Westport, CT: Praeger, 2002, 167–189.

———. *Inventory on Well-Being (IWB)*. Washington, DC: U.S. Copyright Office, 2004, 2006.

———. *Traumatic Experiences Children's and Adolescents' Health (TEACH)*. Washington, DC: U.S. Copyright Office, 2005.

———. *Health and Traumatic Experiences in Adults (HTEA)*. Washington, DC: U.S. Copyright Office, 2005.

Rayburn, Carole A., Lee J. Richmond, and Janice M. Birk. *Religious Occupations and Stress*. Washington, DC: U.S. Copyright Office, 1993, 1996.

Rayburn, Carole A., Steven Handwerker, and Lee J. Richmond. *Children's and Adolescents' Peace Inventory (CAPI)*. Washington, DC: U.S. Copyright Office, 1999.

———. *Peace Inventory*. Washington, DC: U.S. Copyright Office, 1999.

Rayburn, Carole A., and Suzanne Osman. "Women, Peace, and Spirituality: Implication for International Peacework." Symposium, Peace, and Spirituality—Exploring the Multidimensional Relationship in International Peacework." American Psychological Association, Boston, MA, 1999.

Richmond, Lee J. "Religion, Spirituality, and Health: A Topic Not So New." *American Psychologist* 59 (1) (2004): 52.

Chapter 4

Women, Science, and Spirituality

Kathleen Reedy

What gets us through the day? What nourishes us, feeds us? What motivates us to move forward and accomplish? How do we measure our forward motion? What challenges us? What is our essence, our spirit?

These change as time passes, as our lives evolve, as we learn and experience, and as our responsibilities alter. When I was an exploring teenager, in the 1950s in upstate western New York, the realities and challenges of my life in no way resembled the situation in the late 1960s, in the Midwest, when I was raising five young sons, working a job, and helping my husband start a business. A different set of circumstances, and much more living experience, accompanied me in the 1980s, when I was building a career as a scientist in a government agency; I was single and living alone in the nation's capitol.

Different again from my Irish immigrant forbears, who migrated to the most accepting fields of work and crafts in western New York, or the German American ancestors who toiled in the coal mines in Pennsylvania. Even my parents, who survived the Depression, had intermittent work in the steel mills and stayed where they found financial security, had vastly different experiences, wants, and needs than mine.

Now, having recently retired, my needs, motivations, and rewards are all changing again. I work at my own timetable, set my own deadlines, and develop strategies to reach my own goals, without an employer or bureaucratic involvement. A hard-earned, hard-won freedom! My learned work ethic and my natural and scientific curiosity propel me to accomplish, and it emerges as a spiritually satisfying sensation of completion.

SPIRITUAL JOURNEY

I was seven years old, returning with my mother from Confession at our Catholic church, the same church she attended as a child in parochial school. I had heard her stories of walking miles to school with her brothers, carrying a lunch of cold pancakes left over from breakfast. My parents did not send me to the parochial school, as they wished for me to have a broader, more diverse, public school experience. I asked my mother for her wisdom on the premise that all non-Catholics would go to hell after death. I stated that I didn't believe that God would do that to people. These Protestant people were created by God, just as we were, I insisted. They were certainly living their lives in the manner that they had learned that God required. My mother agreed that hell didn't seem fair or reasonable. I was satisfied, felt justified, and I have continued to believe that I understand God's intent, regardless of any dogma.

As a young mother, I avoided sending my undeveloped, impressionable children to religious education classes at a Catholic church, as I didn't want their pliable minds to be frightened by dire consequences for simple infractions of etiquette. I relied upon our family dynamics—love, understanding, communication, and modeling—to convey the standards and ethics I hoped to instill.[1] Then we moved to Oklahoma and found a Catholic church whose doctrine of theological education conformed to general educational concepts. Parents attended classes to discuss and formulate personalized and age-appropriate ways to introduce the sacraments of Communion and Confession to their children, and decided when the children seemed best able to understand these concepts. I was grateful to find a church where we could be comfortable bringing our children.

Our move to West Virginia brought us back to a more fundamentalist, less-adaptable dogma in the Catholic Church. However, in the early 1970s, with the Vatican throwing open the windows, women were permitted to be readers at Mass. I was concurrently on a soapbox, raising consciousness about feminism, so of course I took the opportunity and volunteered to read. It was two years before anyone noticed that I read the New Testament epistles in gender-neutral language. I was warned to read "the word" as it was written.

Later, when my sons were in college, they began to explore their own spiritual paths. A number of my friends were attending a Unitarian Universalist (UU) fellowship, and I began again to question rigid practices and investigate alternate spiritualities. I spent more than a year pondering the differences on my Sunday morning runs, and would shower, dress, attend a Catholic Mass, prepare breakfast for my family, and then attend the UU fellowship. I felt at home there. UUs do not espouse a doctrine, but encourage followers to build their own theology, structured around logic, reason, and social action. I found confirmation for my inquiries and attitudes as a seven-year-old. I've been an active Unitarian Universalist ever since, taking a leadership role in the small fellowship, then in a very large congregation in the Washington, DC, area.

The first and the seventh UU principles:

1. *The inherent worth and dignity of every person.*
7. *Respect for the interdependent web of all existence, of which we are a part.*

These resonated with my own long held ideas, and inspired me to explore the simple Earth-based religion, paganism, and my already deep interest in the environment.

THE EARTH PATH

I follow the Earth Path, the ancient religion of the Goddess. I am woman, goddess, and spiritual, one with the earth, which holds the secrets of science. I am the Earth Spirit Rising, the center of life and science on this planet. I am a wise woman and a scientist.

Earth-based spiritual traditions celebrate the seasonal cycles: the natural flow of light and dark, warm and cold, seeds and harvest, and the cycle of birth, life, death, and rebirth. Earth-based spirituality awakens the broader dimensions of consciousness, an awareness that we are a sacred manifestation of the living being of the earth, nature, culture, and life. Humans are interconnected with the cosmos, the interrelationship making us part of one living organism; not just people, but part of soil, air, water, energy, plants, and animals. So it is natural to protect and conserve the natural world of which we are a part.

My curiosity and awareness of the pagan, earth-based values coincided with my activism in the feminist movement. Ecofeminism refers to the feminine character of the earth, Mother Earth. It produces new life, as women do. It is nurturing, protecting, and healing, as are mothers. Ecofeminists act to heal the earth that is suffering from human misuse of nature, the pollution of the soil, water, and air, and the destruction of plant and animal life. Ecofeminism is active political engagement, combining spirituality and politics. In contrast, the patriarchal side of politics is the interplay of power and gender; male domination over and violence to the earth and women, the conquering, warlike position.[2]

SCIENCE

I continually encounter the spiritual wonder of life, the interdependent web of all existence, the exciting discovery of how things function, the tantalizing mystery just beyond our reach, and the quest for the next bit of knowledge. We scientists are seeking the answers to the question, "How do things work?"

We are residents here on this planet that we call Earth. These are the most basic components of life, of the planet, of science, the elements that preceded humans: earth, air, water, and fire. All elements are products found on, in, and around the planet. The science we practice is the process of learning about what is present in our universe, and how it works. We scientists have combined some of the elements in an artificial way, and this is part of the science we have discovered and created. No matter is ever lost or destroyed; it simply changes form.

All sciences, earth science, atmospheric science, and biological science, are integrated systems, interrelated and interdependent. (For example, humans breathe the air in our atmosphere. Our major requirement is the oxygen, which the body uses, processes, and expels as primarily carbon dioxide. The trees require carbon dioxide from the atmosphere, and process it by photosynthesis, giving off oxygen, which replenishes what humans need.) These same trees require the soil and nutrients to exist and grow. Earth produces plants that humans and animals eat, digest, and produce as waste. The waste products become the fertilizer that enriches new plant life. The cycle of birth, life, death, and rebirth is repeated in the interdependent systems of the sciences.[3]

EARTH SCIENCE: ANTARCTICA

A chunk of my professional life as a scientist was spent doing research in Antarctica, and was preceded by research in the Arctic. The severe limitations of life in the polar regions, as well as life's richness, are unique, beautiful and inspiring, fascinating and awesome in their simplicity and starkness, excitement, and danger.

The Antarctic continent is isolated, surrounded by the Southern Ocean, where the Atlantic, Pacific, and Indian Ocean come together as one body of water. Antarctica's surface is 98 percent covered by ice that is from two meters to two miles thick. Antarctica is nearly totally in its natural state. There is no vegetation, no exposed earth, and the subzero temperatures and fierce winds would not permit or support flora.[4] Therefore, no animal life is possible, except that which lives in or feeds from the ocean. For the same reason, no indigenous life and no humans could have inhabited this continent.

Our presence there is forced. We must transport with us everything we need to survive. Antarctica can be reached by sea and air during just a few months of the year, during the period of the austral summer from October through February. Summer temperatures can reach the vicinity of −20° F. When the sea ice thins due to warmer temperatures and the return of constant sunlight, an icebreaker is able to cut a lane in the ice to the shore. This permits the arrival of two supply ships.

Airplane fuel and engine parts can function at these temperatures without freezing, and air transport of people, materials, mail, and some fresh food is possible.

There are a multitude of scientific studies in progress on the Antarctic continent, not only at the three U.S. stations but at a couple dozen other countries' research stations. The pristine condition of this unreachable continent gives scientists the opportunity to study phenomena untouched by anyone. Oceanic circulation, marine ecosystems, glaciology, earth science, meteorite studies, climatology, ozone changes, global warming, atmospheric studies, astronomy, astrophysics, neutrinos, and UV radiation are some of the scientific fields of study made possible by this continent in its natural, unaltered condition.

I land in an airplane on the ice sheet at McMurdo Station on the edge of the Antarctic continent. Deplaning into the stark, white, icy, and silent majesty of the ice is breathtaking! It is truly an awesome moment. I am immersed and enfolded in the spirituality of the closeness of the universe, the planet, and, at the same time, the remoteness of this incredible place that I am privileged to encounter. Each time I land and take off from the ice in a plane, I am overcome with the awe, wonder, and splendor of this place, and I feel wrapped in the spiritual safety as well as defenseless to the physical danger of this desolate polar outpost.

My work, the only biological human study at the U.S. stations, is to comprehend and describe the mechanism of the human body's adaptation to cold climate. The integration of the function of several systems in the human body to adapt and preserve a person in these extreme conditions is truly amazing. There are three of us scientists, an endocrinologist, a psychologist, and myself, a physiologist. I am female, they both are male, as are four consultant scientists who work with us.

The human body reacts to cold temperatures by setting several endocrine and physiological systems into accelerated performance. This work is activated by the endocrine system, specifically, the thyroid, that regulates all the systems in the body.[5] The cold temperature sets these adaptations in motion, and the chemical and physiological changes that take place in the body create adverse modifications in the central nervous system, resulting in psychological alterations. These typically include short-term memory loss and depression, as well as attention deficit.[6, 7] The human body's response to the atmosphere and the physical surroundings, specifically the cold temperature, result in biological transformation. This adaptation illustrates the interaction and interdependence of the systems in atmospheric, physical, and biological science.[8–10]

One of the tasks that I execute in managing the studies is recruitment and retention of the human volunteers. Whether due to my extroverted, empathic personality, or feminine nurturing traits, I am capable and proficient at persuading people to volunteer their bodies and blood to the protocol. They do so because they are curious about what is happening to them in this milieu, and they are eager to learn and to contribute to the science and the future of humans working in this hostile environment. Our retention rate is very high, as I maintain relationships with them throughout the project. Few drop out or quit.

The flight to the South Pole, another 1,000 miles inland and at an elevation of 10,000 feet, is yet another thrilling experience to savor. I can look out the tiny windows of the cargo plane and see the Antarctic mountain ranges: the ice, the vertical rock outcroppings, the huge crevasses in the ice sheet, and the glaciers that look like frozen rivers flowing to the sea. The temperature there is the coldest on the planet. On the polar plateau, I can see the horizon in every direction across the flat expanse of ice. It appears to be the edge of the earth; I feel that if I walked far enough across the ice, I would experience the curvature of the globe. I feel alone and isolated, yet in a unique spiritual space, suspended in the presence of the past and the future.

One hundred eighty million years ago, this continent was a part of an enormous supercontinent called Gondwana. It began to break apart, with sections drifting away to form what are now Africa, India, Australia, and Antarctica. Forty million years ago, the continent was covered with vegetation, and was still above the 60th parallel. Twenty-eight million years ago, Antarctica had drifted below the 78th parallel, was surrounded by strong ocean currents, and began to get colder.[11]

Here I am, at the center of the Antarctic continent, at the southernmost point of planet Earth. The remnants of vegetation of millions of years past are lying several miles below my feet. The open sky above and all around me is twinkling with stars and heavenly bodies that are thousands of light-years away. I am clearly in the present, with the past above and below me. I am reaching toward the future. I am afloat in our universe, pondering the direction of my grasp. What lies beyond my reach, my vision? The power of this aberration, in this place, is astounding, humbling, and spiritual.

I witnessed a solar eclipse at the South Pole, in the summer when the sun is always high in the sky. The moon passed between the sun and the Earth, and it was dark for the only time in the six-month summer. I am engulfed with a sensation of mysticism, a breathtaking awareness of the power that created this universe, and me a tiny dot. This wonder is followed by the frightening perception that I am not in control. Despite the capability and preparation required to be in such a remote and dangerous frontier, there is a limit to what we have power over in this environment. We are indulged at the benevolence and the whim of the universe, a spiritual and vulnerable position.

The Antarctic Treaty requires that all countries with research stations on the continent must share their scientific findings. Antarctica is a model of international cooperation. It is satisfying to know that it is possible for many varied geographic and political entities to interact and create alliances and collaborate around the science.[12]

It is also comforting to know that peace and cooperation are working well somewhere on our planet. It gives hope that it is possible elsewhere in the world. The Antarctic Treaty prohibits military presence, business, mining, and any profit-making enterprises. Forty-five countries subscribe to the treaty, though fewer have a presence on the continent. Italy and France are building a joint research station, an example of the collaboration that science promotes on this stark continent.

EARTH: THE GRAND CANYON

Several years ago, I whitewater rafted the Colorado River through the Grand Canyon. We entered the river where its surface is at ground level and paddled for ten days, each day cutting deeper and deeper into the earth, as the river has done, cliffs rising higher and higher on the sides of the river. I saw millions of years of layers of earth, rock, and silt as we paddled through rapids, farther and farther down the river. We eventually reached a narrow canyon, the Vishnu Schist, where are there no longer regular layers of the millions of years of crust and accumulation of detritus. At this point, we see gray rock in random, irregular formations, as though it had been mixed in a blender two billion years ago. We are in the core of the Earth, where the boiling rock solidified and the layers of earth, rock, and vegetation formed around and over it, creating the planet and the North American continent.[13]

I was enveloped with wonderment and a feeling of knowledge, a spiritual sense of knowing. At this moment, I realize that the planet and the universe existed long before people inhabited the earth, and that both will continue long after humans are extinct.

This realization is confirmed when I later visit the Smithsonian National Museum of Natural History, and see, in the dinosaur hall, a column approximately thirty feet tall, with the ages of the earth scored and labeled on the side. The presence of humans is marked as the top two inches of the column.

EARTH: CONCERN

In the twenty-first century, there is a serious threat that the advancements of the twentieth century endangered our existence on this planet. Industrial and economic growth and development, in the quest of the enhancement of the quality of life, threaten to ruin life itself. The misguided continuing development of wealthy industries in the United States and around the world, with disregard for environmental warnings, are clearly emanating; the warming climate and fouled air and seas threaten to ruin our very earth, air, water, and environment, rendering it uninhabitable by humans. We cannot ignore the spiritual component of our planet that is in rapid and perilous transformation, possibly toward destruction.[14] Perhaps our feminine qualities of nurturing and caretaking can impede this slow annihilation.

SCIENCE: THE NATURAL WORLD

All that is natural around us is the basis for science. The connection is undeniable. Nature holds the key, and science is the attempt to discover, understand, and unlock the secrets. Humans have made enormous strides in understanding our bodies, our surroundings, our planet, and our universe. Our discoveries enhance the sense of the spirit, the wonder of the unknown, the excitement of the search, and the triumph of progress.

Science is the opportunity to stumble upon spirituality, to meet and connect with our spiritual selves and appreciate the spirituality of the known and the undiscovered that challenges us.

WOMEN IN SCIENCE

Life and survival are not easy for a woman scientist. She encounters skeptics who would question her skills based on her gender. I have been upstaged, dismissed, marginalized, disagreed with, and ignored. Often, in the end, I was right, my method correct, my protocol more exact, my predictions accurate, and my warning of mishap did occur. Sometimes my correct diagnosis or prediction was acknowledged, occasionally with an apology.

Women were not permitted to go to Antarctica until the late 1950s. Now about 30 percent of the scientists in Antarctica are women, and approximately the same percentages of employees and support staff are women.

Gaining the trust and respect of volunteers and collaborators is an elementary exercise that I am able to do well. I trust the Goddess; have faith in my own Goddess-given ability; and my spiritual trust, poise, and conviction create an aura. I feel a spiritual certainty that enables my assertion and assurance in the scientific field.

WOMEN AND SPIRITUALITY

What gets us through the day? I can sit on my deck, in the comforting shade of a big tree, and inhale the scent of flowers, noting the color of iris, impatiens, and mums. I breathe the fragrant air, listen to the birds and crickets, and see the squirrels and rabbits scurry under the bushes. I might be reading an entertaining book, or talking to a friend or family member on the phone and sipping a glass of wine. The thought of these oases as a reward keeps me focused and anticipating these relaxing moments. But what's going on here is arboriculture, floriculture, viticulture, atmospherics, and mammal and human physiology.

What nourishes us? We are literally fed by the fruits of the earth, such apples, peaches, broccoli, and corn. First their bounty in their natural habitats, the trees or fields; then their beauty displayed on the farm stand or in grocery stalls. We enjoy their scents and textures as we wash, peel, cut, and prepare them. Finally, there is the sensuous taste and feel in the mouth and on the tongue. The sciences present are agronomy, nutrition, and digestion.

What motivates us to move forward and accomplish? When I see the mountains and rocks, and wonder about the layers of ancient life beneath the surface, I am inspired to learn, find, reach for new ideas, and dig. Think of geology or archeology. When I stand on the ice, white and still in every direction, silent but for the wind, and blue sky overhead, I feel suspended in time and space, and wonder about polar magnetism. Is it less strong here that I feel ungrounded and drifting? I am experiencing meteorology, glaciology, and magnetic poles.

How do we measure our forward motion? I am certainly more informed than I was a year ago, or five years ago. I am profoundly more experienced and knowledgeable than when I was younger. I look back at my adventures and the events of those years and wonder how I survived, knowing only what I knew then. How much better I could have handled things if I was as smart as I am now. However, I think of my life experience as preparation for whatever has come later. The accomplishments I can count are satisfying measures of forward motion. The experiences are imbedded in psychoneurology and memory.

What is spirituality? Is my spirit similar to that of the planet? Would I recognize the spirit of the earth? Have I connected with the natural world? Can I, do I commune with it? What can I do to retain the spirit of the earth? Can I help the planet to survive the abuse it has endured? What is my role in conserving our habitat? Please ask yourself these questions. I am challenged to search, research, and follow the clues to nurturing and ensuring our world's continued existence. Science is about life, subsistence, and survival.

SUMMARY: WOMEN, SCIENCE, AND SPIRITUALITY

As I sit composing this, I look out the window at a huge tree whose leaves are turning yellow, orange, bursts of red, and even brown. The leaves are falling on the ground and onto my deck. When I began thinking about writing this, the tree had skeletal black branches with tiny but bursting green buds. This illustrates the spirituality that surrounds us and in which we live. It is there, it happens, and we don't control it; it is spiritual and natural. It is certainly scientific, as we wonder if it is the temperature, the light, or the nutrients in the soil, or simply a cyclical, time-related causation. We look at the big picture, not just the leaf, stem, or branch.

We connect. Women connect with one another. I had lunch with a friend, a former coworker and fellow scientist whom I hadn't seen in months. We talked incessantly and caught up on one another's lives, family, and work. Women are weavers, connecting and entwining people, friends, family, events, incidents, places, facts, ideas, concepts, and other things. We're creating whole cloth out of strands and threads, a valuable asset to a scientist.

My experience as I encounter the wonders of the world and recognize its spirituality is to advance the pursuit of science as the whole integration of life.

NOTES

1. Nelson, 2007.
2. Reuther, 1992.
3. Starhawk, 1989.
4. Hooper, 1991.
5. Do, Mino, et al., 2004.
6. Shurtleff, Thomas, et al., 1994.
7. Palinkas, Reed, et al., 2001.
8. Reed, Reedy, et al., 2001.
9. Reedy, Reed, 1997.
10. Case, Reed, et al., 2006.
11. Hooper, 1991.
12. Antarctic Treaty, 1959.
13. Stevens, 1987.
14. Gore, 2006.

BIBLIOGRAPHY

The Antarctic Treaty. Washington, DC: United States Government, 1959.

Case, H. S., H. L. Reed, K. R. Reedy, N. V. Do, N. S. Finney, R. Seip, and L. A. Palinkas. "Resting and Exercise Energy Use in Antarctica: Effect of 50 Percent Restriction in Temperate Climate Energy Requirements." *Clinical Endocrinology* 65 (2) (2006): 257–264.

Do, N. V., L. Mino, G. R. Merriam, L. M. Homer, H. S. Case, L. A. Palinkas, K. Reedy, and H. L. Reed. "The Elevations in Serum Thyroglobulin during Prolonged Antarctic Residence: Effect of Thyroxine Supplement in the Polar T3 Syndrome." *Journal of Clinical Endocrinology and Metabolism* 89 (2004): 41529–41533.

Gore, Albert. *An Inconvenient Truth: The Planetary Emergency of Global Warming and What We Can Do About It.* New York: Rodale Books, 2006.

Hooper, Meredith. *A for Antarctica: Facts and Stories from the Frozen South.* London: Piccolo Books, 1991.

Nelson, Roberta. "Even Secular Parents Are Religious Educators." *UUA World*, 21 (3) (2007): 14–15.

Palinkas, L. A., H. L. Reed, K. R. Reedy, N. V. Do, H. S. Case, and N. S. Finney. "Circannual Pattern of Hypothalamic-Pituitary-Thyroid (HPT) Function and Mood during Extended Antarctic Residence." *Psychoneuroendocrinology* 26 (4) (2001): 421–431.

Palinkas, Lawrence A., Kathleen R. Reedy, Marc Shepanek, Mark Smith, Mihai Anghel, Gary D. Steel, Dennis Reeves, H. Samuel Case, Nhan Van Do, and H. Lester Reed. "Environmental Influences on Hypothalamic-Pituitary-Thyroid Function and Behavior in Antarctica." *Physiology and Behavior* 92 (2007): 790–799.

Palinkas, Lawrence A., Kathleen Reedy, Mark Smith, Mihai Anghel, Gary D. Steel, Dennis Reeves, David Shurtleff, H. Samuel Case, Nhan Van Do, and H. Lester Reed "Psychoneuroendocrine Effects of Combined Thyroxine and Triiodothyronine versus Tyrosine during Prolonged Antarctic Residence." Submitted to *Psychoneuroendocrinology*, December 2007.

Palinkas, Lawrence A., Kathleen Reedy, Mark Smith, Christian Otto, Will Silva, Gary D. Steel, Mihai Anghel, Dennis Reeves, David Shurtleff, H. Samuel Case, Nhan Van Do, and H. Lester Reed. "Effectiveness of Thyroid Supplement and Tyrosine in Prevention of Decrements in Cognitive Performance and Mood during Prolonged Antarctic Residence: A Randomized Clinical Trial." Presented at Scientific Committee on Antarctic Research, June 2006.

Reed, H. L., M. M. D'Alesandro, K. R. Kowalski, and L. D. Homer. "Multiple Cold Air Exposures Change Oral Triiodothyronine Kinetics in Normal Men." *American Journal of Physiology* 263 (*Endocrinology and Metabolism* 26) (1992): E85–E93.

Reed, H. L., K. R. Kowalski, M. M. D'Alesandro, R. Robertson, and S. B. Lewis. "Propranolol Fails to Lower the Increased Blood Pressure Caused by Cold Air Exposure." *Aviation Space and Environmental Medicine* 62 (1991): 111–115.

Reed, H. L., K. R. Reedy, L. A. Palinkas, N. Van Do, N. S. Finney, H. S. Case, H. J. LeMar, J. Wright, and J. Thomas. "Impairment in Cognitive and Exercise Performance during Prolonged Antarctic Residence: Effect of Thyroxine Supplementation in the Polar T3 Syndrome." *Journal of Clinical Endocrinology and Metabolism* 86 (2001): 110–116.

Reedy, K. R., and H. L Reed. "Measuring Metabolic Change in Humans Residing in Antarctica: A Thyroxine Supplement Placebo Control Trial." *Antarctic Journal of the United States*, Review Issue. National Science Foundation: Government Publication, 1997.

Ruether, Rosemary R. *Gaia and God: An Ecofeminist Theology of Earth Healing.* New York: HarperCollins, 1992.

Shurtleff, D., J. R. Thomas, J. Schrot, K. Kowalski, and R. Harford. "Tyrosine Reverses a Cold-induced Working Memory Deficit in Humans." *Pharmacological Biochemical Behavior* 47 (4) (1994): 935–941.

Starhawk (aka Miriam Simos). *The Spiral Dance: A Rebirth of the Ancient Religion of the Great Goddess.* New York: HarperCollins, 1989.

Stevens, Larry. *The Colorado River in Grand Canyon, a Guide.* Flagstaff, AZ: Red Lake Books, 1987.

PART II

The Healing Power of Spiritual Expression

Chapter 5

My "Friendship" with Women Saints as a Source of Spirituality

Oliva M. Espín

In the course of a life full of dramatic change and uncertainty, two strands have remained constant, shaping the backdrop against which I have made decisions and into which I have woven other strands of my life. One is the guiding force of faith and spirituality; the other is the sustaining force of feminism, present in my life even before I had a word for it. Recently, reflecting about the women saints[1] of my childhood, I have woven these two strands together for the first time.

Why have the lives of women saints created this peculiar point of convergence of two main strands of my life? Because I have seen how, in the lives of these women, faith and heroism have worked together. I have been captivated by the intricacies of these women's lives, their courage as well as their weaknesses, their childishness as well as their maturity, their loves and fears, and, above all, their focus on doing what they believed was right or what God wanted from them regardless of the opinions of others, including the male authorities of church and family. And, even though they could not fully subtract themselves from the influence of their cultural milieu—as no one fully can—they used the tools of their culture to implement their own will in the name of God. In rather contradictory ways, they used negative cultural and religious gender norms to challenge what was expected of them as women.

It must have been the paradox at the center of the saints' lives that attracted me. I remember having an inkling that even the most apparently submissive among them had challenged authority. Most of the stories and narratives about saints, particularly those presented to little girls as role models, portray them as compliant, obedient, self-sacrificing masochists, faithful to the dictates of authority. Most of these stories completely neglect or deny the fact that the saints' behavior frequently challenged the norms and expectations placed on them as women. But once I grasped that they understood their lives through the lenses of their historical and cultural contexts, these women's stories had the opposite effect on me. They were examples of the effects a "passionate spirituality"[2] could have on the development of a "radical wisdom"[3] unique to women's spirituality. Reflecting on their capacity to alternatively accept and rebel against patriarchal dictates of the Roman Catholic Church, I found that their experiences, despite the differences in historical circumstances, were frequently close to mine. Their femaleness, like mine, presented specific limitations and provided distinct avenues to spiritual achievement. They became models of self-assertion and rebellion against arbitrary dictates of authority.

The central focus of my spirituality, based in large part on my "friendship" with some women saints, who have been my role models, has grown against the grain of traditional beliefs and has helped me develop a relational perspective on "the life of the spirit" that, in turn, has brought me closer to God and to my fellow human beings. True spirituality is, by definition, relational, since it is fundamentally about a relationship with whatever we understand God to be. And this, in turn, determines our relationships with other people. Spirituality is "embodied in ways that activate memory, deeply felt emotion, social connectedness, and meaning."[4] In other words, there is a profound "materiality" to spirituality. My personal and professional choices have been guided by this relational spiritual perspective, perhaps not always consciously. In these pages, I make my own memories available as a tool to better understand the transactions between these women's stories and my own, as well as their possible significance for the spirituality of everyday human life.

When I was a girl of eight or nine, *los Tres Reyes Magos*—the Three Kings, or the Wise Men who bring presents to children on January 6, the feast of the Epiphany, in many Catholic countries—brought me a small book: *Niños Santos*. It was bound in red velvet, fuzzy to touch, and small enough to fit in my hands. I was already an avid reader; *Niños Santos* became my constant companion. I read its stories so often that I could recite from memory the lives of the young people it contained. Around the same time, a film on the life of Rose of Lima, the first canonized saint of the Americas, became a theatrical success in Latin America. *Rosa de América*, a Black-and-White feature film, further triggered my fantasies about sainthood. Watching Rosa on the screen after reading about her in *Niños Santos* made saints even more real to me. I was mesmerized by Argentinean actress Delia Garcés playing the role of Rose of Lima. Garcés was a beautiful woman, as Rosa was supposed to have been. She played many other glamorous parts in Argentinean cinema but none made her as famous to the Latin American public as her role as Rosa. Her beauty made sainthood seem like an attractive possibility. Her long dark curly hair, so much like mine, made me think I could be like her if I tried. Maybe if I behaved like her I could become as beautiful and as good as she was. Rosa was particularly attractive to many others because she was Latin American, not European like the other saints I was hearing or reading about.[5]

When I was ten or eleven, I watched the now-legendary film in which Ingrid Bergman played the role of Joan of Arc. For days after I passed the time jumping on furniture while carrying my banner, a broomstick with a rag tied on one end, pretending to be Joan of Arc conquering fortresses. While Joan of Arc evoked fantasies of achievement in my childish mind, Rosa had built her sanctity through acts of self-mutilation. Many decades later I learned that because women's bodies were seen as sinful, impure, and imperfect, many women equated sanctity with controlling and reducing their bodies. Such control was the best demonstration of the strength of their souls. Therefore, women who aspired to sainthood showed the power of their spirit through the mutilation or even annihilation of their bodies.[6]

In addition, for centuries, Catholic Church authorities claimed the Apostle Paul's injunctions denied Christian women the right to teach others. Learning and teaching became dangerous activities for women. Deprived of their ability to serve God and the church via their words, many women expressed their faith through that which they could (to some degree) control, namely their bodies. Rosa, who is reputed to have been a beautiful young woman, actively struggled against the dangers of her own beauty by cutting her hair, burning her hands, putting garlic in her eyes, and other similar activities. Yet, taking into account that our knowledge of Rosa comes from interpretations of men writing about her, it is next to impossible to determine what her real motivations were for her extreme self-destruction. But what is certain is that she took it upon herself to control the destiny of her body, including inviting death, rather than leave that power in the hands of others. She did so in the only and rather "contorted" way available to her in her specific cultural and religious context. In this endeavor, no matter how submissive to authority she appeared to have been, she presumed to have a life, a body, and an identity apart from male authority and cultural definitions of what should constitute femininity. Her efforts at "fooling" parents and confessors alike into allowing her to perform ever more extreme penances, although baffling to us, show her self-determination to pursue her own goals, perceived by her and presented to others as God's will.

Rosa engaged in forms of accommodation and resistance characteristic of women saints. She appeared as virtuous and obedient while actively disobeying the authority of parents and confessors and acting as an independent agent. Considering the limited options available to her, she created relatively independent strategies in her self-styled search for sanctity. Rosa was what Kathleen Norris calls a "fierce holy little girl"[7] intent on reaching God in her own way, even in the face of the opposition of her family and the norms for women in her own society. In doing so, she challenged authority and became a role model for other women. At the same time, through her extreme behaviors, she reinscribed the all-encompassing equation of women with the body. Because she focused on her body as the instrument of her sanctification, she underscored the importance and problematic nature of women's bodies. As was to be expected, she shared her contemporaries' constructions of women's bodies and sanctity. To some extent, her predicament is similar to conflicts women face today concerning their bodies and their desires for self-realization.

During my childhood, imitating Rosa could mean hurting my body. Feminist awareness and gender analyses of women's relationships to their bodies were decades in my future. I was lucky enough not to wear a veil that could hide a crown of nails or clothes that might conceal a locked iron chain around my waist as Rosa did. Instead I filled my school shoes with beans, knelt on pebbles to pray whenever possible, and ate foods I strongly disliked. I even went long hours without drinking water in the Cuban heat, while dreaming about founding a religious order named after St. Rose of Lima. I spent hours designing the habit my nuns would wear, making it as beautiful as possible: white pleated chiffon, trimmed with black velvet at the neckline, the sleeves, and the waist. I guess I wanted to be a fashionable saint!

All through my childhood, I read other stories and fairy tales and saw films about young female heroines. Indeed, Disney's *Snow White* was the first movie I saw. But the stories of young women so deeply devoted to God that they reached the Catholic Church's pinnacle of sanctity captivated my imagination with a stronger force than fairy-tale heroines. Transforming the world or the lives of others looked a lot more attractive than marrying an unknown prince. What I wanted most in the world was to be a saint. I fantasized about being some self-sacrificing martyr or heroic holy person, playacting the roles on a daily basis.

Yet, the saints weren't the only catalysts in my life. My childhood memories are also full of "snapshots" of my budding feminism. One anecdote remains vivid. I was five; my sister and I were playing with my two cousins on the porch of my paternal grandmother's house, and being watched closely by one of my father's sisters. The four of us were about the same age, three girls and one boy. In the course of our play talk, I referred to the four of us as "*nosotras.*" My aunt corrected me, saying the right form to use was the masculine "*nosotros*" because my male cousin was part of the "we." Although at the time I had no idea of what sexism was, I quickly responded to her that it did not make any sense: Manoly was only one boy and we were three girls, so we were the majority; the feminine form should prevail! How my aunt responded, I cannot remember, but I imagine she probably said the rule was the rule regardless of what I thought.

Indeed, as far as I can remember, the problems created by rules and rule-makers were major themes in my life. Since my early childhood, my family had lived in genteel poverty, no less harsh because it was hidden beneath the trappings of the middle-class life that my parents had known in their youths and wanted to believe they still enjoyed. Before I was born, my father had been a lawyer in the Cuban navy, a position he had earned after years of study and days of written examinations. Armed with his shiny white uniform and newly acquired credentials, he had married my mother shortly before the beginning of World War II and had had two daughters, thinking himself securely employed.

As a toddler, I lived half a block away from my mother's family in Santiago, in a house with a central courtyard full of trees around a gurgling fountain. I vaguely remember being placed in a big tin bowl that served as my boat as I floated around the fountain. I have a picture of myself—two years old, perhaps—sitting very properly at the fountain's edge.

Then, in December 1941, Fulgencio Batista—who had been elected president for the first time the previous year after several attempts at seizing power—"reorganized" the Cuban armed forces, and that was the end of my family's middle-class life. Batista fired my father and all other officers in the military known to be unsympathetic to his government. My father was left without a job and with a young wife and two daughters to feed—in Santiago, a city where the chances of employment were next to zero.

He had a teaching credential, and, with more hope than understanding, my father decided to start his own elementary school and commercial academy. Barely six months after Batista's action, we moved to Havana, to a flat above a house-painting store in a commercial district. There my father started his school. The patio with its trees and its fountain disappeared from my life, and I found myself, not knowing how, in a cramped space amid the bustling traffic of Havana.

The rest of my childhood unfolded there. My two brothers were born there. My sister and I had our first periods there. And there I built a world of fantasy in my head to compensate for the dreary and limiting surroundings in which I felt imprisoned. I spent my childhood surrounded by desks and blackboards, eating lunch and dinner quickly because our dining room had to be turned into a classroom for afternoon and evening classes. I spent hours staying as quiet as possible behind forbidden doors so that my father's classes wouldn't be disrupted by any sense of our presence. And during vacations and on weekends, when all the students were gone, I played at being Joan of Arc, conquering castles for France or another saint engaged in some other heroic activity.

From the distance and vision provided by five decades, I believe I do not exaggerate when I think Joan of Arc not only saved France but also saved me. Being Joan of Arc, flying over desks and chairs with my broomstick banner and ruler sword, trying to imitate her or some other heroic saint in one way or another, gave me a taste for personal power and helped me recognize that I could do anything and go anywhere without a chaperone. It also taught me graphically that sometimes women pay dearly for daring to be all they can be.

Fantasy and spirituality nurtured my childhood soul. Sharing what I know and understand about women saints has become my passion in adulthood. I want my own appreciation of women saints to open doors for others as it has for me, enabling others to recover, as I have, some of the meaning and spirituality I had lost because of the rigidities of church positions about women. I want to share my struggle against the indoctrination in sanctimony and docility I received through the distortions of these women's stories. And I want to share my struggle to develop strength from the presence of these women in my childhood imagination and the ways in which they led me to believe that many things were possible. In other words, I want to share my personal quest with other women.

Needless to say, my understanding of both spirituality and feminism has changed dramatically over the years. Both could have developed very differently or not at all were it not for the jarring changes and transformations of my life. In 1961, I left Cuba and started a life as an immigrant in Spain, Panama, and Costa Rica. Later circumstances brought me to Belgium and Canada at different points in my life. Finally, I came to reside in the United States. Although I have been a citizen of the United States for almost thirty years, I feel deeply that my life has been marked by the experience of migration: I possess the vague certainty that I could have been another person were it not for the particular circumstances that immigration brought into my life. I do not know and will never know the person I could have been had I not left my birth country. The only me I know is the one who incorporates the consequences of migration. Even though my life has been rich in experiences that may not have been possible otherwise, and I have never felt particularly deprived, I know that whatever I have succeeded in creating and living has been developed at the expense of some significant losses. Migration for me, as for most immigrants, has provided a dual and contradictory legacy. It has given me safety and success, and opened new doors I did not know even existed, but it also has brought losses and silence about them. Talking about these losses is easily confused with ungratefulness to the new country. Life being what it is, most immigrants prefer to focus on what they have gained and forget what they have lost ... as do their hosts.

In my previously published work, I have written about immigrants/ refugees and Latina women from psychological and gendered perspectives.[8] Working as a professor at state and private universities, I have lived most of my adult life in the world of the secular academy, researching women's lives and studying the psychology of women of ethnocultural backgrounds less frequently considered as subjects by psychology. My teaching positions have been supported by public funds or by student tuition at private institutions for the training of psychologists. The professional institutions to which I have belonged have been committed to the nonsectarian study of psychology and women's studies. Therefore, when I have taught courses about women saints and presented this material at professional conferences, it has not always felt acceptable in those settings to speak of the significance of this material in my own life. But there is no denying that my professional activities have been influenced by reflection on the spirituality and life experiences of these women.

For the first time, I have given myself permission to write as a spiritual person, even as I also write as a scholar. Thus I speak in several voices. I speak directly and unabashedly about some of the implications that this material has for my spiritual life. The seemingly small stories of my childhood and my encounters with these women saints create the thread that ties all these stories together. But I also speak as a women's studies scholar recovering the rich and complex legacy of our foremothers; as a woman, I am interested in what these experiences might have meant to them and might mean to us.

As a psychologist, while I am interested in the developmental vicissitudes and experiences that shaped these women's lives, I am also aware that the field of psychology has usually not been particularly friendly to conceptualizations of spirituality as part of healthy development. The association between pathology or immaturity and religious beliefs has been paramount in the field of psychology. However, this trend is being progressively reversed, as the findings of recent studies "seem to indicate that among those with spiritual beliefs, maturity of personality goes with an attitude to religion which is undogmatic and nonrestrictive."[9] Indeed, it is becoming more evident that "maturity of personality goes with a desire to answer fundamental questions rather than with the need to use religion as some form of psychological crutch."[10] By the same token, "it is only recently that the old style of hagiography has been modified and we begin to see presentations of holy persons, warts and all—something that reflects a whole new idea of what holiness may mean, and how grace and nature are intertwined in spiritual growth,"[11] thus helping us understand these historical role models as true human beings immersed in their specific psychological and cultural contexts like the rest of us.

As I write in my multiple voices, I try to reach others like me who have been searching for ways to weave together their feminism and spiritual beliefs. Many women mistrust and reject traditional religion because its patriarchal positions have been a powerful source of women's oppression. Alternative forms of spirituality, such as goddess worship and nature-oriented rituals, have been developed or rediscovered in the context of the women's movement. Yet, many women—feminists included—do not find adequate spiritual fulfillment in these approaches. For some, more traditional religious beliefs continue to serve as a source of inspiration in their struggles for liberation. For them, as for me, such traditions remain a source of strength. The question of what to do with spirituality in a secularized world, of how to preserve spirituality without falling into the trap of fundamentalism that denies and suppresses the insights of feminism, remains alive for many women. The need to recover, revitalize, and breathe life into faith traditions continues to be felt by many women, myself included, as this writing demonstrates.

In the early nineties, when I started teaching women's studies full time, my interest in women's stories and their lives crystallized in more expansive ways that took me beyond psychology or purely psychological interpretations of lives. Not coincidentally, as I started using women's stories more actively in my teaching, I started remembering the saints' stories of my childhood and wondering about the meaning of my favorite saints' life stories. As women's studies scholarship recovered the stories of women's lives in history, literature, anthropology, and as psychologists understood women's emotional experiences and psychological conflicts to be healthy reactions to oppression rather than pathological responses to individual mental health challenges, I began reading Teresa of Avila again.

Although it would be anachronistic to say that Teresa was a "feminist," her sharp understanding and critical interpretation of the constraints of women's circumstances remain relevant today. I began to see that Teresa was not the obedient nun described to me as a child, and rediscovered in Teresa the story of a woman of stature in early modern Europe tenaciously struggling against church authorities to fulfill what she believed to be God's will. Her efforts at providing spaces where women could gather and feel valuable still impact communities of women today. The importance she attributed to women's togetherness and their spiritual strengths is as relevant today as in the sixteenth century.

Reading Teresa's writings with this new understanding made me want to explore the stories of the other women saints of my childhood.

My interest in these tales was further fueled by the importance of narrative and storytelling evident in the last few decades of research and writing in many academic fields. My understanding of who some of these women were and my "relationship" with each one of them started developing in a new light, not only spiritual but also feminist. In addition, my psychology training helped me understand them from a developmental perspective that helped explain some of their decisions and the twists in their lives which might have looked rather puzzling without the lens provided by psychology.

I realized that some of the apparent renunciation of human comforts was, in fact, a strategy for self-preservation. For example, sexuality of the sort encountered in marriage gave most of their women contemporaries very little fulfillment. It had to do more with the husband's desires than with the woman's. Moreover, the consequence of sexuality was one pregnancy after another in rapid succession, often leading to death from childbirth at a very early age. Catherine of Siena made her vow of virginity in childhood, immediately after one of her older sisters died in childbirth. Teresa of Avila makes explicit comments on the topic in some of her writings. Rosa of Lima and many others who chose not to marry were not this explicit about their fears of the consequences of sexuality, but there is no doubt this concern was present in their minds. Indeed, the struggle to integrate sexuality and spirituality continues to be present in many women's lives.[12]

As I searched women's lives and writings, I found multiple examples of their indomitable resolve to achieve what they believed was important: Little, quiet, unassuming Thérèse of Lisieux—the most popular female saint in the Catholic church—had spoken to the Pope in public after a specific injunction to remain silent in his presence; she never hid her ardent desire to become a priest even though she was female. Rosa of Lima played her confessors against each other and pitted them against her own mother to get what she wanted. It didn't seem to matter that women saints had rebelled against authority figures because they wanted to become cloistered nuns or self-mutilating fiends. Their rebellion was a way to get what they wanted rather than what others dictated, no matter how misguided I now might perceive them to be. I also discovered that what I had gathered from their example during my childhood reading was focused on the positive qualities they embodied. What I learned from Joan of Arc was not martyrdom but her feisty attitude and her strong belief that she had a mission to accomplish that, indeed, changed the course of European history. She taught me defiance and courage to risk all for well-defined ideals. What I learned from Rosa of Lima was not to punish my body but to get in touch with my right to be visible and known and respected by peers and others. Together, Joan of Arc and Catherine of Siena showed me that it is possible for women to have political influence despite the discriminatory practices that may still be prevalent. To this day, Teresa of Avila and Edith Stein[13] show me the value and power of intellectual pursuit. Rosa of Lima, Mariana Paredes of Quito, and Teresa of Los Andes demonstrate alternative ways to be Latin American despite racial tensions, social injustice, and political upheaval. Their experiences point out the pitfalls of relying on individual, personal spiritual development in the face of our unique mixture of historical circumstances.[14] Rosa's and Mariana's influences on the development of a beginning Latin American identity in their respective cities in early colonial Latin America persists to this day; through their behaviors we can see the social construction of women's bodies and roles in early colonial Latin America and its implications for the development of popular culture and national identity. In particular, Rosa's role in the creation of Peruvian national identity is a demonstration of the importance of saints. Her canonization was the first successful attempt at acknowledging the possibility of holiness in the New World.[15]

Because I am a psychologist, I see human behavior through the lens provided by developmental, social, and clinical psychologies. Because I am a feminist, I read all historical information about these women with a certain "hermeneutical suspicion" (interpreting these women's lives through a feminist lens and not simply accepting others' interpretations) that helps me see important information in the interstices, in what is not said by them as well as by other writing about them. Because I live in the modern era, I have access to knowledge of gender and women's lives that was not prevalent before. Although the human developmental journey is widely different in different historical and cultural settings, I believe that in many ways, saints are like us—down to earth. Their gritty resistance to authority and sometimes-stubborn conformity can illuminate our own lives' struggles. I have learned my spirituality from their engagement with their embodiment, their cultures, and their personal limitations and successes.

I have not saved any countries from invaders. And I am still here so, clearly, I have not had to pay for my challenging of societal norms by being burned at the stake. I'm far from being a saint. Yet both the triumph and the pain of many of these women's struggles have been present throughout my life. Even though I don't climb desks and chairs anymore, I continue to reach for the possibilities of personal power that some of these saints introduced to me. And I am committed to sharing with other women whatever insights I may have gathered in the process. This is how I understand true spirituality. I see it as a commitment to live one's professional and personal life in light of the depth of dimensions and hunger for transformation that we experience as human beings.[16] I see it as a conscious process of sharing with others what we have been able to gather through our personal search and professional learning. Indeed, spirituality is nothing more and nothing less than "the life project of self-integration through self-transcendence."[17] From these saints' lives have I intuited that "a defining characteristic of Christian mysticism is that it impels a person towards an active rather than purely passive inward life."[18] Indeed, true Christian mysticism "is founded on the practice of common human everyday life rather than on private experiences or on purely devotional or ascetical excercises"[19] and it has nothing to do with political domination or right-wing perspectives that seem to be associated with the word "Christian" these days. In fact, as Michel de Certeau[20] asserts, saints, like the mad, stand for a kind of otherness and live on the social and even religious margins. Their otherness gives them the ability to defy conventional sources of power and privilege. Women saints are, in their own unique ways, culturally and politically subversive. They may have "mouthed" and believed in culturally approved norms, but they lived their lives acting against those norms. For them, as for us, spirituality is a center from which to challenge structures of power and privilege, particularly as they affect women.

That is why I believe that a fuller understanding of women's lives that includes a spiritual dimension could enrich the study of the psychology of women. A mature spirituality can be a source of liberation and freedom as has been the case for women saints. Spiritual beliefs have provided forms and outlets of expression for people who were otherwise excluded from the mainstream. Latin American liberation theology, the Black church in the United States, and the medieval European women mystics have much in common, regardless of differences in centuries, geography, and social context. For me, as for many other people, a relationship with the divine—whatever it is and however it is interpreted—is a source of life and freedom, not a constricting force that stifles my inner being. It is not belief in God (or whatever name we have for whatever that might be) that damages people psychologically or creates useless destructive guilt. The damage comes from "half-baked" and limited religious education interpreted by sexist, racist, and/or heterosexist authority figures. Further understanding of the psychology of women could benefit from appreciation of the self-reliance provided by healthy spirituality and its attendant encouragement of women's personal development. Observing the lives of women for whom spirituality has been a creative force should be a means to achieve this goal.

Despite the distortions and limitations created by sociocultural and historical contexts in the lives of women saints and in ours, ultimately "spirituality is not about a personal 'inner life' that in any way downplays or denigrates the 'outer life' of embodiment, community, tradition, political [and professional] responsibility and so on. Rather, lived spirituality is what we do with these things as we struggle, alone and with others, to construct meaning."[21] And, I would add, to create a better world.

NOTES

1. I am aware that the word "woman" is a noun, not an adjective. In several languages other than English (for example, Spanish, French, Italian, German, and Slavic languages), the grammatical gender of the noun "saint" provides a feminine form, rendering the qualifier unnecessary. In those languages, the word "female" is usually a term reserved for animals or a derogatory term for sexualized women. Therefore, I am opting consciously to use the word "woman" as a qualifier, rather than "female," a term that sounds pejorative to my ears and perhaps those of others.

2. Dreyer, 2005.

3. Lanzetta, 2005.

4. Schneiders, S. M. "A hermeneutical approach . . .," 49–60.

5. Rosa was the only canonized Latin American women saint from 1671 until 1950, when Mariana de Jesús Paredes of Quito—almost her contemporary—was canonized. The third Latin American woman to be canonized was Chilean Teresa de Los Andes in 1993.

6. Espín, O. M. "Rosa de Lima and Mariana de Quito: Women, Body, and Sanctity in the Sixteenth and Seventeenth Centuries," April 1998.

7. Norris, 203.

8. See, for example, Cole, E., O. M. Espín, and E. Rothblum, eds. *Refugee Women and their Mental Health: Shattered Societies, Shattered Lives.* New York: Harrington Park Press, 1993; Espín, O. M. *Latina Healers: Lives of Power and Tradition.* Encino, CA: Floricanto Press, 1996; Espín, O. M. *Latina Realities: Essays on Healing, Migration, and Sexuality.* Boulder, CO: Westview Press, 1997; Espín, O. M. *Women Crossing Boundaries: A Psychology of Immigration and the Transformations of Sexuality.* New York: Routledge, 1999; and Kawahara, D. and O. M. Espín, eds. *Feminist Reflections in Growth and Transformations: Asian-American women in Therapy.* New York: Haworth Press, 1997.

9. Fontana, 135.

10. Ibid., 135.

11. Principe, 42–48.

12. Mahoney and Espín, 2008.

13. On Stein, see for example, Espín, O. M. *"The Destiny of this People is my own . . ." Edith Stein's Paradoxical Sainthood.* Lipinsky Institute for Judaic Studies, San Diego State University, San Diego, CA, 1997.

14. Espín, "Saints in the Cuban heat."

15. Espín, O. M. "Rosa de Lima, first saint of the Americas: Women, sainthood, and community in early colonial Latin America." International Hagiography Society Conference on Saints and Communities. Groeningen, The Netherlands, July 2000; Espín, O. M. "Rosa de Lima, first saint of the Americas: Sainthood, women's bodies, and the building of national identity." Association for Religion in Intellectual Life, New York, July 2005; Hampe-Martínez, T. Los testigos de Santa Rosa. (Una aproximación social a la identidad criolla en el Perú colonial) [Santa Rosa's witnesses. (A social approximation to *"criollo"* identity in colonial Peru)]. *Revista Complutense de Historia de América*, 23 (1997): 113–136.

16. The importance of this idea is broadly presented by the contributors of E. A. Dreyer and M. S. Burrows, eds. *Minding the Spirit: The Study of Christian Spirituality.* Baltimore: Johns Hopkins University Press, 2005.

17. Schneiders, "A Hermeneutical Approach . . ." 53.
18. Sheldrake, P. F. "Christian spirituality as way of living publicly," 282–298.
19. Ibid., 283.
20. De Certeau, 21.
21. Frohlich, 65–77.

BIBLIOGRAPHY

Cole, E., O. M. Espín, and E. Rothblum, eds. *Refugee Women and Their Mental Health: Shattered Societies, Shattered Lives*. New York: Harrington Park Press, 1993.

De Certeau, M. *The Mystic Fable*. Chicago: University of Chicago Press, 1992.

Dreyer, E. A. *Passionate Spirituality: Hildegard of Bingen and Hadewijch of Brabant*. Mahwah, NJ: Paulist Press, 2005.

Dreyer, E. A., and M. S. Burrows, eds. *Minding the Spirit: The Study of Christian Spirituality*. Baltimore: Johns Hopkins University Press, 2005.

Espín, O. M. *Latina Healers: Lives of Power and Tradition*. Encino, CA: Floricanto Press, 1996.

———. *Latina Realities: Essays on Healing, Migration, and Sexuality*. Boulder, CO: Westview Press, 1997.

———. *"The Destiny of This People Is My Own:" Edith Stein's Paradoxical Sainthood*. San Diego, CA: Lipinsky Institute for Judaic Studies, San Diego State University, 1997.

———. "Rosa de Lima and Mariana de Quito: Women, Body, and Sanctity in the Sixteenth and Seventeenth Centuries." International Psychoanalytic Conference, At the Threshold of the Millennium, Lima, Perú, April 1998.

———.*Women Crossing Boundaries: A Psychology of Immigration and the Transformations of Sexuality*. New York: Routledge, 1999.

———. "Rosa de Lima, First Saint of the Americas: Women, Sainthood, and Community in Early Colonial Latin America." International Hagiography Society Conference on Saints and Communities, Groeningen, the Netherlands, July 2000.

———. "Rosa de Lima, First Saint of the Americas: Sainthood, Women's Bodies, and the Building of National Identity." Association for Religion in Intellectual Life, New York, 2005.

———. "Saints in the Cuban Heat." In I. Lara and E. Facio, eds. *Fleshing the Spirit, Spiriting the Flesh: Expressing Our Spiritualities*, forthcoming.

Fontana, D. *Psychology, Religion, and Spirituality*. Malden, MA: BPS Blackwell, 2003.

Frohlich, M. *Spiritual Discipline, Discipline of Spirituality*. In E. Dreyer and M. S. Burrows, eds. *Minding the Spirit: The Study of Christian Spirituality*. Baltimore: Johns Hopkins University Press, 2005.

Hampe-Martínez, T. "Los testigos de Santa Rosa." (Una aproximación social a la identidad criolla en el Perú colonial) [Santa Rosa's witnesses. (A social approximation to *"criollo"* identity in colonial Peru)]. *Revista Complutense de Historia de América* 23 (1997): 113–136.

Kawahara, D., and O. M. Espín., eds. *Feminist Reflections in Growth and Transformations: Asian-American Women in Therapy*. New York: Haworth Press, 2007.

Lanzetta, B. *Radical Wisdom: A Feminist Mystical Theology.* Minneapolis, MN: Fortress Press, 2005.

Mahoney, A., and O. M. Espín, eds. *Sin or Salvation: The Relationship between Sexuality and Spirituality in Psychotherapy.* New York: Haworth Press, 2008.

Norris, K. *The Cloister Walk.* New York: Norton, 1996.

Principe, W. H. "Broadening the Focus: Context as a Corrective Lens in Reading Historical Works in Spirituality." In E. Dreyer and M. S. Burrows, eds. *Minding the Spirit: The Study of Christian Spirituality.* Baltimore: Johns Hopkins University Press, 2005.

Schneiders, S. M. "A hermeneutical Approach to the Study of Christian Spirituality." In E. Dreyer and M. S. Burrows, eds. *Minding the Spirit: The Study of Christian Spirituality.* Baltimore: Johns Hopkins University Press, 2005.

Sheldrake, P. F. "Christian Spirituality as Way of Living Publicly: A Dialectic of the Mystical and Prophetic." In E. Dreyer and M. S. Burrows, eds. *Minding the Spirit: The Study of Christian Spirituality.* Baltimore: Johns Hopkins University Press, 2005.

Chapter 6

Illuminating the Black Madonna: A Healing Journey

Lillian Comas-Díaz

Yet mystery and manifestations arise from the same source.
This source is called darkness.
Darkness within darkness,
The gateway to all understanding.

—*Tao Te Ching*

I travel an inherited path. My ancestors—deeply spiritual people—followed a road to illuminated darkness. Accepting their traditions helped me to view my psychotherapist role as a calling. Such spiritual journeys enabled me to embrace multiple ways of knowing. Although I was raised Catholic, I endorsed a syncretistic orientation comprising indigenous, African, Western, and Eastern spiritual elements. Consequently, I baptized my spirituality as Spirita.[1] A way of being, Spirita is a spirituality of protest, resistance, evolution, and revolution that promotes global social justice. Centered on feminism of color, Spirita is not male or White; instead, she has dark skin.

As I struggled with the meaning of darkness, I developed a special connection with the Black Madonna. The term "Black Madonna" refers to the hundreds of icons of the Black Virgin Mary. Called *Vierges Noires*, or Black Virgins in France, they are known as Black Madonnas in other countries.[2] An iconic vestige of the Mother Earth worship, the Black Madonna has been associated with ancient goddesses such as Isis, Black Artemis, Demeter, Cibele, Tara,[3] Kali[4] Inana, Lilith, Astarte, and other dark goddesses. Indeed, she is an emanation of the ancient divine female. Thus, the Black Madonna emerged as a syncretism of the goddess worship into Christianity. When the patriarchy usurped the goddess, early misogynist Christian writers split her into the Virgin Mary (immaculate conception) and Mary Magdalene (wrongly designated as a whore).[5] Such Madonna-whore division repressed female sexuality and excluded it from spirituality. Thus, the Black Madonna reclaimed female sexuality and became associated with Mary Magdalene, who appeared to have been an Astarte priestess.[6] Today the Black Madonna echoes the indigenous goddesses and embodies the hidden feminine qualities of healing, intuition, and ancient wisdom. She reigns over creation, destruction, sensuality, sexuality, fertility, mystery, esoteric knowledge, magic, revolution, evolution, and transformation.

As a Puerto Rican, I contend with historical and contemporary colonization. Therefore, my initiation into sacred darkness began with my struggle against oppression, racism, sexism, and elitism. Since the Black Madonna releases us from enslavement and oppression,[7] I internalized her as a subversive warrior. People all over the world struggling for liberation favor the Black Madonna.[8] For me, her darkness represents the strength, resilience, and transformative power of the oppressed. Invoking her alleviates my thirst for equality and justice. The mother of all, the Black Madonna protects the persecuted, consoles the unloved, and empowers the oppressed. As a feminist of color, I have joined others[9–11] who reinterpret the Black Madonna as a source of justice, reconciliation, and empowerment.

My healing journey was born out of paradoxes. Most Puerto Ricans call themselves the rainbow people, indicating their mixed racial ancestry. Simultaneously, they harbor internalized racism. As part of this paradox, they pray to a Black divinity. Consequently, the Black Madonna was omnipresent during my Caribbean childhood. She graced churches, cemeteries, houses, street corners, hospitals, bodegas (markets), and even *galleras* (cock-fighting establishments). Children caressed her scapulary, women nested her medallion in their breasts, drivers adorned their car dashes with her image, and politicians paraded her effigy during festivals.

I eagerly welcomed a *morena* (dark-skinned) divinity that looked like me. Fierce and loving, the Black Madonna made me comfortable with contradictions. Our Lady of Monserrat, the most popular icon in Puerto Rico, was my first Black Madonna. Originally from Catalonia, the Virgin of Monserrat is known as *la Moreneta* (the Dark One). She immigrated to our island and transformed herself into Monserrate of Hormigueros (a small town that witnessed several miracles by the Puerto Rican Black Madonna). She found a Puerto Rican home where she was honored as a matriarch during family fiestas. However, she did more than attend celebrations. As the Black Madonna stands against assimilation and enculturation,[12] La Monserrate presided over the emergence of the Puerto Rican identity during the Spanish colonization. Moreover, since the Black Madonna foments revolution and rebirth,[13] she reappeared on the island to affirm the Puerto Rican identity shortly after the invasion of the United States.[14]

La Virgen de Guadalupe was my second Black Madonna. Known as the patroness and goddess of the Americas, our Lady of Guadalupe— *La Morenita* (the Little Darkling) carved a special niche in my heart. Pregnant with contradiction, Guadalupe provided me with a model of feminine power since she is a petite, brown, poor woman who became a Pan-American liberation warrior. A blend of the Mexican goddess Tonantzin (our mother) with the Virgin Mary, Guadalupe's *mestiza* face reflected my own mixed racial ancestry. When I visited her shrine in Mexico I looked into her eyes and saw my Taíno, European, African, Asian, and Gypsy ancestors. No wonder she helped me integrate my multicultural identity; the Black Madonna calls us to embrace diversity.[15]

LONGING FOR BLACKNESS

Why do I yearn for her? Dislocations punctured my childhood. I was born in Chicago; my family moved back to their native Puerto Rico when I was six. A few years later I "lost" my parents and my toddler brother when they moved back to the continental United States. Due to financial reasons, I stayed with my maternal grandparents on the island. Contradictions colored that period of my life. On one hand, it was an idyllic time. I became Alicia in Mangoland, growing up with loving grandparents and an extended family. On the other hand, my mother's absence shadowed my heart. I retreated into a dark space where I encountered the Black Madonna. She inhabited my mother's shadow. The Black Madonna soothed what was burnt, wounded, and broken. In other words, she showed me how to alchemize pain into compassion.

I reunited with my parents and younger brother when I was ten years old. During my adolescence and youth I "forgot" the Black Madonna. Instead, I affirmed my Blackness in a sociopolitical way. The women's and civil rights' movements arrived to Puerto Rico during the late 1960s and early 1970s to find a nation with a collective internalized oppression. Contradictions fostered my development. These sociopolitical movements helped me to reformulate my identity as a Third World woman. I discovered the literature on psychology of the colonized, pedagogy of the oppressed, and liberation theology—later to be transformed into liberation psychology. Frantz Fanon taught me to analyze behavior in a geopolitical way, Paulo Freire raised my critical consciousness, and Ignacio Martín-Baró—a liberation priest and psychologist—reaffirmed my solidarity toward oppressed people all over the world. Even though these teachers were males, albeit being men of color, my constant mentors were women. Female teachers, relatives, saints, friends, colleagues, neighbors, politicians, artists, literary figures, historical personalities, and many other women became my compasses during my healing journey.

My training as a psychologist further distanced me from the Black Madonna. I became a conceited professional who favored science over wisdom.[16] Furthermore, my scientific socialization trained me to neglect matters of the soul. In short, I forgot who I was. Such negative internalization separated me from my ancestors and thus from myself. Notwithstanding my cultural amnesia, the Black Madonna repossessed me. As I matured, I frequently "stumbled" onto her sacred places in Belgium, Brazil, France, Italy, Russia, Spain, Sicily, Poland, and other countless locations. Millions of her devotees around the world visit her sacred sites in search of illuminated darkness. Interestingly, these same places were the original sites of ancient goddesses. As the proverbial saying goes, I didn't find the Black Madonna, she found me. I became conscious of my search for Blackness. When I arrived to Monserrat's basilica in Catalonia, her enigmatic face mesmerized me as I tried to figure how she balanced the world on her hand. As I performed the ritual of touching the ball/world resting on her hand, I fortified my commitment to global solidarity.

> *Do not fear any illness or vexation, anxiety, or pain. Am I not here who am your Mother? Are you not under my shadow and or protection? Is there anything else you need?*
>
> Our Lady of Guadalupe's words to Juan Diego,
> December 9, 12, 1531 (Shrine of Nuestra Senora de Guadalupe)

Death provided an opportunity to deepen my connection with sacred darkness. The Black Madonna releases us from grief, bereavement, and suffering. Paradoxically, she calls us to grieve in order to learn from suffering.[17] I traveled to India after my mother's death. A motherless daughter, I grieved for everything I had lost. In a mourning state I entered Kali's temple. The Black one, Kali is an ancestral Hindu goddess of creation and destruction. She transformed herself into a Black Madonna when the gypsies brought her from India to the West.[18] A mix of fury and love possessed me as I met Kali. I requested consecration and her priest opened my third eye. In my initiation I saw an illuminated darkness.

My mother's death converged with the birth of my oldest niece, Antonia. Three weeks separated Mami's departure from Antonia's arrival. My path to darkness took me to Nepal, where Kumari cemented my bond with the Black Madonna. The living goddess of Nepal, Kumari is believed to be Kali's human incarnation. I encountered Kumari-Kali on my first day in Katmandu. She looked into my eyes and claimed me. In a trance, I followed Kumari into her temple. Her guards stopped me with a "No foreigners allowed" order. That night, I witnessed the premature birth of my niece Antonia in a dream. Today, when I look into Antonia's face, Kumari stares back at me.[19]

Family illness further illuminated my inner Black Madonna. When my husband Fred developed cancer, we traveled to Mexico searching for hope. We found Marcelo, a Sufi healer who blended Christianity, Judaism, and Islam. A physician, Marcelo developed a psychospiritual approach to the treatment of cancer and psychological trauma. After working with Fred, Marcelo trained us on his psychospiritual healing. Thanks to a combination of Western and holistic healing, Fred remains in remission. We continue to work within a psychospiritual healing approach. Years later, my father-in-law's death facilitated a Buddhist pilgrimage. Since he always wanted to visit Asia, we took his ashes to Thailand, Bhutan, and Cambodia. While Fred scattered his father's ashes, I integrated Tara into my Black Madonna/Kali/Kumari. The Tibetan female Buddha, Tara is a bodhisattva of compassion identified with Kali and the Black Madonna.[20] Years later, Tara accompanied me as I journeyed into Tibet, where I witnessed how spirituality sustains Tibetans in their struggle against political oppression and cultural genocide. I found that many Tibetan women are named Tara after their guiding divinity. In China I met her as Kuan Yin. In this manifestation she sits enthroned in my bedroom. While I dream, Kuan Yin infuses me with compassion toward myself.

On my healing path I met Bill, a psychiatrist and a psychic who became my teacher. Bill facilitated the awakening of my inner Black Madonna. Through this process, he helped me to honor my prophetic abilities. During a guided imagery session, he asked me:

"How have you forgotten who you are?
"By not acknowledging my power."
"How can you own it?
"Stop being afraid."

My trepidation represented a fear of power. Theologian Matthew Fox[21] argues that the throat chakra (energy center) relates to our ability to prophesize because it manifests the expression of one's truth and wisdom. According to some Eastern practices, chakras are energy centers reflected in our bodies.[22, 23] I had previously channeled universal wisdom, but only in the sanctity of my psychotherapy office. Indeed, many of my Latino clients call me the Latino term *bruja*. Although translated as witch, bruja refers to a psychic healer. Healing runs though my veins and chakras. Petra, my paternal grandmother, earned a living working as a psychic. Hopscotching from island to mainland, Petra was very successful in her spiritual profession. As a Sybil, a woman who prophesizes, she acknowledged her Christian, Native, and

African spiritual guides. Likewise, my maternal grandmother Antonia was a devout Catholic who had powerful psychic abilities. Although she did not earn a living via her spiritual gifts, she was a compassionate and altruistic woman. My mother also had psychic and healing abilities and used them in her nursing profession. Notwithstanding this ancestral heritage, my deepest fear was to own my powers of prophecy.

This fear appeared to be related to karma. I was born with a cleft palate that was surgically repaired when I was four. I stammered until age seventeen, when I realized that success in college required the ability to engage in articulate conversation. Consequently, I developed an anti-stammering therapy and treated myself.[24] Years later, an international expert on cleft palate surgery examined me at the Mayo Clinic. She told me that my cleft palate was one of the top three repairs she had ever seen. "Your doctors did not know what they were doing when they operated on you," she said. Her eyes filled with tears. "At that time we did not have the correct technology to repair cleft palates. Yet your operation was a triumph." The doctor grabbed a tissue. "Divine intervention made your operation a success."

Notwithstanding the surgical victory, my throat chakra had a spiritual wound. Known as the fifth chakra, the throat energy center is usually associated with communication and with lessons related to will and self-expression.[25] According to Bill, I am a warrior who carried a mighty sword. The spiritual act of accepting the sword fissured my palate.

"You don't have to carry the sword all the time," Bill reassured me.

I reviewed the literature on warriors of the light and gained a conceptual understanding of my purpose in life.[26] However, it took sustained psychospiritual practice and guidance from my inner Black Madonna to accept my life's task: To balance the scepter with the light, and to integrate my warrior into my healer. I learned to wield the sword and to rescue my creativity. As a child, I loved to write stories. My family and friends circled around me as I told my tales. I stammered my words into *cuentos* (stories) of wonder. Today, I see myself as a healing *cantadora* (story teller). I encourage others to tell their stories. Just like my loving circle did for me, I witness my patients' healing as they rescript their life stories.

MY PATIENT, MYSELF

The healing influence of the Black Madonna is extending into psychotherapy. In Jungian psychology, she embodies the feminine principle manifested in consciousness and inner transformation. Moreover, the Black Madonna represents the feminine in man and the self in woman.[27] She awakens a collective consciousness wherein the individual connects with all. The integration of the Black Madonna empowers us to fight against oppression, racism, and materialism.[28] Therefore, healing with the Black Madonna entails reconnecting with inner guidance, awakening our liberation warrior, and fostering transformation. My path to the Black Madonna helped me to access my intuition as a therapist. Healers help by simply aiding patients to commune with their spiritual natures.[29] Likewise, I try to assist my patients in their healing journeys. I have found that it is important for the psychotherapist to commit to a spiritual practice in order to witness her client's transformation. However, I am careful not to suggest any particular spiritual approach. Instead, I wait for cultural resonance to emerge. I use this concept to describe the ability to understand clients through clinical skill, cultural competence, and intuition.[30] In multicultural psychotherapy, intuition refers to a collectivistic nonverbal communication that relies on internal cues, hunches, and vibes as a means of problem solving.[31] If I have cultural and spiritual resonance with a patient, I intuitively work within an experiential mode to allow her to awaken her inner divinity.

In the following vignette, I discuss my therapy with Amparo, using a feminist psychospiritual approach. I present how Amparo uncovered her inner Black Madonna as a process of healing, reconciliation, and transformation.

Amparo was a thirty-year-old single Mexican American woman. She came to psychotherapy complaining of concentration problems. The first in her family to graduate from college, Amparo worked as an architect. Her parents divorced when she was six. Afterward, Amparo, her mother, and her younger brother Sebastian moved in with Dona Flor, Amparo's maternal grandmother. Tragedy visited the family. When she was eight, Amparo witnessed Sebastian's death. A car killed five-year-old Sebastian when he ran into the road chasing their pet dog. Blinded by grief, Dona Flor blamed Amparo's mother, who in turn blamed Amparo. Sebastian's death became the common denominator between the three women. His absence permeated their relationship. Consequently, Amparo left home at seventeen to work as a waitress. She saved enough money to go to college. Amparo described her relationship with her mother as cordial but distant. However, she felt betrayed by Dona Flor because, prior to Sebastian's death, Amparo and her grandmother were very close. "*Abuela* lost her spirit after Sebastian died," Amparo said of her grandmother. As a result of these experiences, Amparo developed posttraumatic stress disorder (PTSD). I suggested a trauma therapy to help her with the memories around her losses. We used eye movement desensitization reprocessing (EMDR) therapy.[32] After completing EMDR, Amparo's grandmother passed away. "I want to work on my relationship with mothering," Amparo stated.

I suggested a holistic approach. After teaching Amparo relaxation techniques, I used experiential techniques to help her initiate a conversation with herself. She responded well to guided imagery and mental visualization. Additionally, she learned to meditate. Around this time Amparo left her job and founded a Latino architectural firm. "I'm designing my own life," she announced. During an experiential session, Amparo "saw" her mother dressed in black crying over a grave. Upon closer examination, Amparo realized that the grave bore her own name. She became agitated by this dream. We worked on her feelings of loss, guilt, and anxiety. Paradoxically, her fear of dying connected Amparo with her self-healing capacities. To illustrate, Amparo began to revisit old traumatic memories and to recreate and reprocess them into positive experiences. For instance, she mentally rescripted several conflicts with her mother by being assertive and letting go of her guilt. "I have internalized the trauma therapy," Amparo explained. She gained an increased sense of agency. Notwithstanding this progress, an event changed her life dramatically.

Amparo discovered she was pregnant. Alberto, an ex-boyfriend and classmate from graduate school, visited her. Both of them realized that they still had feelings for each other. "I'm keeping the baby, but I'm not getting married," Amparo asserted.

We worked on Amparo's complicated bereavement. "I would like to talk with my unborn child," she stated. I suggested an experiential healing exercise—the inner guide. While physicians have used this technique for treating cancer,[33] psychotherapists have used the inner guide or wise-mind technique to work with trauma.[34, 35] During the exercise, I asked Amparo to concentrate on her abdomen:

"I feel relaxed," Amparo said.
"Anything else?"
"No—wait, I see a woman."
"Who is the woman?"
Amparo began to sob. "My grandmother loved her."
"Can you tell me more?" I inquired.
"Yes, she is our Lady of Guadalupe. Abuela was her devotee," Amparo said.
"What's happening now?" I asked.
"She is telling me not to worry. Guadalupe is pregnant. She will help me with my baby."

We processed this experience during regular psychotherapy sessions. Amparo worked out her complicated grief, guilt, and bereavement. She wrote a letter to her grandmother and initiated the mother-daughter-granddaughter healing. She invited her mother to accompany her to the cemetery. Amparo read the letter to her Abuela while her mother embraced her. Amparo felt more connected to her mother after performing this ritual. During meditation, Amparo realized that her child was a son and decided to name him Sebastian. Months later, Amparo completed treatment. Eventually, I received a birth announcement in the mail. Amparo had decided to reunite with Alberto, who was working at her architectural firm. Furthermore, the letter stated that Amparo's mother had moved in to help her raise Sebastian.

CONCLUSION: THE ENIGMA OF THE JOURNEY

My healing journey takes me to places of sacred darkness. These pilgrimages illuminate the enigma of my journey—to see darkness out of light. The Black Madonna is my departure and arrival. In the process of awakening my inner sacredness, I accompany others in their healing journeys. Together we seek illuminated darkness.

NOTES

1. Comas-Díaz, "Spirita: Reclaiming Womanist Sacredness into Feminism," 2008.

2. Begg, The Cult of the Black Virgin, 1985.

3. Galland, Longing for Darkness: Tara and the Black Madonna, 1990.

4. Boyer, The Cult of the Virgin: Offerings, Ornaments, and Festivals, 2000.

5. Pagels, The Gnostic Gospels, 1989.

6. King, The Gospel of Mary of Magdala: Jesus and the First Woman Apostle, 2003

7. Dumars and Nyx, The Dark Archetype: Exploring the Shadow Side of the Divine, 2003.

8. Teish, "The warrior queen: Encounters with a Latin lady," 1996.

9. Castillo, Goddess of the Americas/La Diosa de las Americas: Writings on the Virgin of Guadalupe, 1996.

10. Cisneros, "Guadalupe, the sex goddess," 2001.

11. Rodriguez, "Guadalupe, The feminine face of God," 1996.

12. Dumars and Nyx, The Dark Archetype, 2003.

13. Gustafson, The Moonlit Path: Reflections on the Dark Feminine, 2003.

14. Negretti, La Buenaventura (The Good Adventure), 2005.

15. Fox, "The return of the Black Madonna: A sign of our times or how the Black Madonna is shaking us up for the twenty-first century," 2003.

16. Comas-Díaz, "Becoming a multicultural psychotherapist: The convergence of culture, ethnicity, and gender," 2005.

17. Gustafson, The Moonlit Path, 2003.

18. Comas-Díaz, "The Black Madonna: The psychospiritual feminism of Guadalupe, Kali, and Monserrat," 2003.

19. Comas-Díaz, "In Search of the Goddess," 2006.

20. Gallard, Longing for Darkness, 1990.

21. Fox, Sins of the Spirit, Blessings of the Flesh: Lessons for Transforming Evil in Soul and Society, 1999.

22. Anodea, Eastern Body, Western Mind: Psychology and the Chakra System as a Path to the Self, 1996.

23. Myss, Anatomy of the Spirit: The Seven Stages of Power and Healing, 1996.

24. Comas-Díaz, "Becoming a multicultural psychotherapist: The convergence of culture, ethnicity, and gender," 2005.

25. Fox, *Sins of the Spirit, Blessings of the Flesh: Lessons for Transforming Evil in Soul and Society,* 1999.

26. Coelho, *Warrior of the Light: A Manual,* 2003.

27. Gallard, *Longing for Darkness,* 1990.

28. Quispel, *The Secret Book of Revelations: The Last Book of the Bible,* 1979.

29. Karasu, *The Art of Serenity: The Path to a Joyful Life in the Best and Worst of Times,* 2003.

30. Comas-Díaz, "Cultural variation in the therapeutic relationship," 2006.

31. Comas-Díaz, "Cultural variation in the therapeutic relationship," 2006.

32. Shapiro, *Eye Movement Desensitization and Reprocessing: Basic Principles, Protocols, and Procedures,* 1995.

33. Simonton, Matthews-Simonton, and Creighton, *Getting Well Again,* 1978.

34. Comas-Díaz, "Our inner Black Madonna: Reclaiming sexuality, embodying sacredness," in press.

35. Linehan, *Cognitive-Behavioral Treatment of Borderline Personality Disorder,* 1993.

REFERENCES

Anodea, Judith. *Eastern Body, Western Mind: Psychology and the Chakra System as a Path to the Self.* Berkeley, CA: Celestial Arts, 1996.

Begg, Ean. *The Cult of the Black Virgin.* London: Arkana/Penguin Books, 1985.

Boyer, M. F. *The Cult of the Virgin: Offerings, Ornaments, and Festivals.* New York: Thames & Hudson, 2000.

Castillo, Ana, ed. *Goddess of the Americas/La Diosa de las Américas: Writings on the Virgin of Guadalupe.* New York: Riverhead Books, 1996.

Cisneros, Sandra. "Guadalupe, the Sex Goddess." In M. Sewell, ed. *Resurrecting Grace: Remembering Catholic Childhoods.* Boston: Beacon Press, 2001.

Coelho, Paulo. *Warrior of the Light: A Manual.* New York: HarperCollins Publishers, 2003.

Comas-Díaz, Lillian. "The Black Madonna: The Psychospiritual Feminism of Guadalupe, Kali, and Monserrat. In L. Silvestein and T. J. Goodrich, eds. *Feminist Family: Empowerment and Social Location.* Washington, DC: American Psychological Association, 2003, 147–160.

———. "In Search of the Goddess." In M. L. Tompkins and J. McMahon, eds. *Illuminations: Expressions of the Personal Spiritual Experience.* Berkeley, CA: Celestial Arts, 2006.

———. "Becoming a Multicultural Psychotherapist: The Convergence of Culture, Ethnicity, and Gender." *In Session* 61 (2) (2005): 973–981.

———. "Cultural Variation in the Therapeutic Relationship." In C. Goodheart, R. J. Sternberg, and A. Kazdin, eds. *The Evidence for Psychotherapy: Where Practice and Research Meet.* Washington, DC: American Psychological Association, 2006.

———. "Spirita: Reclaiming womanist sacredness into feminism." *Psychology of Women Quarterly,* 2008, 32(1), 13–20.

———. "Our Inner Black Madonna: Reclaiming Sexuality, Embodying Sacredness." *Women & Therapy,* in press.

Dumars, Denise, and Lori Nyx. *The Dark Archetype: Exploring the Shadow Side of the Divine.* Franklin Lakes, NJ: The Career Press/New Page Books, 2003.

Fox, Matthew. "The Return of the Black Madonna: A Sign of Our Times or How the Black Madonna is Shaking Us Up for the Twenty-first Century." In F. Gustafson, ed. *The Moonlit Path: Reflections on the Dark Feminine.* Berwick, ME: Nicolas-Hays, 2003.

———. *Sins of the Spirit, Blessings of the Flesh: Lessons for Transforming Evil in Soul and Society.* New York: Three Rivers Press, 1999.

Galland, China. *Longing for Darkness: Tara and the Black Madonna.* New York: Compass/Penguin Press, 1990.

Gustafson, Fred. "The dark mother, the dark earth, and the loss of native soul." In F. Gustafson, ed., *The Moonlit Path: Reflections on the Dark Feminine.* (pp. 3–16). Berwick, ME: Nicolas-Hays, 2003.

Karasu, T. Byram. *The Art of Serenity: The Path to a Joyful Life in the Best and Worst of Times.* New York: Simon & Shuster, 2003.

King, Karen L. *The Gospel of Mary of Magdala: Jesus and the First Woman Apostle.* Santa Rosa, CA: Polebridge Press, 2003.

Linehan, Marsha M. *Cognitive-Behavioral Treatment of Borderline Personality Disorder.* New York: Guilford Press, 1993.

Myss, Carolyn. *Anatomy of the Spirit: The Seven Stages of Power and Healing.* New York: Three Rivers Press, 1996.

Negretti, Vionette. *La Buenaventura (The Good Adventure).* Bogota, Colombia: Ediciones Yagrumo, 2005.

Pagels, Elaine. *The Gnostic Gospels.* New York: Vintage Books, 1989.

Quispel, Gilles. *The Secret Book of Revelations: The Last Book of the Bible.* San Francisco: McGraw-Hill, 1979.

Rodriguez, Janette. "Guadalupe: The feminine face of God." In A. Castillo, ed., *Goddess of the Americas/La Diosa de las Américas: Writings on the Virgin of Guadalupe* (pp. 25–31). New York: Riverhead Books, 1996.

Shapiro, Francine. *Eye Movement Desensitization and Reprocessing: Basic Principles, Protocols, and Procedures.* New York: Guilford, 1995.

Simonton, O. Carl, Stephanie Matthews-Simonton, and James Creighton. *Getting Well Again.* New York: Bantam Books, 1978.

Teish, Luisa. "The Warrior Queen: Encounters with a Latin Lady." In A. Castillo, ed. *Goddess of the Americas/La Diosa de las Americas: Writings on the Virgin of Guadalupe,* 137–146. New York: Riverhead Books, 1996.

Chapter 7

View of Women, Spirituality, and Tibetan Buddhism

Renate Wewerka

Tibetan Buddhism, with its different schools and lineages, postulates that there is suffering in every human life, simply through living in our world. On the basis of our physical existence, we experience much suffering: birth, sickness, old age, and death. On a different level, we may suffer from disappointments when we get what we do not want or we do not get what we want. Buddhism strives to end suffering. Its goal is an understanding of the real nature of our minds. Negative thoughts and feelings are not seen as inherent to our psyches, but are perceived as obstacles that keep us from the true nature of our basic goodness. The inherent natures of ourselves, these absolute truths, are clear, luminous, and completely nonjudgmental. Not directly or easily accessible, our real selves are hidden like the sun behind the clouds. All of the "chatter" that goes on in our minds could be compared to the clouds keeping us from experiencing the true nature of mind.

Buddhism is not a "belief system, or a set of intellectual exercises, or something that applies just to Buddhists. It is a meticulously reasoned analysis of life, which places great emphasis on watching the mind."[1] To overcome one's obstacles and suffering, one can train one's mind, through meditation, the development and practice of compassion, and knowledge of the true nature of mind. Here, "compassion can be roughly defined in terms of a state of mind that is nonviolent, nonharming, and nonaggressive. It is a mental attitude based on the wish for others to be free of suffering and it is associated with a sense of commitment, responsibility, and respect toward others.... In developing compassion, perhaps one could begin with the wish that oneself is free of suffering, and then take that natural feeling towards oneself and cultivate it, and extend it out to include and embrace others."[2]

How do these concepts relate to my own life? I was raised in Vienna, Austria, mostly by my mother and grandmother from the former Czechoslovakia. When I was three, my beloved grandfather died. He was until then the source of my emotional support, accepting me as the child I was. Looking back, it seemed that after my grandfather's death, I was never seen as the child I had been, but instead had to carry the projections of my parents and grandmother. Going through a divorce in my late thirties, I was somewhat surprised to hear my therapist say that without my grandfather, I probably would have died. At first I took this as an exaggeration, but upon further consideration, I had to agree with her. Overall, my family was clearly dominated by its Slovakian, not Viennese, women, with a grandmother who had owned a small business and a mother who appeared more fulfilled when circumstances forced her to work outside the home. Therefore, I was a member of at least two minorities. My mother, coming from another culture, and having her own standards and rules, brought me up differently than other children were raised. One of her standards was, "You must always tell the truth." When in my late teens I read one of the key novels of Austrian literature from the twentieth century and encountered a sentence that, as far as I remember, stated something like, "Vienna is the city where people think differently than they talk, and talk differently than they think." (from *The Man without Qualities*, Robert Musil, 1930, 1933, 1943). I experienced a sense of relief that somebody else, and not only anybody, but one of the most famous Austrian writers of his time had written about a reality that quite often I had trouble understanding and handling. Although I always had a few friends, overall I felt alienated and not fitting in, quite often without knowing why and what it was that I contributed to the situation.

I also grew up as a Protestant in a Catholic country. There were a few of us in each class and at summer camp. Although religion was usually not an issue that came up in our talks or interactions, we Protestants had to participate in certain Catholic ceremonies in school. At summer camp we had to attend Catholic mass to "earn" some time on our own and to experience some freedom. Therefore, soon I knew all Catholic prayers by heart and could not avoid reciting them in my head, even when the content was contrary to what I was taught about my religion. This made me feel like I betrayed my faith. During my early childhood, I faithfully said my prayers before going to sleep. Later, I participated in religion classes in school and in Sunday school the year before my confirmation. From the fifth to the twelfth grade, religion was taught by a teacher who was also a historian. She familiarized us with the Bible from a historical point of view, letting us work out the way it related to our lives in the late 1960s. Having been an unhappy child and teenager, I became an agnostic in my late teens. This was due to a lack of understanding where all the suffering in my life and in the world was coming from if there was a benevolent God.

I later realized that, as a woman in a very patriarchal society, I also had a different status and therefore was excluded from certain areas of society. It was all right to get a PhD, so a woman could be a more interesting hostess for her husband's guests, but apparently wrong to pursue a "real" job. After my graduation in 1977, during job interviews I was usually asked, "Do you really want to take away a job from a man?" I was also informed that I would have children and leave the job, which would be too big of an inconvenience for the company. It should be noted that statistics at the time showed that women usually changed jobs less frequently than men. When a friend of mine graduated in communications and pursued a position in the marketing department of a huge organization, she was told by the director of the department that he would do anything to keep her from getting any job in his department.

At the time of the women's movement in the United States, my life in Vienna meant dealing with the culture of a more conservative, patriarchal, and traditional society than in the United States. It appeared to me that the U.S. women's movement was wider spread and encompassed a larger variety of women from more sociodemographic groups than in Vienna, where a small movement took place mostly at the universities.

Coming from a family dominated by strong and controlling women and from a background where I felt sometimes unprepared for the dynamics of society, I experienced strong feelings of "not fitting in." Maybe not surprisingly I had to deal with feelings of depression, anger, frustration, and rejection. Fortunately, with the help of friends in the United States, by then I had encountered ideas and concepts of female writers in the United States, which made me feel less ostracized and estranged from the culture that had surrounded me while growing up, and I was therefore open for my emigration to the United States.

The experiences as a woman in a predominately patriarchal society came back to me many years later when I came across a chapter in Taigen Daniel Leighton's book *Bodhisattva Archetypes*.[3] A bodhisattva is usually described as an individual who relinquishes complete Buddhahood or full enlightenment with the help of his/her compassion, love, and practice of virtues. Leighton writes about the bodhisattva Vimalakirti, a wealthy follower of the historical Shakyamuni Buddha, who was born around 566 BCE into an aristocratic family in Nepal.

In a sutra, a prose text that relates to the Buddha's teachings, the main character Vimalakirti is described as a quite wealthy person who lived a privileged life. He practiced Buddhism as a layperson demonstrating that spiritual practice can happen outside a monastic environment.

The sutra tells of Vimalakirti's abilities of teaching other bodhisattvas, especially about insight in "emptiness."

According to Buddhist teachings, all beings, all thoughts, all feelings, all perceptions, all things, and therefore all phenomena we are experiencing are essentially empty. This does not mean that nothing exists; it rather means that all phenomena are free of fixed qualities, identities, and the judgments we usually associate with them. They are recognized as themselves only in relation to other things. For instance, we might put a judgment on an object that it is really long. The object might be quite long compared to one object, but really short compared to another. To put it differently, we see everything as real, but in an absolute sense, nothing actually is. In an absolute reality all phenomena are illusions. On an absolute level the "long" object initially judged that way is free from any permanent judgment, along with our ideas and perceptions that we had about it; the object is what Buddhism calls "empty." However, emptiness is not nothing, but is filled with compassion.

We are used to perceiving all phenomena, all sensations (forms, sounds, smells, tastes, thoughts, etc.) as different from ourselves. An internal "I" perceives these objects. Thus, a duality is experienced. Between its two poles, thoughts of attachment and repulsion are created. But objects perceived as external do not have any self-existence and lack essence. They do not have independent existence that we may prescribe to them, but are only the illusions and projections of our minds.

Going back to Vimalakirti's sutra, it was interesting for me to read that one of the most spectacular examples of Buddhist teachings was performed by an unnamed female bodhisattva who had been living with Vimalakirti for several years. After this female bodhisattva gave a demonstration of her powers and teachings, she was asked by the male disciple, Shariputra, why she did not transform herself into a man. Giving instructions about emptiness, namely, that all phenomena, including gender, are only illusions, the female bodhisattva used her magical powers and switched her body with Shariputra: "She is transformed into Shariputra, and he finds himself in her body. Shariputra is shocked and distraught to find himself a woman, and he admits that he does not know how to change back into a man. The goddess explains to Shariputra that the gender distinction is not ultimately real, that the Buddha has said that beings are not, in essence, limited to being either male or female.

"The goddess changes Shariputra and herself back to their previous forms. She clarifies that just like Shariputra's temporary femininity, which he neither produced nor could transform, all qualities, including gender, are not really created."

In another story, Tara, the female bodhisattva of compassion, was the daughter of a king before becoming a bodhisattva. Her name was

Wisdom Moon. After years of offerings to the Buddha of her time and his monks, she decided to take the bodhisattva vow, thus declaring her intent to seek enlightenment not only for herself but also for the sake of all sentient beings. With their congratulations, the monks counseled Wisdom Moon to pray to be reborn as a man so she could be of greater benefit to all sentient beings. Concerned about the monks' limited understanding of Buddhist teachings, she responded:

"Here, no man, no woman,
no I, no individual, no categories.
"Man" or "woman" are only denominations
created by confusion of perverse minds
in this world."[4]

Thus, Wisdom Moon, who later became the bodhisattva Tara, answered from an absolute point of truth. As an enlightened deity, her mind is absolute, beyond any duality as existing and nonexistent. Her awakened mind is the true nature of our own mind. Tara is also sometimes referred to as the "perfection of knowledge" (prajnaparamita). This perfection of knowledge is emptiness, one of the most important concepts in Buddhism. Also often called "mother of all Buddhas," it refers to the source from which everything originates, not literally to a birth mother. In earlier stages of Buddhism, prajnaparamita, the feminine principle, was not represented as a Buddha as it happened later.

Interestingly, many of the great practitioners and teachers of history were female: Machig Lapdron, who lived in the eleventh century and reportedly was an incarnation of Guru Padmasambava's consort, Yeshe Tsogyel, taught the Chod practice, which aims to "cut through" all attachments and the ego. In this practice, ego should be understood as one's attachment to thoughts, emotions, and sensations, and, according to Buddhism, the false perception of a split between an I and others.

The protector of the Tibetan Buddhist Drikung lineage is Achi Chokyi Drolma, who lived in the eleventh century. Her birth is described as auspicious, because her body radiated rays of light. As an infant she was reciting the mantra of Tara and at the age of three she was teaching it to others. Reportedly, she was very beautiful, but refused many marriage proposals, stating that she would marry a certain yogi with whom she would found a lineage. She was able to lead her followers to enlightenment.

Thus, according to Buddhist teachings, gender is empty; in essence there are no differences between men and women. In a public talk in July 2007, Gochen Tulku Rinpoche pointed out that differentiations between men and women are created by the culture in which the teachings are given and not by the teachings themselves.

However, perhaps all of us Buddhist practitioners might have encountered situations wherein the teachings challenged our ordinary everyday lives. Female practitioners have been refused access to the highest teachings or, because of their "inferior" bodies, had to sit behind monks with less experience and fewer teachings, to name only two of such experiences by ordained female practitioners. The book *Cave in the Snow* by Vicki Mackenzie[5] describes how, at a Western Buddhism conference in Dharamsala, India, a German laywoman asked the invited participants, including His Holiness the Dalai Lama, to participate in a visualization: "Please imagine that you are a male coming to a Buddhist center. You see the painting of this beautiful Tara surrounded by sixteen female arhats (arhats work towards their own enlightenment in contrast to bodhisattvas who aim to free all sentient beings from suffering) and you have the possibility to see too Her Holiness the fourteen Dalai Lama, who, in all of her fourteen incarnations, has always chosen a female rebirth.... Remember you are male and you approach a lama, feeling a little bit insecure and a little bit irritated, and ask, 'Why are there all these female symbols, female Buddhas?' And she replies, 'Don't worry. Men and women are equal. Well, almost. We do have some scriptures that say that a male birth is inferior, but isn't this the case? Men do have a more difficult time when all the leaders, spiritually, philosophically, and politically, are women....' And then the male student, who is very sincere, goes to another lama, ... and says, 'I am a man, how can I identify with all these female icons?' And she replies, 'You just meditate on Shunyata (emptiness). In Shunyata no man, no woman, no body, nothing. No problem.'

"So you go to a tantric teacher and say, 'All these women and I am a man. I don't know how to relate.' And she says, "How wonderful you are, beautiful Daka, you are so useful to us practitioners helping raising us our kundalini energy. How blessed you are to be male, to benefit female practitioners on their path to enlightenment." Reportedly, this mental exercise gave male participants, including His Holiness, some new perspectives.

Maybe the young (and female) Venerable Kandro Rinpoche said it best when advising Judith Simmer-Brown in her book *Dakini's Warm Breath*, "If being a woman is an inspiration, use it. If it is an obstacle, try not to be bothered."[6]

One might also consider the Buddhist concept of karma. Karma, which means action, initiates cycles of cause and effect: when we act (and here one has to bear in mind that Buddhist philosophy considers attaching to one's thoughts as action) based on negative emotions such as anger, hatred, or ignorance, we create negative conditions for ourselves; when we act based on positive motivation, for instance, because we can have compassion, we create positive conditions. Since karma does not follow an immediate timetable, consequences are never lost; it only may appear so.

After the age of three, having grown up with the very subjective feeling of having to accomplish everything on my own without the support from my immediate family, my preference of Buddhism became clear to me when in a social situation a minister questioned my practice of Buddhism instead of accepting that Jesus Christ died for me and my sins. Apparently, it is easier for me to follow a philosophy and practice in which I am responsible for everything that happens in my life than have somebody else responsible for it. As a psychologist, another attraction of Buddhist teachings is their similarity to cognitive psychology as the Dalai Lama and H. C. Cutler demonstrate in their book *The Art of Happiness*.

In my work as therapist, I have seen clients who try to avoid their suffering with some form of addictive behavior, related to substances, sex, work, or other addictions. Clients also use psychological defense mechanisms such as denial and projection to avoid dealing with their pain. Sometimes a client gets so entangled in her or his story that the person does not allow her/himself to feel his or her pain, anger, or shame. Having Buddhist philosophy in mind, I may choose to communicate to clients that they do not have to feel sorry for themselves, but can allow surrendering to feelings of pain, shame, or anger, acknowledge them, thereby allowing their thoughts and feelings to pass through and then to release them. This might lead to the clients' courageous steps of letting go of their pain and suffering from the past, and undergoing a process requiring time and courage. Since I try to remember that Buddhism is a philosophy that does not blame anybody and does not judge, I work on accepting others (including my clients) as they are without blaming and judging, being with them where they are in each moment, accepting their willingness or unwillingness to confront their pain, and at the same time aiming to facilitate changes in behaviors, feelings, and cognitions. Sometimes teaching my clients a simple form of meditation, like focusing on an object, for instance, one's breath, and bringing one's mind back to the object when thoughts, feelings, or sensations arise, might allow the client to become aware of thoughts coming up, to acknowledge them without judgment, and to let them go. This could lead to the ability to let go of one's ideas and perceptions about the past and the future, and makes it possible that one is fully present in the here and now. According to Buddhism, mindfulness, the state of being in the present moment and consciously experiencing and performing all activities, even mundane ones like breathing and walking, is a step toward recognizing the true nature of the mind; it makes it possible to control one's mind and to experience a state where the mind is at rest. During therapy, most likely I will not explain this or other concepts; however, I truly believe that being able to experience every moment mindfully and consciously might benefit almost everybody.

Now working again in a patriarchal environment and having to deal with "old-boy's networks" leaves me little time to do a formal practice or to meditate. My practice these days consists of working on remembering the Buddhist teachings and watching every thought that comes to my mind. Ideally, I would allow thoughts and feelings to come up and let them go. Realistically, I get angry more often than I want to and struggle to let go of my anger. Far from being able to let go of my anger or other negative thoughts and feelings as soon as they arise, I also have been unable to practice unconditional compassion with people who lie to me or try to manipulate and/or undermine me in different ways. Nevertheless, I consider exercising mindfulness of my cognitions and/ or feelings every moment and not reacting to them as my current practice. Thus, Buddhist teachings have become a very integral part of my daily life and have enabled me to find a philosophy and practice that helped me to organize the world I live in and my perceptions of it. Interestingly enough, during my attendance of teachings and retreats, I have encountered people who continue to follow other religions but find Buddhist concepts helpful on their spiritual paths. For instance, Catholic women friends of mine with a strong connection to the Virgin Mary also have strong connections to one of the manifestations of the female bodhisattva Tara.

Buddhist teachings taught me to be respectful of every religion or spiritual path others might follow. I learned that if I were living with somebody who does not share my beliefs, I have to avoid chanting loudly or display any rituals that might offend others. I am not supposed to try to convert anybody to the teachings either, since, not surprisingly, Buddhists believe that the religious or spiritual path one follows is determined by one's karma.

I was lucky enough to be able to hear the Dalai Lama twice. On both occasions he was asked about possible military actions by Tibet against China. Each time he explained that active violence is not acceptable and thus will not be considered as a possibility. Having grown up in a country that was still devastated by World War II, I think that Buddhism's emphasis on nonviolence is one aspect that has drawn me to it.

In my daily life I continually strive to maintain an orientation toward the principles of basic goodness and compassion. At times this is difficult since it is so easy for me to get angry or see others as annoying and frustrating. However, the more I can maintain a nonaggressive, compassionate mind, the happier and more content I am.

NOTES

1. Gyaltsen, 1996.
2. Dalai Lama, and Cutler, 1998.
3. Leighton, 1998.

4. Rinpoche, 1999.
5. Mackenzie, 1998.
6. Simmer-Brown, 2001.

BIBLIOGRAPHY

Dalai Lama, and Howard C. Cutler. *The Art of Happiness.* New York: Riverhead Books, 1998.

Gyaltsen, Rinpoche, and Khenpo Konchog. *Transformation of Suffering.* Frederick, MD: Vajra Publications, 1996.

Leighton, Taigen Daniel. *Bodhisattva Archetypes.* New York: Penguin Putnam, 1998.

Mackenzie, Vicki. *Cave in the Snow.* New York: Bloomsbury, 1998.

Rinpoche, Bokar. *Tara, the Feminine Divine.* San Francisco, CA: Clear Point Press, 1999.

Simmer-Brown, Judith. *Dakini's Warm Breath.* Boston, MA: Shambhala, 2001.

Chapter 8

American Indian Women and Spirituality

Rose L. Weahkee

American Indian women are very spiritual people. It is impossible to talk about Indian women and culture without considering Indian spirituality.[1] Spirituality is an integral part of the American Indian way of life.[2] Indian spirituality permeates every facet of Indian women's daily lives. Traditional spirituality and practices are integrated into American Indian cultures. It is not seen as a separate part of life or confined in any way. It is not separate for the physical, social, mental, or emotional aspects of self.[3]

Indian women are members of a community that includes all beings. Each has its proper role, and each has its sense of responsibility and obligations to others.[4] A woman's identity in traditional Indian life is firmly rooted in her spirituality, extended family, and tribe.[5] Indian women see themselves in harmony with the biological, spiritual, and social worlds. They are valued for being mothers and raising healthy families. They are considered to be the extensions of the Spirit Mother and contribute to the continuation of their people. They also serve as transmitters of cultural knowledge and as caretakers of children and relatives.

American Indian spirituality is much broader than what we think of as religion. Those that follow the traditions, the beliefs, and rituals of old culture find it very difficult to define or explain religion.[6] It encompasses our relationship to our family, our community, those living, our ancestors, and the yet to be born or "seventh generation." The concept of the seventh generation refers to a core philosophical value that cuts across many American Indian tribes. Embodied within this philosophical perspective is the notion that the responsibility for the well-being of future generations rests with the generations that come before them. Therefore, the actions and decisions that we make today are guided by what is best for the seventh unborn generation. As such, we will make decisions and take actions that will ensure a healthy future for generations to come.

Indian spirituality includes the relationship of a particular tribal group with a respective land. The majority of Indian tribal religions have a sacred center at a particular place. This sacred center can be a river, mountain, plateau, valley, or other natural feature.[7] This spiritual place enables the tribe to relate to historical events on that particular land. These sacred lands provide tribal groups with cultural and spiritual meaning and understanding. Indian people have responsibility for these sacred lands. They must live in harmony and balance with the land. Many Indians derive their identity from their homelands no matter how far away they may live.[8]

Spirituality includes our relationship to the unseen world of spirits. Specific beliefs, practices, and relationships with the spiritual world differ from tribe to tribe, family to family, and person to person. Spirituality deals with beliefs, how one conducts her life, and with what happens. It is broad and encompasses religion, psychic, visionary, telepathic, and synchronistic experiences.[9] Indian spirituality is circular, feeling, and being.[10]

Indian spirituality encompasses "all my relations" and all those living things that possess a spiritual nature. Spirituality is at the core of all living things and humans.[11] It is seen and understood as a fundamental reality of all life and people. This interconnectedness between all things is inseparable. It is continuously interacting.[12] Worship in traditional religions was out-of-doors among nature. There is the widespread belief that all creatures, all things, both animate and inanimate, possess a spiritual being.[13] There is a spiritual side to all living and natural things, not only to humans. Spirituality is interwoven into all aspects of life and affects all of it.

Spiritual activities bring family and friends together. For example, the sweat lodge brings people closer in this feeling of connectedness. When participants leave the sweat lodge ceremony, they are reminded to say "all my relations." This affirms the relationship that humans share with all aspects of creation and nature. Creation and nature include living things, those in the waters, the plants, the wind, the sun, and all inanimate objects such as the rocks and the earth. The expression of "all my relations" affirms the relationship that humans share with the spirit world. The spirit world coexists with the physical world; elders often refer to this as a transformation through "connection to spirit."[14] The belief is that all creation and nature have spirit.[15]

One of the most important values of many Indian people is a sense of responsibility. Placing the needs of the group before others is a fundamental aspect of Indian spirituality. Along with the belief that all things are connected comes the responsibility to take care of and respect all creation.[16] There is a basic goodness in all creation, nature, and people. As such, we have the responsibility to take care of each other and all aspects of life.

Spiritual life is of great importance to Indian people. Most Indian people approach spiritual events with great care and respect.[17] American Indian cultures share an attitude of respect toward the world around us and for spiritual forces. This includes respect for those who lived before us and honoring our ancestors. This respect is emulated in the way we conduct ourselves every day and it is taught to our youth. Elders are also highly respected as the keepers of traditions. Elders serve as guides to traditional culture.[18]

The concept of spirituality for many American Indian women is personal and private.[19] Privacy serves many purposes for Indian spirituality. Privacy preserves one's special relationship to a spiritual being, it avoids ridicule or persecution from non-Natives, it deflects potential misuse of spiritual knowledge, it avoids the loss of spiritual power, and, most importantly, it demonstrates respect.[20] There are many American Indian spiritual beliefs and practices that are considered sacred and are not to be shared publicly or with outsiders.

Many American Indians believe that not only are some spiritual phenomena not understandable or explainable, but that it is inappropriate to attempt to do so.[21] Often, tribal spiritual leaders cannot explain Indian culture or spirituality in a simplistic way. Indian people commonly believe that taking spiritual matters lightly leads to harm.[22] They believe spiritual matters are powerful and largely unknown. Some spiritual forces are good, some are bad, and some are neutral. It is thought inappropriate to play with spiritual powers without proper commitment or guidance. Proper spiritual training carries responsibility and builds character.[23] Because there is a quality of danger associated with some spiritual practices or beliefs, there are often prohibitions and taboos that are observed. It is thought that disharmony is a dangerous and vulnerable state of being.

Indian spirituality is very different from Christian belief systems in that many Indian people seek assistance from medicine men and women whether they may live on their homelands or in urban areas. The causes of illness are sometimes attributed to an imbalance in one's body, mind, or spirit, or to the breaking of taboos or to witchcraft.[24] Spiritual beliefs and perceptions of the world and the meaning of life are very diverse among regions, tribes, and/or individuals. Specific practices such as ceremonies, prayers, and religious protocols will vary among different American Indian communities.[25]

Spirituality and religion are pervasive in tribal settings. They affect worldviews and belief systems, family and community relationships, health, wellness, illness, ways of healing, and ways of dealing with grief.[26] Spiritual ways of dealing with grief help the family of the deceased to complete a period of mourning and resolve their grief.[27] Spirituality is closely connected to physical, social, and emotional well-being. Many Indian people have a holistic view of the world and of the person. Indians tend not only to focus on physical or medical causes of illness but also to examine the context of the person. They focus on understanding the broader relationship of the person to his or her total environment, including his or her family, significant others, creation, and nature.[28] The idea of balance and harmony or of being in the right relation to the world is of central importance in most Indian cultures. Spiritual well-being is dependent upon living in harmony with all beings, including human, animal, and spiritual beings.[29]

Most tribal groups acknowledge that certain persons have special knowledge, healing, or spiritual powers or gifts.[30] Many Indian people believe that the spirit must be healed in order to heal the mind. Family participation is an important aspect of the healing ceremony and is often a prerequisite. Prayer is an Indian's way of putting himself or herself in balance with the universe. Music, drumming, songs, and speaking one's own tribal language have a special significance to many tribal people as forms of prayer. Those who speak traditional languages are highly respected. Many Native people believe that healing is not possible unless we "connect to spirit" first.

Indian women have a special role spiritually. There is a history of spiritual female figures reflecting their sacred and central positions in their tribal communities.[31] All Indian women have the inherent right to a distinct identity, history, and culture.[32] The role of Indian women in the family and community, now and in the past, differs from tribe to tribe. Historically, there was a point in time when there was greater equity between Indian men and women.[33] Today, Indian women's power is manifested in their roles as sacred life givers, transmitters of cultural knowledge, caregivers of relatives, socializers of children, healers, warriors, and leaders. With the respect that comes with these powerful roles, Indian women define and describe their history. It is a history not of mere survival but of resiliency and strength. Indian women have formed the core of Native resistance to colonization.[34] The health and spiritual well-being of tribal communities in many ways depends upon Indian women who are the forefront of restoring harmony and balance among their tribal groups.

The subordination and suppression of tribal communities in the United States have taken many forms. The U.S. government has implemented policies of genocide, ethnocide, and assimilation, including the outlawing of traditional Indian spiritual practices, forced removal and relocation of Natives from their traditional lands, disproportionate placements of Native children into non-Native custodial care, assimilation through government and church-run boarding schools, and the disempowerment of Native women.[35]

In the 1800s, Indian religion, spiritual practices, and healing were outlawed. It was not until 1978 that the Indian Religious Freedom Act was passed, officially repealing the ban on Indian religious beliefs and practices.[36] Native people were fined and jailed if they practiced their traditional beliefs. As a result, some traditional practices went underground, some Indians made public conversions but practiced traditional beliefs privately, while others were converted to Christianity by missionaries in the latter part of the 1800s.[37] For many, however, this suppression of Indian religion and spirituality led to losses of healing knowledge and practices. Native healing practices and belief systems were damaged by this attack on tribal religions. The loss of these practices resulted in Indian women and tribal communities experiencing unresolved grief from historical and present-day traumas. The unresolved grief is what they experience when they incur a loss that cannot be openly acknowledged, publicly mourned, or socially accepted, such as the abuse experienced in government and church-run boarding schools.[38]

Throughout the United States, education was a means of assimilation and Christianization. Thousands of Indian children were brought up in government and church-run residential schools. Child abuse and neglect occurred including physical, emotional, and sexual abuse which led to student depression, resentment, bitterness, and at times death.[39] As late as the 1950s, students were whipped when they spoke their Native languages. They were taught to despise the way of life of their parents as pagan, savage, and uncivilized. The belief was to "kill the Indian to save the child."

Another goal of the colonizers was the disempowerment of Indian women who are the foundation and backbone of Indian families and communities. A major tactic of colonization was to destroy the family by targeting Indian women.[40] Colonizers made attempts to crush and dominate tribal sovereignty by destroying women's sovereignty. Indian women experienced violence and sexual assault because it was believed that hurting women would destroy the Indian Nation.

The repetitive and cumulative effects of these injustices and the tremendous cultural, spiritual, emotional, and economic losses have been characterized as a "soul wound" among Native peoples and constitute considerable "historical trauma" or "multigenerational trauma."[41] The historical and current traumas that impact Indian women, such as domestic violence and sexual assault, affect the health and well-being of Indian women, their families, and their communities. This historical trauma and unresolved grief originated from the loss of lives, land, spirituality, and vital aspects of Native culture as a direct result of colonization. This trauma and grief has contributed to the pain and destructive coping styles of American Indian individuals and families. The trauma and grief can become so pervasive that it impacts the community and may result in community-level trauma.[42] Community-level trauma and its negative impact on the well-being of the group are of particular importance given the nature of Native extended and well-integrated family and clan systems. Family is described in terms of an extensive kinship system of relationships to people who are not always related by blood.[43] Community is sometimes a larger culture in which people share values and a sense of responsibility for each other. Indian people share and maintain a strong community of culture, relationships, shared history and experiences, and kinship.[44]

The effect of physical and cultural genocide directed at American Indians is transferred across generations like the transfer of trauma to descendents from Jewish Holocaust survivors. The effects of historical trauma are passed on from generation to generation, creating a cycle of disharmony and imbalance or the multigenerational trauma cycle.[45] When there is disharmony and imbalance, the spiritual self becomes weak. As a result, one is more vulnerable to the effects of historical and current traumas.[46] It has been said it takes four generations to heal one act of violence.[47] Many Indians feel that their personal and cultural strength is based in their spirituality. The survival of Indian people and the ability to break out of the cycle of historical trauma require that harmony and balance be restored.[48] Restoring harmony and balance will stop the multigenerational trauma cycle and allow Indian people to heal future generations.[49]

Communities have taken many approaches to healing from historical trauma that include the wellbriety movement (such as White Bison), historical trauma groups, community-healing models, and by restoring and revitalizing traditional spiritual and cultural practices. For example, community healing from mutigenerational trauma is a central theme of the Gathering of Native Americans (GONA) curriculum. At the core of these healing approaches is the focus on tribal identity, language, culture, and spirituality. This includes an understanding and healing of self, family, and community and an understanding of the historical context of Native people and communities.

The most powerful country in the world has made numerous attempts to totally eradicate Indian spirituality and its worldview through wars and multiple federal policies of genocide, ethnocide, and assimilation specifically designed to destroy tribal sovereignty. Facing religious persecution from the U.S. government, Indian people experienced social alienation, psychological confusion, and a loss of traditional belief systems.[50] After four centuries of assimilation, many tribal religions have disappeared. Some perished because the tribes were destroyed or reduced to so few members that the survivors accepted the practices of the larger tribes they joined.

Every religious and spiritual variation possible has resulted from colonization.[51] This includes acceptance of Christianity, rejection of Christianity and acceptance of traditional religious beliefs and practices, revitalization movements, new religions, blending of Christian and traditional Indian religious practices and beliefs, and embracing both Christianity and traditional or new religions.[52] As a result of colonization and the impact on spirituality practices and belief systems, Indian people tend to recognize that spirituality is not confined to only one church. A number of Indian people actively participate in both a formal religion and a traditional spiritual system.

In addition, the traditional spiritual practices and rituals that went underground in the early twentieth century began to reemerge in the 1930s. As the civil rights movement gained momentum, American Indians became more outspoken against an oppressive system that continued to attack the identity, culture, and spirituality of Indian people.[53] Indians were oppressed by the trust relationship between the tribes and the United States. Indian people believed that the U.S. government had and continues to renege on its promises to protect tribal territories, access to sacred sites, and be sensitive to tribalism and to traditional spiritual leadership. During the civil rights movement, Indian people criticized programs that undermined spirituality, including culturally insensitive educational programs, forced relocation to cities, and a variety of other policies designed to assimilate and terminate tribal communities.[54]

The Native American Church is a religion created by Indians to meet modern Indian needs. As powerful as peyote and the Native American Church has been in addressing the spiritual needs of American Indians, it has not displaced or replaced traditional spirituality.[55] Peyote has helped Indian people to reorient their lives. "Peyote is an alkaloid plant containing mescaline which is an important plant used as a sacrament and healing plant in the Native American Church. This plant is valued because of its healing properties. Peyote is also valued because it can be used to teach the person via vision about the cause of his or her illness or imbalance. The Peyote Way emphasizes the care of the family, a strong work ethic, and abstinence from alcohol. The Native American Church peyote ceremony usually lasts one night and is used for a broad range of illnesses and blessings (Champagne, 1994)." The Native American Church has affirmed cultural identity by preserving old worldviews of interconnectedness and traditional ritual practices. It has affirmed Indian identity by valuing being American Indian. At the same time, it has eased the conflicting demands of traditional spiritual belief systems and Christianity.[56] The Native American Church has helped Native people resist cultural assimilation. Unfortunately, just as the U.S. government has made attempts to suppress traditional religious practices, it has also attacked the use of peyote.

Despite the suppression of Indian spirituality, tribal people have fought to maintain traditional lifestyles and value systems and have prevailed.[57] Native languages are still spoken and tribal sovereignty remains strong.[58] Many beliefs and practices have continued, are being taught, and continue to affect the worldview of many tribal people.[59] Even the most acculturated continue to use traditional knowledge to inform their lives. This knowledge and interconnected view of the world have survived. Though there are significant cultural differences among the more than 500 distinct tribal groups, there is a fundamental understanding among traditional Indian people that everything is related and that all living things play important roles in keeping the earth in balance and harmony.[60] Each tribal community derives its unique spiritual and cultural identity from a shared history, land base, values, knowledge, stories, and relationships with one another and creation. Music, drumming, and songs have particular significance for most Indian people as a form of prayer and ceremony.[61] The ceremonies remind Indian people of their place in the universe and their responsibilities as human beings (Mankiller, 2004).[62]

Spirituality defines Indian people and their worldview as being members of a specific tribal community. Spirituality also interconnects Indian people across cultures throughout the United States and the world.[63] North American Indians have the only nature-based religion that is indigenous to the Americas.[64] The spiritual beliefs and value systems come from the indigenous areas where Indians originally lived. Creation and nature served as the outdoor classrooms that formed Indian people's worldview. The significance of their land cannot be understated. It not only supplied food, water, and shelter, but it also determined the clothing, architecture, ceremonies, and life patterns that defined Indian identity and culture.[65]

Of most concern to Indian people is the loss of identity, culture, and traditional spirituality.[66] This sense of identity and culture is conceptualized and articulated through Native languages. Restoring harmony and balance involves developing a sense of who we are in relation to our history, nature, land, time, and our physical and spiritual world.[67] It is the women who are responsible for continuing the culture to the next generation and who serve as the transmitters of culture and knowledge.[68]

Indian women leaders focus on the strengths, resiliency, and positive attributes of their tribal communities instead of on the tremendous amount of economic and social problems that may exist. There are common values among Indian women leaders. These include a sense of duty and responsibility to others, tremendous tenacity, unwavering ability to not only survive but to succeed despite all obstacles, and an unwillingness to give up.[69] Indian women leaders include grandmothers, mothers, daughters, aunts, friends, and sisters. Some Indian women have buried their husbands and children, faced racism and oppression, confronted daunting health problems, and experienced social conditions and problems caused by extreme poverty.[70] Despite all these struggles, Indian women have led their tribal Nations, their families, and their communities with dignity, strength, enthusiasm, and optimism.[71] This sense of belonging to a tribal group comes from knowing who you are and where you come from.[72]

As Indian women conduct themselves in a way that will benefit future generations, they are embraced by the memory of their ancestors. Often Indian people are told to forget about the history and the past and the historical trauma that has been endured by their ancestors. It is difficult to forget when our history is woven into the very fabric of our daily lives.[73] Our past is the premise of who we are and how we make decisions today. Even our history, which has always been told from the colonizer's perspective, is finally being expressed from our point of view.[74] Each time we continue to experience oppression or hear the stories of the historical trauma that has plagued Native people, the pain and anger is raw and fresh.[75] What our ancestors endured and what we have gone through is as real as it was in the past, so the grieving process continues.

Our ancestors have left us a legacy, and we have the responsibility to pass this legacy on to our great-grandchildren and beyond, as far as to the seventh generation.[76] Future generations take on this responsibility to restore the harmony and balance to tribal communities and to become strong leaders in the face of tremendous adversity.[77] Harmony and balance in tribal communities can be recovered through a reintegration of our traditional ways,[78] and starts with us as Indian women. We have the responsibility to teach our children to be proud of who they are and where they come from. We must teach our children to respect themselves and respect creation. We have the duty to learn and to teach our children to speak in our Native languages. We have the responsibility to break out of the mutigenerational trauma cycle. These responsibilities have been given to us by the creator.

NOTES

1. Swinomish, 1991.
2. Champagne, 1994.
3. Swinomish, 1991.
4. Champagne, 1994.
5. LaFromboise et al., 1994.
6. Champagne, 1994.
7. Deloria, 2003.
8. Mankiller, 2004.
9. Champagne, 1994.
10. Deloria, 2003.

11. Swinomish, 1991.
12. Ibid.
13. Champagne, 1994.
14. Ibid.
15. Schiff and Moore, 2006.
16. Ibid.
17. Champagne, 1994.
18. LaFromboise et al., 1994.
19. Swinomish, 1991.
20. Ibid.
21. Ibid.
22. Ibid.
23. Ibid.
24. Ibid.
25. Ibid.
26. Champagne, 1994; Swinomish, 1991.
27. Swinomish, 1991.
28. Ibid.
29. Ibid.
30. Ibid.
31. Walters and Simoni, 2002.
32. Clark and Johnson, 2007.
33. Mankiller, 2004.
34. Ibid.
35. Walters and Simoni, 2002; Champagne, 1994.
36. Swinomish, 1991.
37. Ibid.
38. Johnson, 2006.
39. Swinomish, 1991.
40. Walters and Simoni, 2002.
41. Johnson, 2006; Yellow Horse Braveheart and DeBruyn, 1998; Duran and Duran, 1995.
42. Johnson, 2006.
43. Mankiller, 2004.
44. Ibid.
45. Johnson, 2006.
46. Ibid.
47. Mankiller, 2004.
48. Johnson, 2006.
49. Swinomish, 1991.
50. Champagne, 1994.
51. Ibid.
52. Ibid.
53. Ibid.
54. Ibid.
55. Ibid.
56. Ibid.
57. Mankiller, 2004.
58. Ibid.

59. Swinomish, 1991.
60. Mankiller, 2004.
61. Swinomish, 1991.
62. Mankiller, 2004.
63. Ibid.
64. Ibid.
65. Ibid.
66. Ibid.
67. Deloria, 2003.
68. Mankiller, 2004.
69. Ibid.
70. Ibid.
71. Ibid.
72. Ibid.
73. Ibid.
74. Ibid.
75. Ibid.
76. Champagne, 1994.
77. Deloria, 2003.
78. Mankiller, 2004.

BIBLIOGRAPHY

Champagne, D. *The Native North American Almanac.* Detroit, MI: Gale Research Inc., 1994.

Clark, R. L., and C. L. Johnson, "Overview of Issues Facing Native Women who are Survivors of Violence in Urban Communities." In S. Deer, B. Clairmont, C. A. Martell, and M. L. White Eagle, eds. *Sharing Our Stories of Survival: Native Women Surviving Violence.* Lanham, MD: Alta Mira Press, 2007.

Deloria, V. *God Is Red: A Native View of Religion.* Golden, CO: Fulcrum Publishing, 2003.

Duran, E., and B. Duran. *Native American Postcolonial Psychology.* Albany, NY: State University of New York, 1995.

Johnson, C. L. "An Innovative Healing Model: Empowering Urban Native Americans." In T. Witko, ed. *Mental Health Care for Urban Indians.* Washington, DC: American Psychological Association, 2006.

LaFromboise, T. D., J. S. Berman, and B. K. Sohi. "American Indian Women." In L. Comas-Díaz and B. Greene, eds. *Women of Color: Integrating Ethnic and Gender Identities in Psychotherapy.* New York: Guilford Publications, Inc., 1994.

Mankiller, W. *Every Day Is a Good Day.* Golden, CO: Fulcrum Publishing, 2004.

Schiff, J. W., and K. Moore. "The Impact of the Sweat Lodge Ceremony on Dimensions of Well-Being." *American Indian and Alaska Native Mental Health Research Journal.* 13(3): 2007.

Swinomish Tribal Community. *A Gathering of Wisdoms Tribal Mental Health: A Cultural Perspective.* Mount Vernon, WA: Veda Vangarde, 1991.

Walters, K. L., and J. M. Simoni. "Reconceptualizing Native Women's Health: An 'Indigenist' Stress Coping Model." *American Journal of Public Health* 92 (4) (2002): 520–524.

Yellow Horse Brave Heart, M., and L. M. DeBruyn. "The American Indian Holocaust: Healing Historical Unresolved Grief." *American Indian/Alaska Native Mental Health Research Journal* 8 (2) (1998): 60–82.

Chapter 9

Spirituality and Resilience of Filipinos

Asuncion Miteria Austria

Perhaps the most well known global event that comes to mind when thinking about the relationship between the spirituality and resilience of Filipinos was the peaceful revolution of the Filipino people after decades of dictatorship under Ferdinand Marcos. The Filipinos' fearless overthrow of Marcos' dictatorship in 1986 showed the international community that nonviolent struggle for freedom is possible. Propelled by their deep faith in the Virgin Mary, the Mother of God and the patroness of the Philippines, and their unparalleled resilience in the face of an oppressive government, the Filipino people mounted an unusual opposition against a repressive dictatorship. The unarmed revolution has since been called "people power." It was a revolution in which men, women, and children, armed only with their rosaries, crucifixes, images of the Virgin Mary, and prayers, made themselves into human barricades and faced heavily armed soldiers and tanks. In fact, a book entitled *People Power*, which documented the nonviolent revolution, was dedicated to the Virgin Mary.[1]

This revolution taught the modern world that there are effective alternatives to violent revolts. This unparalleled and historic event showed the powerful influence of spirituality, faith, and prayers among Filipinos determined to live in peace. At the core of Filipinos' personalities is the virtue of spirituality.[2] In turn, it is their spirituality that is at the center of Filipinos' ability to be resilient in the face of adversity.

This chapter will trace the context of the sociopolitical dynamics of the Philippines that underlies Filipinos' spirituality, the use of spirituality as a coping tool, as well as my own spiritual journey as a Filipina.

SOCIOPOLITICAL HISTORY

The Philippines is a country that smiles with graciousness and hospitality. The people are like the bamboo plant: graceful, bending back against a raging storm, and swaying forward again as straight as can be. The Filipino people's indomitable spirit helped them fight colonizations by several countries.

A brief history of these colonizations includes the following: long before the Philippines was a colony of Spain from 1521 to 1898, it already had its own commerce with other eastern countries, and possessed its own culture and religious and political systems. The conquest of the Philippines led to more than 350 years of oppressive Spanish rule, under which the Spaniards divided the country into several tribes and dialects to subvert the development of a sense of nationalism and pride. Undaunted by the ruthlessness and avarice of the *conquistadores*, who taught the Filipinos to think of their own culture and of themselves as inferior, the Filipinos revolted and declared their independence from Spain. Unfortunately, Philippine independence was short-lived, as Spain ceded the country to the United States after the Spanish-American War and the United States became the country's new ruler.

The U.S. military ruled first, and then a civilian form of government was instituted. English was introduced and as a result, the Philippines became the third-largest English-speaking country in the world. The Philippines became a commonwealth of the United States in 1935 and independence was scheduled in 1945. In 1942, during World War II, Japan invaded and occupied the country. For three years, the Filipino people suffered miserably under the brutalities of the Japanese forces. The country was razed to the ground, buildings were destroyed, and the identities and dignities of Filipinos were buried under the ruins of the buildings and corpses of hundreds of thousands of men and women who had perished. The United States, with the Philippines as an ally, subdued the Japanese; and in 1946, the Filipinos' long-sought independence was finally attained.[3]

The struggles of the Filipinos continued under Ferdinand Marcos, the sixth president of the republic, who declared martial law in 1972. After fourteen years of social, political, and economic hardships, and following the 1983 assassination of Benigno Aquino, the political rival of Marcos, the time was ripe for the Filipinos to revolt against the repressive dictatorial regime. But what surprised the world was a nonviolent revolution that overthrew the Marcos' oppressive dictatorship in 1986. Strengthened by Filipinos' deep faith in the Virgin Mary and their remarkable resilience in oppressive circumstances, they mounted an unusual opposition against a dictatorship. Historically, the Filipino people have longed to live in peace, justice, and as a Christian nation.

Driving their struggles in oppressive and often violent circumstances was the Filipino virtue of spirituality.

THE FEMINIST SPIRITUAL CULTURE OF FILIPINOS

As previously stated, Filipinos possessed a distinctive religious, political, and cultural system long before the colonization of the West. For example, in the southern part of the Philippines, they believed in good and bad spirits. Interestingly, the only person who could communicate with these spirits, called a *babaylan*, is a woman. Only she can give thanks to the spirits for a good harvest or catch. Under the rule of the Spaniards, the Filipino people learned the ways of Christianity and they began to worship and love the supreme being. They asked for the help of saints, and instead of many Gods, one God alone was worshipped. Filipinos now pray to God through women saints and the Virgin Mary for inner strength and empowerment. They celebrate their blessings by holding town fiestas with processions to honor their saints or patronesses, such as *Nuestra Senora de Guia* (Our Lady of the Way), reputed to be the oldest statue in the Philippines. Other patronesses of the Filipinos are *Nuestra Senora de Paz Buen Viaje*, *La Naval de Manila*, *Our Lady of Perpetual Help*, *Virgen de los Desamparados*, and *Our Lady of Immaculate Conception*. Specific months are dedicated to honor each Virgin patron.

FILIPINO WOMEN AND SPIRITUALITY

As research shows that social support seeking takes place within one's social context, we find Filipina women seeking support and guidance through their spirituality within the private confines of their worship of God through the Virgin Mary, in a place where no shame, criticism, and poor evaluation is made by others. Spirituality provides meaning and purpose in the lives of Filipina women, and provides the relationship with the transcendent being.[4] Filipinos' spirituality is manifested in their behavior, beliefs, and experiences[5] and practiced through prayers, the Bible, and other sacred texts, study, novenas, rituals, and cumulative traditions[6]; all of these are part of their being and deepen their sense of connectedness, developing a collaborative relationship with God for empowerment in the face of adversity.

The following is a case that clearly illustrates the power of spirituality as it affects resiliency. This case involves a sixty-seven-year-old woman, Mrs. V, who is now celebrating her twenty-first anniversary as a breast cancer survivor. In 1986, she was diagnosed with breast cancer that had metastasized. Her doctor's prognosis was that she had only a 30 percent chance of survival. She would cry as soon as she woke up in the morning and again when she went back to bed. She also prayed and read as much as she could about cancer. Besides her three young children and her husband, no one else knew, for she kept silent about her condition, consistent with her Filipino cultural values. She concealed her illness and kept her suffering to herself and her husband. Her young children were not even aware of the seriousness of her medical condition. She did not want to burden them or anyone else with her problems. She had feelings of shame and felt responsible for having the disease.[7–9] Her behavior was consistent with studies that show that stigma prevented women with cancer from seeking assistance or social support. "No one tells anything about this secret illness to others. They all kept it a secret, and this is a family affair."[10]

Mrs. V prayed and joined a Bible-study group. Her abiding faith in God provided her with a sense of meaning and peace within herself. She viewed God as a caring, dependable, and compassionate model. Her relationship with God was collaborative and secure. The feeling that one has a positive relationship with God can give one a sense of self-acceptance and belonging as well as provide a source of emotional comfort when faced with life-threatening illness.[11] Gall and Cornblatt found that women breast cancer patients who were asked to describe how their religion and spirituality aided them to cope with their illness said that God was their ever-present support and personal control throughout their illness.[12]

Mrs. V reflected on the meaning and purpose of life and retained her sense of humor and appreciation for beauty. She felt a surge of strength and her purpose in life was clarified. Throughout her illness and her treatment, she continued to teach young children in a public school. She did not have time to feel sick from chemotherapy as she continued to devote her life to teaching, parenting her children, and taking care of her family. Research data indicate that religious faith can enhance a person's ability to cope with negative life events and that negative life events can lead to enhanced religious faith.[13] The love for her profession as a teacher deepened and the purpose to continue as a model teacher heightened. Gall et al. found that this ability to make meaning when faced with a stressful event promotes successful coping, adaptation, and well-being.[14]

Mrs. V recently retired from teaching but she continues to pray, read, and discern the scriptures with a group of like-minded friends who share the same interests and passions. She continues to engage in spiritual and religious activities such as attending church, meditating, and repeating the Virgin Mary's name. She is also engaged in meaningful community activities that provide support for the sick. Studies of South and East Asian women find they experience spirituality by helping others.[15] Mrs. V's religiosity and spirituality appear to buffer the impact of her disease. As Powell, Shahabi, and Thoresen[16] stated, regular churchgoing is associated with the ongoing experience of positive emotions that contributes to one's health. Mrs. V's spirituality have empowered and provided hope to her. Fowler[17] found in his work with the elderly and persons with Parkinson's disease that spirituality enhances their adaptive capacities. Indeed, Mrs. V's spirituality has expanded her awareness, her purpose has clarified, and her inner demons have been transformed.[18]

MY PERSONAL JOURNEY OF SPIRITUALITY

I was born and raised a Catholic in the Philippines, a predominantly Catholic country. We are devoted to the Virgin Mary. The main altar in my church has a statue of the *Virgen de los Desamparados,* to whom we pay homage. The Virgen de los Desamparados stands for compassion and provides empowerment to the distressed and desperate. The image is the center of our annual town fiesta in May. As a young woman, I belonged to the Legion of Mary, the Catholic women's prayer group. Our home in Manila is a typical Filipino home; we had an altar in the master bedroom which contained a big crucifix, statues of the Sacred Heart of Jesus, the Immaculate Conception encased in glass with a couple of rosaries draped over the enclosure, and a framed picture of the Virgen de los Desamparados. This is where the family gathered for afternoon prayers and other occasions. I grew up in a family that glorified God and prayed to the Virgin Mary. My parents demonstrated kindness, impeccable character, high moral values, and considerable respect for others. They instilled in us the symbol of God as the point of reference for understanding experiences, life, and the world. Although we had a low income, we were taught to praise God for all the rich blessings provided to us.

In my current home, we have an altar located in the master bedroom. It is, however, not the central place for our family's worship. When my out-of-town children come home to Milwaukee, no matter how short their stay is, and no matter how busy our schedules are, we all hear mass on Sundays. Prayers and relaxation techniques that incorporate beliefs have kept me moving forward on the road of spiritual wholeness. There is not a day that goes by without a prayer and spiritual connection with God. Spirituality has given me unlimited strength. A sense of connectedness with God and my patron saint, Virgen de los Desamparados, has consistently enhanced my adaptive capacities.

My spiritual life provides me with values to treat people with respect, compassion, and kindness. My spiritual beliefs are a source of strength to find meaning in my experiences and empowerment to ward off daily hassles of prejudice and discrimination. My early life, family values, and the traditions associated with growing up in a religious and spiritual home were all salient factors in the development of my spirituality.[19] Just as my parents, my children acclaim God as beneficent, nurturing, and compassionate.[20]

THE FILIPINOS, THEIR SPIRITUALITY, AND RESILIENCY

Like other people of color, Filipinos' resilience can be observed in the context of their experiences with racism, discrimination, and prejudice. There have been many studies on the effects of racism and prejudice on people of color.[21] There is also a growing body of research on the coping abilities of racial and ethnic minorities in the United States; it shows their remarkable adaptability and fortitude to succeed in life despite persistent prejudice and discrimination from the majority culture.[22-24] Studies of Asian Americans show that they use spirituality and religion as important means of coping with daily stressors and problems.[25-29]

The capacity for adaptability, perseverance, and hospitality is at the core of the Philippine national personality. Centuries of contact with conquerors and other cultures and the intermingling of races through marriage have produced a Filipino personality possessed with a spiritual approach to life. Filipinos' identity and spirituality are inextricably linked. We have a rich tradition of rites associated with birth, marriage, and death. It is not uncommon to find houses with *santos* or statues of the Sacred Heart of Jesus, the Virgin Mary, in the living rooms or bedrooms of Filipino homes. These statues provide Filipino families protection as well as serve as a source of strength, comfort, and peace in both good times and bad. Just like the Latino culture,[30] we have communal activities such as *novenas* for the sick, novenas for the departed, and nine days of early morning masses, *Misa de Gallo*, to prepare for the birth of Jesus Christ.

For Filipinos, their ability to grow, flourish, and even thrive despite overwhelming conditions reflects their remarkable resiliency and spirituality. Their spirituality mitigated the socially oppressive effects of racism and discrimination suffered under various rulers and conquerors, and continues to be a coping strategy used to face daily challenges as well as societal prejudice and discrimination. Prayers, rituals, and ceremonies have provided the essential ingredients in their struggles for peace. Their spirituality and religiosity have indeed been the major sources of their strength and survival, and for the healing of their country.

ACKNOWLEDGMENTS

I thank A. Marie M. Austria for her invaluable assistance in the preparation of the manuscript.

NOTES

1. Mercado, Monina A., ed. *People Power: The Philippine Revolution of 1986. An Hyewitness History*. Manila, Philippines: The James Reuter, S. J. Foundation, 1986.

2. Austria, Asuncion Miteria. *The Psychology of Peace in Filipino and Asian Cultures*. Paper presented at a symposium, The Psychology of Peace: Its

Meaning, Goals, Impediments, and Achievements. American Psychological Association Annual Convention. Boston, MA, August 1999.

3. Goncillo, Teodoro A. *A Short History of the Philippines*. New York: The New American Library, 1969.

4. Hodge, David R., and Charlene C. McGrew. "Spirituality, Religion, and the Interrelationship: A Nationally Representative Study." *Journal of Social Work Education* 42 (3) (2006): 637–654.

5. Miller, W. R, and Thoresen, C. E. "Spirituality, Religion, and Health: An Emerging Research Field." *American Psychologist* 58 (2003): 24–35.

6. Fukuyama, Mary A., and Todd D. Sevig. *Integrating Spirituality into Multicultural Counseling*. Thousand Oaks, CA: Sage, 1999.

7. Austria, Asuncion Miteria. Symposium on Women, Cancer and Coping. Discussion at American Psychological Association Annual Convention. Boston, MA, August 1999.

8. Austria, Asuncion Miteria. "People of Asian Descent: Beyond Myths and Stereotypes." In J. D. Robinson and L. James, eds. *Diversity in Human Interaction: The Tapestry of America*. New York: Oxford University Press, 2003.

9. Bolger, N., A. Zuckerman, and R. C. Kessler. "Invisible Support and Adjustment to Stress." *Journal of Personality and Social Psychology* 79 (2000): 953–961.

10. Cavendish, Roberta, Barbara K. Luise, Karen Horne, Maria Bauer, Judith Medfindt, Mary Ann Gallo, et al. "Opportunities for Enhanced Spirituality Relevant to Well Adults." *Nursing Diagnosis* 11 (2000): 152–163.

11. Burkhardt, M. A. "Becoming and Connecting: Elements of Spirituality for Women." *Holistic Nursing Practitioner* 8 (1994): 12–21.

12. Gall, Terry L., and M. W. Cornblatt. "Breast Cancer Survivors Give Voice: A Qualitative Analysis of Spiritual Factors in Long-Term Adjustment." *Psychooncology* 11 (2002): 524–535.

13. Pargament, Kenneth I. "God Help Me: Towards a Theoretical Framework of Coping for the Psychology of Religion." *Research in the Scientific Study of Religion* 2 (1990): 195–224.

14. Gall, Terry L., Claire Charbonneau, Henry C. Neal, Karen Grant, Anjali Joseph, and Lisa Shouldice. "Understanding the Nature and Role of Spirituality in Relation to Coping and Health: A Conceptual Framework." *Canadian Psychology* 46 (2) (2005): 88–104.

15. Chiu, Lynn, Marina Morrow, Soma Ganesan, and Nancy Clark. "Spirituality and Treatment Choices by South and East Asian Women with Serious Mental Illness." *Transcultural Psychiatry* 42 (2005): 630–656.

16. Powell, Lynda H., Leila Shahabi, and Carl E. Thoresen. "Religion and Spirituality: Linkages to Physical Health." *American Psychologist* 58 (2003): 1, 36–52.

17. Fowler, S. "Hope and a Health-promoting Lifestyle in Persons with Parkinson's Disease." *Journal of Neuroscience Nursing* 29 (1997): 111–116.

18. Brussat, Frederic, and Mary Ann Brussat. *Spiritual Literacy*. New York: Simon and Schuster, 1996.

19. Kiesling, Chris, Gwendolyn T. Sorell, Marilyn J. Montgomery, and Ronald K. Colwell. "Identity and Spirituality: A Psychosocial Exploration of the Sense of Spiritual Self." *Developmental Psychology* 42 (6) (2006): 1269–1277.

20. Austria, Asuncion Miteria. "Spirituality in Women Alive Today." Paper presented at the Women's Commission, Women—Called and Gifted.

Spirituality for the Third Millennium. Archdiocese of Milwaukee, Milwaukee, WI, February 1997.

21. Jones, James. *Social Psychology of Prejudice*. Upper Saddle River, NJ: Prentice Hall, 2002.

22. Lee, Richard M. "Resilience against Discrimination: Ethnic Identity and Other Group-Orientation as Protective Factors for Korean Americans." *Journal of Counseling Psychology* 52 (1) (2005): 36–44.

23. Pargament, Kenneth I. *The Psychology of Religion and Coping: Theory, Research, and Practice*. New York: Guilford Press, 1997.

24. Stone, A., L. Helder, and M. Schneider. "Coping with Stressful Events: Coping Dimensions and Issues." In L. Cohen, ed. *Life Events and Psychological Functioning: Theoretical and Methodological Issues*. Newbury Park, CA: Sage, 1988.

25. Leong, Frederick T. L., Angela G. Inman, Angela Ebreo, Lawrence H. Yang, Lisa Kinoshita, and Michi Fu. *Handbook of Asian American Psychology* (2nd ed.). Thousand Oaks, CA: Sage, 2007.

26. Stone, A., L. Helder, and M. Schneider. "Coping with Stressful Events: Coping Dimensions and Issues." In L. Cohen, ed. *Life Events and Psychological Functioning: Theoretical and Methodological Issues*. Newbury Park, CA: Sage, 1988.

27. Langer, Niele. "Resiliency and Spirituality: Foundations of Strengths Perspective Counseling with the Elderly." *Educational Gerontology* 30 (2004): 611–617.

28. Masten, A. S. "Ordinary Magic: Resilience Processes in Development." *American Psychologist* 56 (2001): 227–238.

29. Fukuyama, Mary Ann, and Todd D. Sevig. "Spirituality in Counseling across Cultures." In P. Pedersen, J. Draguns, W. Loner, and J. Trimble, eds. *Counseling across Cultures*. Thousand Oaks, CA: Sage, 2002.

30. Comas-Díaz, Lillian. "Latino Healing: The Integration of Ethnic Psychology into Psychotherapy." *Psychotherapy: Theory, Research, Practice, Training* 43 (4) (2006): 436–453.

PART III

Individual Journeys

Chapter 10

Stepping Stones in a Full Life

Jane Simon

As long as I can remember I've been searching for order and an ultimate explanation of what life is about. Why are we alive? What is our purpose on earth? My parents tried to help. My mother voiced what the popular psychologist, Wayne Dyer, wrote in his best-selling self-help books many years later: "We're here to have a good time."

I didn't find my mother's answer satisfactory nor did my observations of how she led her life coincide with her words. She didn't pursue a life of hedonism. On the contrary, she worked with diligence; a single parent, she put her five children through college and two of us through graduate school. She loved music and science and began a second career as a seismologist and traveled the world to set up seismographs. She wrote a teaching primer for students of seismology that achieved wide circulation. She joined a writing class, completed a memoir, and, a few years later, began to help nursing-home residents write their own stories. She read serious books, such as Eric Kandel's *In Search of Memory: The Emergence of a New Science of Mind*, until her dying day. Hardly a hedonist, her belief in science sustained her and she had no need to posit the existence of a being beyond humans.

My father possessed a marvelous memory and dedicated himself to a career in medicine. He was an avid reader of politics, law, and languages, and, in his later years, focused on the study of Arabic. He passed away at the end of 1999 and I often wonder if he had a premonition about 9/11 and if his beliefs would have changed after this world-shaking event.

My parents encouraged learning but in no way fostered beliefs in God or the pursuit of religion. They believed in the goodness of humans and the scientific process to solve the world's problems. In fact, they pointed to religion as a source of conflict and wars.

I would say my parents were spiritual but not religious. The "spirit" of love (and caring for one another) exists in both organized religion and spirituality, but not all religions or individuals espouse love as a cornerstone of connectedness among us (theory and practice often diverge). Spirituality is an individual matter as opposed to a definition by a religious community, and is idiosyncratic as opposed to organized. It consists of positive, transcendent beliefs that an individual constructs to aid her to solve problems and use in times of crisis. Spirituality has a fluidity which allows change or modification in accordance to the situation: that is, to feel one with the ocean, the sky, the woods, the fields, or any aspect of nature. Religion is an organized, well-defined body of beliefs, practiced by a group of people, at the head of which are leaders trained in the traditions. The boundaries, more or less rigid, tend to promote the concept of insiders and outsiders.

From an early age I longed for a belief beyond what I experienced in daily living. Shut out from the sanctity of my parents' living room during their weekend meetings with like-minded friends (young idealists who called themselves communists in the 1940s and 1950s), I eagerly searched for my own territory. One Sunday a friend invited me to a local Christian church. After my parents heard I wanted to return, they forbade it.

In grammar school, the only Jewish boy in our class advised my brother and me to stay home from school on the Jewish holidays. Without a synagogue to attend, we were at a loss about what to do, and decided to attend school in spite of our friend's disapproval.

My pre-med curriculum in college didn't allow time to take religion courses, so I read on my own: Pierre Teilhard de Chardin (*The Phenomenon of Man*, 1959), Bishop Fulton Sheen (*The World's First Love*, 1952), and Thomas Merton.

One bright afternoon as I studied intensely in the science library at Columbia, I glanced up from my book to see a golden beam of light pouring through the window onto the table. To my surprise, a perfect miniature figure stood within the beam. She was about three inches tall, dressed in a blue gown, and wore a polished gold crown on her head. Self-possessed and serious, she didn't speak but remained motionless for what seemed like an eternity. Then she melted away slowly, never to return. Once was enough to convince me of powers beyond everyday experience. I vowed never to negate the existence of a superior force or being. Years later I saw a movie that featured the mother of Jesus, dressed in classic blue robes; she balanced a gold crown on her beautiful, blonde head. Then I recognized the tiny figure of my vision as the Virgin Mary. William Nobel had a similar experience and wrote a comprehensive paper on its meaning. In "Reflections on a Vision," he writes, "To have seen this vision is to have been given God's own assurance that all things are securely held together and that we, as an offering, are a part of that whole." The appearance of a Christian figure rather than a Jewish or pagan symbol didn't trouble me. I was reading authors of the Christian faith and concluded God dresses in robes of many colors and designs. (To this day, no one can prove that this phenomenon originates beyond our brain/minds.)

So I might say the first women to teach me about spirituality were my atheistic mother, with her dedication and belief in people and science, and Mary, the mother of Jesus, whose vision inspired me to believe in the presence of a higher being.

Sadly, present-day events bear out my parents' opinions; namely that wars are fought in the name of religion. Our era embodies the clash of civilizations about which Bernard Lewis writes with knowledge and eloquence.[1] To reconcile religious differences, to bring about peace and benefit all humanity, is the huge dilemma of our time.

Nonetheless, my parents' belief in communism (dashed against the shores of history when the abuses of Stalin came to light) contributed to my understanding of dialectics. A concept first introduced by the German philosopher Fichte and expanded by Hegel, dialectics alludes to a process or foundation that underlies all disciplines.[2] The pattern of change unfolds (evolution) revealing the pattern that begins with a thesis out of which arises its opposite, the antithesis. A resolution, or synthesis, eventually integrates these opposites. Over a period of time, the synthesis breaks down and the process repeats itself in unending variations on the theme. In *The History of Philosophy*, Copleston writes, "The emergence of contradiction is the motive force of the dialectical movement. The conflict of opposed concepts and the resolution of the conflict in a synthesis which itself gives rise to another contradiction is the feature which drives the mind restlessly onwards towards an ideal term, an all-embracing synthesis, the complete system of truth ... When philosophy considers ... the history of man, it discovers a dialectical movement at work."[3] According to Copleston, while "... the movement of the dialectic in the world and in human history was regarded by Hegel as the reflection or phenomenal expression of the movement of Thought. For Marx and Engels ... the dialectical movement is found ... in reality ... in Nature and history. The dialectical movement of human thought is simply a reflection of the dialectical process of reality."[4]

An approach to God as the natural order (akin to Einstein's view and the creative process) reveals the pattern of change as it unfolds in the lives of individuals, families, and nations. As the sun, rain, wind, and earth support the growth of crops, so natural catastrophes of volcano eruptions, earthquakes, tornadoes, and hurricanes destroy them. Through destruction, changes occur, and, modified, the process begins again.

DIALECTICS WITHIN OUR CULTURE

If we take Judaism as the thesis, and the Torah, with its focus on mind, justice, and law, as a blueprint for living, Jesus, a Jew, stands out as the embodiment of love, or the antithesis of law. Judeo-Christian culture integrates both and the place of mind, body, and spirit.

DIALECTICS AND THE POWER OF POSITIVE THINKING

Norman V. Peale's mind-altering books changed the lives of many from the 1930s to the present. Dr. Peale is remembered for founding the Blanton-Peale Counseling Center. He recognized that the tool of the power of positive thinking could not reach everyone. The depth of depression in some of his practitioners required psychological know-how. He sought the help of the psychiatrist Smiley Blanton to found a clinic that combined religious and psychiatric approaches. The thesis of religion combined with the antithesis of social science or psychology created the synthesis, or a psychiatric clinic with an awareness and acceptance of spirituality.

THE ESSENTIAL IS MOST DIFFICULT TO ACHIEVE

For me, the processes most essential to navigate life's challenges do not come naturally. First, we have a natural resistance to change that confronts us daily, as if change is akin to a disease.

One day this mantra popped into my mind: "At the heart lies paradox."

I find the concept of paradox useful. Similarly, we make matters more difficult for ourselves when we want to hold on to what we know, and block out how we have to change in changing circumstances. Especially difficult are the situations when change brings loss and the possibility for growth is much less obvious.

At times, life closely resembles a Chinese finger trap. On the surface, it appears we need to pull our fingers free by pulling them out of the trap. But reality belies appearance: to free ourselves, we have to alter our approach: we must push inward to release the woven net, that is, to count our blessings in the midst of disaster.

KEY OF GRATITUDE

Gratitude, an essential ingredient for successful living, requires a great deal of work; we try to tell God what to do instead of opening ourselves to what is, the reality of the moment with which we must deal and try to find some aspect about which to be grateful. No matter how dire a situation, finding something to be grateful for opens doors and creates possibilities for the next step.

I will never forget a patient who insisted there was a key. Since I didn't believe there was a key, I tried to dissuade her of the idea that there isn't a key, but that progress comes a step at a time, and because it is slow, it may be difficult to perceive. Disappointed with my failure to uncover a key, she made some progress and left treatment.

A few years later, she returned for a follow-up session. By then I had discovered the magical key of gratitude that opens doors we never imagined existed. No matter how dire a situation, solutions appear when we find an aspect to appreciate and about which to be grateful. When I told her of my discovery, her mouth broke into a knowing smile. So happy was I for this chance to share our treasure it seemed she had been sent by God.

A variation on this theme relates to finding something we don't even know exists. One of my patients didn't believe she'd find a good husband. But she didn't give up the search and found a man whose positive qualities exceeded her imagination. If we stay open to experience, our findings can outdistance our beliefs. Ideally the psychotherapist removes the psychological blinders from patients' non-seeing eyes which prevent them from perceiving possibilities. Undoubtedly, the tools of Peale and Blanton combined to enhance the vision of many.

DIVIDED TO BECOME WHOLE

Psychotherapy/psychoanalysis teaches us to become our own therapist by developing an observing ego. This observing aspect of self comments on the experiencing of self and allows us to act with more awareness of what we're doing and to ask why. We learn how we get in the way of our own goals and how we can correct our actions to avoid self-sabotage.

Paradoxically, we divide ourselves into two parts (our observing and experiencing selves) in order to become more integrated, authentic, and whole. This process can be viewed dialectically as thesis (experiencing self), antithesis (observing self), and synthesis as informed action of the authentic self.

THE PERVASIVE THEME OF AMBIVALENCE

Another contradiction or paradox is the pervasiveness of ambivalence. We love and hate, trust and doubt, and yet we're surprised when this reality comes to light in the life of one of our heroines. Mother Theresa's doubt in her faith as recently revealed by the press comes as a surprise to many.[5] Our human task is to integrate opposing feelings of love (thesis), hate (antithesis), and action as synthesis in order to apply them in a positive way to heal ourselves and our world.

THE CHALLENGE OF THE MOMENT

What seems obvious is often most difficult to achieve. We live in the moment, but rarely experience it. Yet Buddhists teach us its importance and when we achieve it, we experience its value. Yet most of our (mental) life is spent dwelling on thoughts of the past or the future.

Awareness of our distractedness comes unexpectedly, sometimes in a routine event as it did for me one morning as I jogged in Central Park with my German shepherd. There, a circle of people surrounded a large oak tree where a Black-and-White pointer dog fixed his eyes on a little grey squirrel, who trembled in fear. For the squirrel, the situation embodied life or death, while for the pointer, the game was sport. Mesmerized as if nothing else existed, I too stood still. Then, without warning, the squirrel made a mad dash up the tree. The dog relaxed, breathed a deep sigh, and, like a trooper, shrugged off disappointment as if it were a mere drop of rain. The crowd dispersed silently. I walked home, permeated by the realization that I had stopped and inhabited this moment with its drama. The stillness I experienced stood in stark contrast to my common experience of living as if chased by a pack of wolves. I resolved to slow my pace and imbibe the richness of the moment whenever possible.

Buddhists refer to this awareness of the moment as "awakening" or "enlightenment," which usually comes after hours or even days of meditation. In these moments I realized that the world doesn't revolve around me or my schedule. I exist not to be taken in by life, but to take in life. The poet Wallace Stevens wrote, "We are not at the centre of a diamond." We are not the brightness; the brightness exists in the world outside ourselves. I have free will to live like an atom agitated by a hot flame, or to see myself imbibing the grandeur of the world in each moment.

Today I am aware of how little time I spend in the moment; more often than not my mind carries me into the past and the future. But I experience ecstasy when mind, body, and spirit, my conscious and unconscious, are aligned and alert to the moment; ambivalence resolves, and a sense of well-being and acceptance overcomes the opposing drives of haste and dividedness.

DIALECTICS AND KABBALA

Several years ago I asked my friend and colleague, Leah Davidson, MD, to recommend readings about the meaning of money. She referred me to Nilton Bonder's *The Kabbalah of Money*. Bonder's book of practical applications of the Kabbalah opened my eyes to the multiple dimensions of reality.

Kabbalah means receiving and explores the layers/levels on which giving and receiving function in our world and in worlds beyond our common perception. The study of Kabbalah explores levels of meaning, interconnections, and relationships beyond the visible. These can frighten us or drive us mad if we aren't spiritually prepared to accept them. But the belief can also help us process and deal with terrible events, which make no sense on the apparent level. We can trust that there is meaning beyond our comprehension.

The belief system of Kabbalah also contains thesis, antithesis, and synthesis; esoteric and mystical, it is also practical, guiding us to accept and make the best of a situation. We correct evil by moving forward in the world in a practical way. *Tikkun Olam*, literally to heal the world, is part of the practices of Judaism and Universal Unitarianism. No matter how terrible an event, we cannot reverse something which has happened. Working toward acceptance and assuming there is meaning beyond our comprehension encourages us to process the loss and try to take a positive direction.

An example is the parents' response to the loss of their child from leukemia. Instead of withdrawing from the world in their grief, they might establish a research fund to find a cure for the disease and take comfort in knowing they are helping others.

Not only do we help ourselves in this positive action/attitude but we heal the world. According to the Kabbalah, evil in the world is seen as a reflection of a cosmic rupture, and redemption on earth entails restoration of the divine order with our help.

THE PLACE FOR HUMAN ANGELS

I attended medical school in Puerto Rico, isolated from friends and family. As I studied on the beach and gazed at the aquamarine ocean, I felt high on the fusion of myself with the world, at one with everything. My feelings of isolation dissolved; I had the courage to pursue my studies in a foreign culture.

I had the good fortune to meet two individuals who made a great difference in my life and whom I think of as human angels. The YWCA, a dilapidated old wooden house that looked as if it would be blown away by the next hurricane, provided an inexpensive abode near the medical school. There I met the headmistress, Ms. Rodriquez, who realized immediately that in order to study, I needed the only single room available in this noisy establishment where working women played loud music. In that moment, her empathy seemed life-saving.

A second angel facilitated my return to the United States. A surgeon vacationing in Puerto Rico assessed that I was a person of integrity and wrote me a recommendation letter to his alma mater.

FREE WILL

William James, author of *The Varieties of Religious Experience*, stumbled for years before he found direction. He recognized he had a will to exercise and guide his choices among possible actions. "Life presents us with situations we may not choose but the practice of free will comes as we decide which action of those possible." Kabbalah and free will interdigitate. What we do with what happens is the opportunity to exercise our will. We may not be able to prevent a hurricane, but we can pitch in and rebuild.

Recently I saw Margaret Atwood, the award-winning writer, interviewed on television on the subject of faith. She commented on the allegorical novel, *Life of Pi*, in which a young boy and a tiger cross the seas in a little boat. On shore, the tiger disappears without saying goodbye or even looking back at his companion. The question: did the tiger really exist or was he fabricated, hallucinated, or produced by the child's mind? Atwood says the tiger is like God in whom we choose to believe or not. We exercise free will. Like Atwood, I choose to believe because belief comforts and smoothes life's rough edges. To believe our lives matter gratifies in contrast to the existential viewpoint of the world as an indifferent bystander.

Those who helped dig out ground zero after 9/11, for example, and now suffer serious medical or psychological illnesses as a result, suffer an additional challenge to find God beyond the apparent "punisher." We can't count on good deeds to bring anticipated rewards. To view God as punishing doesn't soothe, but riles and troubles. When a person thinks he does good, but bad things happen, he may conclude that God punishes.[6]

When they were discussing the nature of the atom, Albert Einstein remarked to Niels Bohr, "You can't tell God what to do." This comment demonstrates again how, in many instances, the world operates beyond our comprehension.

GOALS

More important than the specifics of belief systems is how we apply them: to divide or destroy or to foster loving bonds, creativity, and world peace. To negotiate, engage in dialogue, and remain flexible is essential. Not all of us achieve the ability to integrate another's diverse agenda. This most difficult task requires an advanced development of the human brain; the ability to empathize and place one's self in another's shoes or situation. When we can, we're much less likely to kill each other. We no longer view the world in terms of all "Black" or "White" or "them" versus "us." The huge zone of gray makes functioning in a creative and self-protective manner more complex and rewarding.

To further our own and another person's journey whenever possible can be as simple as helping a blind person across the street, or as complex as integrating diametrically opposing philosophies.

As the rabbi in *Fiddler on the Roof* says, "You're right," and to his opponent, "and you're right too."

Rumi, the mystic poet of the thirteenth century, summarizes: "Sometimes visible, sometimes not, sometimes devout Christians, sometimes staunchly Jewish. Until our inner love fits into everyone, all we can do is take daily these different shapes."

NOTES

1. Lewis, 2003.
2. In *The Great Ideas of Philosophy*, Daniel Robinson explains that while Fichte introduced the concept, Hegel developed it.
3. Copleston, 176.
4. Ibid., 315–316.
5. Kolodiejchuk, 2007.
6. Kushner, 1983.

BIBLIOGRAPHY

Bonder, N. *The Kabbala of Money.* Boston: Shambhala Publications, 1996.

Copleston, F. *A History of Philosophy.* Vol. 4. New York: Doubleday, 1994.

Kandel, E. R. *In Search of Memory: The Emergence of a New Science of Mind.* New York: W. W. Norton, 2006.

Kolodiejchuk, B., and Mother Teresa. *Mother Teresa: Come Be My Light.* New York: Doubleday, 2007.

Kushner, H. S. *When Bad Things Happen to Good People.* Waterville, ME: Thorndike Press, 1983.

Lewis, B. *What Went Wrong? The Clash between Islam and Modernity in the Middle East.* New York: Harper Perennial, 2003.

Martel, Y. *Life of Pi.* New York: Harcourt, 2001.

Nobel, W. "Reflections on a Vision." *Journal of Religion and Health* 42 (2) (2003): 133–138.

Robinson, D. N. *The Great Ideas of Philosophy.* Springfield, VA: The Teaching Company, 1997.

Sheen, F. J. *The World's First Love.* New York: McGraw-Hill, 1952.

Teilhard de Chardin, P. *The Phenomenon of Man.* New York: Harper & Row, 1959.

Chapter 11

Spirituality: An Eclectic Force in Life

Aphrodite Clamar

I am Greek Orthodox by birth. I have always taken my religion as a given—a "genetic heritage," much like the color of my hair or eyes. I took the beauty of the Greek Orthodox liturgy and the rich traditions of the church for granted. When I did give it some attention, it was with a clinical eye. Only when the issue arose just before my marriage did I become aware of my commitment to my faith.

My fiancé, who was Jewish, asked me if I would consider converting. After considerable thought and reflection, I chose not to do so. Instead, we maintained a dual-religion household, each of us learning about and participating in the other's religion. However, the discussion served as a pivotal point. To my surprise, I realized how much I am transformed by the beauty of the services, the majesty of the lives of women and men who suffered and died for their beliefs, and the artistry of the Byzantine hymns and icons.

Along with most Christians, the resurrection has profound meaning for me because it addresses the most basic existential concern in peoples' lives. It proclaims that pain, despair, and death are not the sum of our lives; that after this life, there is hope for a new life. For me, the Greek Orthodox faith is like a meadow of beautiful flowers: the more I explore, the more I enjoy its sweet scent and amazing beauty. This image and the path it unfolds sowed the spiritual seeds for my life. They are the foundation that I use to help my patients explore their spiritual concerns and form a foundation for their lives.

"Spirituality" is one of those words that our society tosses about in a myriad of ways to define many kinds of experiences and feelings. In essence, spirituality has been used as a catchall term for our emotional, physical, and mental states. Yet, at its core, spirituality is a very personal and individual experience for each of us; it animates and mediates between our body, our soul, and our self.

For me, spirituality is an eclectic experience, made more profound for me through the two religions that are a part of my life, and in the beauty and spirit of my upstate New York home. Built in the 1660s, its spiritual presence often leads me to feel the presence of the souls of those who lived (and most likely died) in my home. I wonder who they were and how they came to live there. Truly, they deeded a profound calmness and peace to this rambling house, with its garden and elegant, gnarled old trees. I sense, then, that all of life and nature has an innate spirituality.

Besides spirituality imparting a sense of the eclectic force in life, I also feel the ecclesiastic sense of spirituality in the Greek Orthodox Church experience in which I was born and raised. The chanting, incense, flickering candles, and Byzantine vestments and architecture enhance the spiritual for me. Yet, having married into Judaism, I also relate to the Friday night Kabbalah services at my local synagogue. The chanting in Hebrew and the intonations of a long-ago Middle Eastern world are seductive and compelling, relaxing and succoring. Through the spiritual within me, I sense the connecting threads that run through both of these religious and spiritual ties to the holy, the transcendent, and that which is outside ourselves and which leads us to higher thoughts and experiences.

Both of my religious heritages—the one that I was born into and the one that I adopted—as well as the serenity and comfort with myself that I feel in the woods, by the ocean, or when stroking or talking to an animal, are the ballast in my life. Deprived of these life forces, I feel bereft. Fed by these forces, I know balance and contentment—I can touch my inner (and sometimes hidden) self.

Though I am now in private practice in psychology and a practicing psychoanalytic therapist, until recently I worked with senior services in New York City and New Jersey. I learned many spiritual lessons from the population of older women in those settings. Many challenges face the elderly: separation from and loss of significant others; finding a place to fit into a youth-oriented society; serious medical issues, including end-of-life decisions; loss of home and financial independence; decline in intellectual skills and memory—issues that they rarely have the opportunity to talk about with family and friends. Their developmental objective is reaching or maintaining a healthy balance of spirituality, autonomy, and religious beliefs. Senior women seek to connect to the universe, find more meaning in an otherwise mundane world, and achieve more balance and inner peace. They want to understand what lies ahead (besides more aches, pains, and pills) and how to shape their lives more meaningfully. Seniors often instinctively turn to the "magic" of nonattachment, not to be confused with not caring. While appearing to escape into detachment, nonattachment often translates into "I'll do everything possible to put the odds in my favor by trying.

If it doesn't work, that is okay, too." They choose philosophical solutions to resolve an intractable solution. Being nonattached senior women creates an emotional, spiritual freedom. The message is that trying hard and really caring can go together with a willingness to accept an outcome—whatever that may be—in which flexibility prevails. In the process, the spiritual message suggests magic. Either way, regardless of outcome, seniors are the winners. This attitude of acceptance helps lay the foundation to move to the next step in the spiritual path: to reassess situations and play out the deck of cards that they have been dealt in life. Finding and following this road ultimately allows them to tap into their spiritual core.

Since women tend to be more communal than men,[1-3] these senior women seem to be going against the grain in deciding to be less attached and to "go it alone" in less group-affirmed but rather individualistic solutions to their problems. They have switched, then, to a more agentic (acting or exerting power, assertiveness), administrative role. Women tend to use both agentic and communal life choices, depending on a particular situation. The philosophical resolutions to their problems of aging may be more defensive and self-protective devices, as well as blame avoidance for them. It is also refreshing that they are taking charge of life in a more responsible way. Spirituality allows them the flexibility and openness, in any event, to use both communal and agentic solutions to their problems whenever they see either or both as most feasible.

From my eclectic background, I am able to see the benefits of senior women taking the reins to resolve their problems. Their dealings with life often show resilience, strength, hope, and vitality in creative ways that engender inspiring and viable resourcefulness. Life can prove promising, joyful, and vibrant even into later years. Spirituality is what gives the fervor, affirmation, and life force to me now and will with hope continue to do so throughout my life, regardless of my age and condition of health. Women can be as strong, tough, and enduring as the proverbial "steel magnolias," even beyond the Scarlett O'Haras of this world. Whatever the spirit or animated life forces hand to us, they—and we—can be a mighty creation interacting with all of life.

NOTES

1. Rayburn and Osman, 2002.
2. Rayburn, 2002.
3. Rayburn, Hansen, Siderits, Burson, and Richmond, 1999, 2004.

BIBLIOGRAPHY

Rayburn, Carole A., L. Sunny Hansen, Mary Anne Siderits, Phyllis Burson, and Lee J. Richmond. *Life Choices Inventory (LCI)*. Washington, DC: U.S. Copyright Office, 1999, 2004.

Rayburn, Carole A. "Spirituality, Morality, Life Choices, and Peacefulness in North American Women." Presentation at the International Council of Psychologists Annual Meeting, Manila, the Philippines, 2002.

Rayburn, Carole A., and Suzanne Osman. "Spirituality, Morality, Life Choices, and Peacefulness in North American and Filipino Women." Presentation at the International Council of Psychologists Annual Meeting, Manila, the Philippines, 2002.

Chapter 12

Living Kabbalah

Marcella Bakur Weiner

The Jew has the advantage of having long since anticipated the development (the study of) consciousness in his own spiritual development. By this I mean the ... Kabbalah.

—Carl Jung[1]

I was not looking for Kabbalah. Kabbalah found me. For decades I had lived securely encased in theories of psychology. Comfortably settled in, I was not consciously seeking; the nest seemed secure. Yet, the obvious is often not so obvious. Since Kabbalah means "to receive," while it appeared that there was "no receiver," a crack in the door had opened. God had sent me an invitation. Unaware, it had been slipped into my unsuspecting self, prying open the walls of my longtime prison of choice. The crack now open, it widened and widened, the light ever intensifying until I became aware; I was created in the image of God, was now the open vessel, hungry, indeed ravenous, to receive. Kabbalah was the "good-breast" mother.

When I say that Kabbalah found me, it is my strong feeling that we are "found" when we are searching. There has to be a place, deep within ourselves, as there was with me, which was unfulfilled. Some say, it has to be a "death." Not a literal death, but one where there is a longing, a deep desire for something, someone, to fill the hunger. It came about in an unusual way: the office next to mine in New York City was vacated by a colleague. Another professional took it. Unknown to me, he was/is a spiritual leader who gave classes. He invited me. He spoke of the spiritual world that is ours for the asking. God was his frame of reference. I drank it all in, thirsty as one who had been relegated to the desert. I came for a class. I stayed for seven years, the equivalent of my period of psychoanalytic training, during which God was never mentioned, as He was not in all of my doctoral studies—or any others of an academic nature. I devoured it all, to my heart's content, and my life changed. With new "glasses," the worlds were revealed to me, vast, glorious, open, and embracing. I found my place, and, most critically, my objective: to live in truth. As with all seekers, in Judaism and Christianity, it is truth that is the way. Christ said that to "follow him, is the Way."[2]

This is similar to when Moses came down from seeing/speaking with God with the Commandments and gave them to his people for them to follow the way of law that was the truth as related to Judaism. I found the truth in Kabbalah.

WHAT IS KABBALAH?

Kabbalah is one of many forms of Jewish mysticism that arose during its nearly two millennia of development. Since the thirteenth century it has emerged as the most important current, and in subsequent centuries all Jewish mystical expressions were made, with few exceptions, through the symbolism of Kabbalah.[3]

The most characteristic and recognizable symbol of Kabbalah is that of the ten *sefirot* (singular *sefirah*). As cosmological symbols, these ten sefirot express ten extremities or polarities in a three-dimensional world: up, down, east, west, north, and south (the dimensions of space); beginning and end (the dimensions of time); and good and evil (the moral dimension).

In Kabbalah, the sefirot are a series of divine emanations, spreading forth from the godhead and comprising the divine world, which separates the created worlds—the world of angels, celestial bodies, and earth—from the hidden godhead. This system of the ten sefirot is nothing more than a philosophical-cosmological attempt at explaining the world, both earthly and divine—not very different in most respects from similar ideas put forth in the eleventh and twelfth centuries by Muslim, Christian, and Jewish philosophers influenced by ancient Neoplatonic worldviews.

THE FOUR WORLDS OF CREATION

Most of us, deeply connected to this world, are unaware that there are four worlds. For those of us on a conscious spiritual quest, we tip over into the world directly above us, the other two beyond our limited human comprehension. The highest world is that of emanation, God's world, one of limitless light. Creation, the world below, is one whose quality is unconditional love. Moving down to the next one, we are in the world of formation, where deep meditation and dreams take place; all psychic phenomena, such as the feelings of, "I know but can't really tell you how I know" are found here. But, for most of the time, we live in the fourth world, the world of action, our material world. In this world, we function using our five senses: to see, to hear, to feel, to touch, and to taste. This is given to us for divine purposes, to be used with consciousness and fulfill God's intentionality for all human creatures. This is molded into the highest form of intentionality, free choice; humans are the only of God's creatures so bestowed. "I give you life and I give you death. Choose life." (Deuteronomy 29:11, 15[4]) With this, as human beings, we not only choose, but after choosing, we consciously reflect upon the consequences: "Have I hurt someone's feelings, made the same mistake over and over again, not seen the obvious signs all around me?" With this, we move into the desire for atonement with a simple "I'm sorry" or, in self-reflection, choose another road to travel. Sadness and mourning are also parts of this process. Animals also can and do mourn. I remember, one day, in a foreign country, stopping in amazement at seeing an exquisite, elegant, long-necked giraffe. She was standing totally still, like an inhaled breath lasting forever, at the side of her baby who had been shot by one of us, a human being. It seemed a sight of deep, deep mourning, similar to ours, at the loss of a loved one. A true creature of God's, she would not leave her baby, in life or in death. That image has stayed imprinted in my brain for three decades, never to fade.

Has this higher consciousness always been in me? Perhaps yes, on some primitive, unrealized, if deeply felt level. But it was not to bear fruit for many decades. Earlier, I suggested that, unless, in one form or another, we experience a form of death, many will not feel the longing, the deep hunger for something besides this all-too-visible, obvious world of our five senses. For me, the death was real, but not yet consciously in my mind since I was a very small child, barely out of infancy: I had an operation, a routine removal of my tonsils. My loving parents, very financially secure, hired the very best doctor/specialist. The procedure done, I went home. After a week or so, my mother noted that I was swollen in my whole body—all of me was "blown up." She rushed me to a hospital, where she was told that I had blood poisoning. Someone (the doctor?) had used an infected needle/instrument. I had a 1 in 1,000 chance of survival. In other words, as my mother later related it to me, they stated, "your baby will die." I was about eighteen months old. Of course, I have no memories of this. I was hospitalized for many months, with frequent operations to save my life. A great deal of my leg was cut up (this was before antibiotics), and I had to wear a cast for much of my childhood. This kept me at home, out of school, and out of play with other children. But I never felt lost, lonely, neglected, injured, or resentful. Quite the contrary, I had my own guardian angel right there with me for years. School, when I did go, was a huge bore; it could not compare to what I had at home, a doting mother who mirrored me in all we can possibly hope for: she played with me, told me stories, sang to me, and looked at me with such love that I felt no sense of guilt that she had to feel burdened to spend so much time with me. This period was one of freedom. By the time I was in my early teens, books had become exquisite replacements for the parts of my leg that had been taken from me. I got drunk on Goethe, Aristotle, Aristophanes, Tolstoy, Dostoyevsky, Roth, Nin, Keats, Shelley, and the classical music my brother, seven years my senior, supplied: Bach (my favorite), Mozart, Schubert, and Wagner. I had my own private salon and a loving, caring, and devoted family.

My parents were Jewish immigrants, my father from Poland and my mother from Russia. Their story is fascinating: he immigrated to Russia from a farm in his youth; he saw my mother, a political sophisticate active in the prerevolutionary movement. He joined just to be near her, "the most beautiful woman I have ever seen," but was arrested and sent to Siberia, noted as much for its horrendous cold as its brutal conditions. She visited, bribed a guard, and they escaped, he to America, later to send for her. I am the last of their four children. My father became what was called "very rich," while my mother stayed left wing. Neither really practiced their religion, my mother going to synagogue only on the day you mourn those no longer in this world. My father was totally against religion of any kind.

But I felt an absence, a deep longing for something beyond, but I knew not what. One day, at age ten, I said to my eldest sister, thirteen years my senior, married, and with her own children, "Dorothy, I want to go into a convent, to devote myself to God." Not blinking, she merely replied, "You can't. Jewish girls can't go to convents." I still remember my feelings of huge emptiness, a vast hole widening inside of me. I asked, "Where can I go?" She smiled and kissed me. But the hole remained, if later smoothed over by dating, friends, and a joyful existence.

My older son, having become part of a spiritual community after college, introduced me to spirituality. I became ravenous. I read everything I could about Jesus, Moses, and anything related to the world of spirit. I later joined the seminar of the man who shared my office suite for those of us in the healing arts. I could now heal others along with myself. Like climbing Jacob's ladder, I was on the first rung, ready to move up or down, as needed. It was intoxicating, and still is.

HEALING

How do we heal? In our world of materialism, greed, corruption, exploitation, and competition, how do we, the "healers," stay "pure?"

How can we not submit or be seduced by the murky, even dirty side of the world, when it is part of our daily life? How do we rise above it all? Can Kabbalah be a necessary, even glorious accessory? Yes. For healing, like Kabbalah, is a process. Kabbalah (Jewish) and Cabala (Christian) are similar, the major distinction being that, in the latter, the emphasis is on Jesus. In both Kabbalah and Cabala, the emphasis is on attaining balance, similar to the message of the ancient Greeks, and for Jews, the emphasis is on the ability to seek *teshuvah*, forgiveness, if we have gone astray. Moving away from our material world, we advance more deeply into ourselves, our visions, our dreams, and our intuitive selves, where we can find the true meanings of our existence. Therein lies the truth, the ultimate reality that is our inheritance, and which has been and is there for us to enfold. How do we, as women, heal? How has Kabbalah embraced women, or not?

WOMEN AND KABBALAH

Genesis[5] says that God made two great lights: the greater to rule the day, the lesser to rule the night. The sun was designated for the day, the moon for the night. When first created, they enjoyed equal power. According to God, this was so that there would be two worlds. The moon was unsatisfied and pleaded with God to make her the larger sphere. One Kabbalistic version states that the moon was very unhappy with this state, insisting that it would be most fitting for God to make one the larger—preferably she. In this version, God punishes her for this and makes her smaller. In another version, God, most beneficent, tells her that, while she is smaller, she rules both by day and by night, for, if one looks up at the sky, even during daylight, one can see the outlines of the moon. In still another version, God promises the moon that, at some later time, in a future world, her light will be restored so as to equal that of the sun.

If we read the Old Testament carefully, we find tales of women, some of whom lived thousands of years ago: "From Sarah, women can learn when and how to say No." From Rebecca, who struggled to bring heaven and earth together for her descendants, today's woman can find inspiration as she seeks to turn away from "models" in our society who concentrate on materialistic values alone, and look instead for a balance between spirit and body toward a richer and more meaningful life.[6] There are others: Rachel, extraordinarily compassionate, puts aside her own jealousy to do what is right, accomplishing what the greatest man could not do: She gave help to all who came to her in need and compassionately brought them comfort and sustenance.

From the beginning, women were healers. Healing with herbs, they cured the sick, the frail, and the old. They were there when a mother was giving birth; when a mother had no milk to breastfeed a child, another nursing mother took over. They saved lives. Healing and compassion were theirs.

THE *SHEKINAH*

The *Shekinah*, in Kabbalistic writings, is the Heavenly Mother. Still regarded by many as a form of heresy, She is not well known, and if/when mentioned, is considered meek and helpless. In fact, with the rise of the industrial age, almost all references to Her vanished. But some Kabbalists see this as related to a decline in religious beliefs. Others, including prominent theologian Elaine Pagels in her highly popular *The Gnostic Gospels*,[7] showed that ancient Christianity, heavily influenced by Jewish mysticism at the time, embraced a more feminine identity.

THEOLOGY

How does Kabbalah deal with it all today? The term "Shekinah" itself does not appear in the Bible. Yet, the word, translated from Hebrew as "the act of dwelling" implies that this "dwelling" took place in the holy sanctuary of the Jews, said to have been most instrumental in carrying out God's purpose. Indeed, in the book of Job (written about 1,000 to 800 BCE), wisdom is affiliated with the feminine. In the book of Proverbs, wisdom is more closely described as a female entity who has been the deity's "partner" and "delight" ever since the origin of the cosmos.[8]

To the surprise of many, and generally unknown, Shekinah became involved whenever sexual intercourse occurred. This was to become a key feature of the Kabbalah. Kabbalists themselves ascribe great significance to human sensuality as a mirror of the divine structure and vice versa. In an early work of Kabbalah, The Book of Brilliance, the penis and vagina are referred to as earthly counterparts to heavenly forces around us. In other Kabbalistic writings, we find vivid eroticism, where the celestial king and queen unite in sexual ecstasy to sustain the cosmos each day. In fact, Jewish mysticism even stipulates that "married persons carry out love-making at least once a week."[9]

Kabbalah has always recognized sexual desire in women as well as men. Indeed, as far back as the thirteen century, Kabbalah has given credence to women's sexuality, stating that pregnancy is the result of an equal and reciprocal desire between marital partners. Further, Kabbalists stress that how we approach lovemaking is most essential, the chief ingredient being to engage in a mood of reverence, bound with joy. Thus, say the Kabbalists, for both men and women, we transcend the physical world through the exalted paths of our bodies: the woman is equal to the man, much as the Shekinah is the female component of the deity.

LIVING IN CLOSENESS TO GOD

Kabbalists say that there are many levels of being. Some are responsible for galactic developments. These are great spirits or archangels. Others of a lesser nature act as intermediaries, carrying out specific tasks such as watching over planets or species of plants and animals. Still others are involved with routine matters. Or, as Dr. Gerald Epstein, noted spiritual teacher/mentor, humorously states: "Depending on how 'Godlike' you were here on earth, so will your corresponding task be above. Or, simply stated, you could just be an usher bringing bodies down to their new, incarnated lives. One choice would be to live closer to God, another, to stay removed. The choice is yours."

Kabbalah teaches that humans emerge from God. If people have the same essence as God, how do we veer off course? We do when we desire to receive for the self alone. States Michael Berg in his riveting book, *Becoming Like God: Kabbalah and Our Ultimate Destiny*,[10] "When we use our energy for sharing, for giving for the pure sake of giving, we are acting with the light of our Creator. The world is the war of two opposite forces: Light and Darkness. We are either heading toward the Light or we're heading for Darkness. Through our actions, we choose our direction. The source of Light, known as God, is the wellspring of joy, fulfillment. The force of Darkness, better known as ego, is the source of pain, suffering, and death. All the positive things we experience in our lives are manifestations of the Light; the ego is the state of total disconnection from God's Light, thus bringing total Darkness. We navigate between these two forces. Being given free choice, we have the power to choose our reality. All of this is through our actions."

LIVING ON A HIGHER LEVEL OF CONSCIOUSNESS

In all my training and education in clinical psychology, God, of any nature, and/or "higher consciousness"—or indeed, any form of consciousness—was never mentioned. Not at an Ivy League university where I obtained my doctorate and almost immediately thereafter was on staff as an adjunct professor, nor during my postdoctoral training in psychoanalysis at an analytic institute where I also was invited to take, and accepted, a staff position. In my clinical psychology program, I was friendly with a colleague who sometimes quoted Carl Jung. He was dismissed as "brilliant but strange," his comments discarded, though he was allowed to graduate and, I'm happy to say, has now practiced for many years as a Jungian analyst.

Steeped as I was in psychology, I went through various theories as a shopper does with changes in fashion, buying the current styles. Sigmund Freud was the major theorist taught, others coming soon after, all vying for eminence. There was ego psychology, Melanie Klein theory, object relations theory, and finally, the field I most veered toward, self psychology. With a prominent psychoanalyst and soon-to-be dear friend, the late Marjorie Taggart White, I coauthored a book about it *The Theory and Practice of Self Psychology*,"[11] related to Kohutian (Heinz Kohut) psychology. The book became a best seller in psychology, and popular and widely touted. I found Kohut's view of using the empathic approach most appealing, and while I was not fully conscious of it then, it is and was the most closely related to a spiritual approach, though Kohut denied not only his Jewishness but all forms of religion. But then I turned to spirituality and, on a new path, read voraciously. My readings of Judaism and Christianity seemed to hold some profound truths which also led to me to write, along with coeditors Paul Cooper and Claude Barbre, *Psychotherapy and Religion: Many Paths, One Journey*. In the book, ten of us, all trained as psychoanalysts, spoke of our spiritual paths and how to use them in our clinical practices.[12] (Interestingly, our publisher felt that "spirituality" was too broad a term and that "religion" would be more attractive and all-encompassing.) What I learned from reading what my nine colleagues contributed was that truth and consciousness, if considered within a tight interpretation, can also be sought through a diverse variety of paths. Here, feeling deeply, I reflect on the words of Jesus, beautifully spelled out in a book by Raymond E. Brown, *The Death of the Messiah*.[13] The book talks about the trial of Jesus, who at this point, with Pilate as the interrogator, both he and Herod finding him innocent but succumbing to the wishes of "the crowd for execution"—speaks of his role as "truth come into this world."

TRUTH/CONSCIOUSNESS IN CLINICAL PRACTICE

In his most recent book, *Escape Your Own Prison*, a close friend and colleague and sometime coauthor, Dr. Bernard Starr, writes: "I could no longer ignore the gnawing sense that the very principles and techniques that I taught, practiced, and experienced missed the main mark of fundamental change.... Traditional approaches to psychological healing were often helpful, but were rarely, if ever, transformational."[14] I share these feelings.

How do we as clinicians practice truth? For me, truth is to be who I am, as Berg posits: "God-like." God is not an omnipotent judge sitting on high and ordering us around. God is within. It is the Jungian "I" of individuation, a true consciousness, Jung being the only theorist who made this spiritual connection in his work. Neurosis for him was the individual's need to escape from a challenging life event that they feel unequipped to meet. Thus, he would ask: "What task is this person trying to avoid?"[15] But consciousness is not just an individual phenomenon. There is also a collective consciousness, a state of being of any society at a particular time. How then do we work with the individual?

Aware as I am that we are each most unique, having come into this world for our own special purpose, and believing, as I do, in incarnation, this is either our first time around, or, not having attained what we needed in another life, we are here to continue our journey. I am also cognizant of the fact that all we do, as individuals, enter and change global consciousness affecting not only those in our immediate environment but people around the world. So, I may say to a patient who says she feels sad, "You are sad because I know you as a sensitive person and today, as you know, some children have just been found murdered in X (some faraway country), and many of us, feeling this, are sad." That is my truth and, on another level, helps remove the client's sense of loneliness or isolation. A "neurotic response" such as sadness to a sad event is actually a response to a universal happening somewhere and picked by more sensitive, spiritual persons throughout the world. The much over-used and out-dated, nonspiritual DSM fails to take this reality into account.

Even in teaching, I am open, direct, and honest with my students: I tell them I am here to offer them theory, the 500 there are, much to the amazement of us all. But the advice I can offer is that, during this term, I can help them get to know who they are, their purpose for being here, what their task is in life, and how they want to use themselves as clinicians. To accomplish this, we do a lot of role-playing, with a lot of laughter as they take turns being the professional and the person seeking help.

Since I believe there is purpose in all things, not randomness, those who choose to come to see me for professional reasons seem to have been hand picked. For the most part, they are on a path of which they are conscious. When not, I stay with where they are and do not push my view. I do retain my humanity: I go to weddings, bar and bat mitzvahs, and answer calls and questions such as: "Are you married? Did that ever happen to you? Did you see that movie? Do you like opera?" And so on. I share my humanity with them, having overcome the neutrality of my psychoanalytic training a long time ago. Finding joy, glory, ecstasy, and a true delight in being alive after having been so close to death at an early age, I am open to the light of Kabbalah and to the spiritual teachings of other religions as well. One of my closest friends was Sister Jean-Marie, a nun who has since passed on to another life. I found my desire to be in a convent at age ten in her; though she was on a different path, she was so like me. What I offer to those who see me for working out their lives is guidance for the path they choose. I try to make them aware that they do indeed have choices. A woman living with an abusive husband can leave; a young mother who has found that she wants to live with another woman instead of a man can do so if that is her choice; the man who tells me he deeply mourns his dog and talks to his priest is relieved when I tell him that that's a good choice and not to feel stupid about it. Rather, he's showing unbelievable love for all of God's creatures. And so, if Kabbalah means "to receive," I am grateful to receive and hope that, in so doing, I too can give, and help heal our world. In so doing, I also heal myself.

NOTES

1. Stevens, 1998.
2. Brown, 1992.
3. Dan and Keiner, 1986.
4. Van Duzen, 2001.
5. Ibid.
6. Weiner and Feinstein, 2001.
7. Pagels, 1979.
8. Van Duzen, 2001.
9. Hoffman, 1992.
10. Berg, 2004.
11. White and Weiner, 1986.
12. Weiner, Cooper, and Barbre, 2006.
13. Brown, 1992.
14. Starr, 2007.
15. Weiner and Simmons, in press.

BIBLIOGRAPHY

Berg, Michael. *Becoming Like God*. New York: The Kabbalah Center, 2004.

Brown, Raymond E. *Death of the Messiah*. New York: Doubleday, 1992.

Dan, Joseph, and Ronald Keiner. *Early Kabbalah*. Mahwah, NJ: Paulist Press, 1986.

Hoffman, Edward. *The Way of Splendor*. Northvale, NJ: Jason Aronson, Inc., 1992.

Pagels, Elaine. *The Gnostic Gospels*. New York: Random House, 1979.

Starr, Bernard. *Escape Your Own Prison*. New York: Rowman & Littlefield, 2007.

Stevens, Anthony. *Freud and Jung*. Princeton, NJ: Princeton University Press, 1998.

Van Duzen, Grace. *The Book of Grace*. Loveland, CO: Eden Valley Press, 2001.

Weiner, Marcella Bakur, and Blema Feinstein. *A Woman's Voice*. Northvale, NJ: Jason Aronson, Inc., 2001.

Weiner, Marcella Bakur, Paul Cooper, and Claude Barbre. *Psychotherapy and Religion: Many Paths, One Journey*. New York: Rowman & Littlefield, 2006.

Weiner, Marcella Bakur, and Mark Simmons. *Your Problem Is the Solution: A Mirror for the Hidden "I."* New York: Rowman & Littlefield, in press.

White, Marjorie, and Marcella Bakur Weiner. *The Theory and Practice of Self Psychology*. New York: Brunner/Mazel, Inc., 1986.

Chapter 13

African American Women, Religion, and Oppression: The Use and Abuse of Spiritual Beliefs

Beverly Greene

This chapter examines the varied roles of religion and spirituality in the lives of African American women and its influence on my own life. My analysis contemplates the ways that spiritual/religious beliefs, theological doctrine, and religious institutions in African American communities can be used to support behavior that reflects differential uses of spiritual beliefs. Spiritual and religious beliefs can be used to support behavior that reflects a theology of liberation for all members of that community and for all people in ways that promote optimal mental health. However, those same beliefs can be used to support behaviors that constitute internalized oppressions, racism, sexism, heterosexism, scapegoating, and isolation. They may be used to support the social status quo of dominance and subordination as well as individual and family pathology. My emphasis is on the way religious belief is used rather than on the content of the belief per se, the importance of considering both the positive and negative potential uses of such belief systems in people's lives, and the active role that individuals have in making decisions, consciously or unconsciously, about how they interpret or derive specific meaning or intent from scriptural doctrine, what they choose to believe, and what they think their beliefs give them license to do to others and themselves. Psychotherapists can be helpful to clients who use spiritual beliefs in ways that ill serve them and exacerbate their social and personal struggles by making the examination and exploration of those beliefs an active part of their therapeutic inquiry.

African American women have diverse spiritual and religious beliefs. Both historical and contemporary African American women should not be regarded as homogenous groups. While their cultural dispositions and practices varied distinctly from traditional Western models, they also vary greatly within the group. Their spiritual connections have always been important to their survival and continue to be vital. Most contemporary African Americans are members of Christian denominations; however, African Americans may be found in virtually every religious denomination.[1] For the most part, precolonial Africans and African slaves did not practice what we understand as traditional Christian faiths. Furthermore, African slaves were not consistently presumed to have "souls" in the Western religious sense, and it is likely that viewing them as beings without souls facilitated their exploitation. As soulless creatures, they were treated as little more than animals, seen as objects and property whose existence was designed to make life easier for the White population that exploited them.[2] As long as Africans could be viewed as objects, members of the dominant culture would have no need to reconcile the blatant contradiction between their destructive behavior toward Africans and their descendants that comprised American racism and the Whites' espoused Christian beliefs that would make racist ideology and behavior unacceptable, and, moreover, egregiously sinful. Those beliefs would have required that creatures with souls be treated with the respect accorded human beings that Africans were conspicuously denied in a racist society. White slaveholders who espoused Christian values saw no conflict between those religious values and their routine practice of raping Black female slaves. While contemporary African Americans claim Christianity as a significant component of their culture and heritage, it is important to acknowledge that they did not come to the United States as Christians. They came as slaves, objects in a deplorable enterprise that was often officially supported by established Christian denominations and leaders.[3] American churches more often than not reflected rather than challenged the American racial social status quo. When the United States practiced legal racial segregation in ways that mirrored South African apartheid, American churches were segregated as well. Not only was the humanity of African Americans denied, White supremacist groups often used verses from the Bible to argue that God intended for White-skinned persons to dominate dark-skinned persons because White-skinned people were superior beings.[4] Not only did this rationalize racism as God's will, it removed any need for Whites to experience their behavior as destructive and malevolent.

The most potent symbol of domestic terrorism in the nineteenth century, appropriated from Christianity, was the burning cross used by the Ku Klux Klan in its reign of terror over African Americans.[5] Nazi propaganda also used select verses from the Bible to support the quest for Aryan dominance and its vicious anti-Semitism, racism, and elitism. Black nationalists, who are critical of the dominance of the Christian faith in African American communities, suggest that it contributes to their racial oppression.[6] They have argued that Christianity was used to: support the subordination of African descendants by justifying racist behavior as part of God's plan; emphasize scriptural verses that admonished those who suffer that the meek would inherit the earth; encourage oppressed people to pray for and forgive their oppressors rather than openly oppose or want to destroy them; encourage passivity by admonishing those who suffer to look to God and not other human beings for their deliverance; encourage many who suffer to believe that their suffering is what God intended for them because of their own innate inadequacy; convince the oppressed that questioning their abuse is synonymous with questioning God's will and a direct expression of their lack of faith; support the belief that Christians should focus their concerns on the afterlife and not be concerned about their oppression in the here and now.[7]

African descendants who accepted those ideas in unqualified form were less likely to engage in active resistance to their plight or to challenge the ideologies used to support their ill treatment. While Christian beliefs have been used in the ways previously described, they have also served as potent sources of liberation theology that reinforce African Americans in challenging their poor treatment and rejecting their oppressed status. Most leaders of the civil rights movement have their origins in Black churches; indeed, many, including Rev. Martin Luther King, Jr., were ministers (for example, Andrew Young, Jesse Jackson, Ralph Abernathy, Rev. Wyatt Tee Walker, Rev. Adam Clayton Powell, and Rev. James Daughtry). Clergymen from other Christian churches were powerful allies in that struggle as well (for example, Frs. Daniel and Philip Berrigan and Rev. James Reeb).

EARLY PRACTICES

Initially, the spiritual practices of African slaves were more consistent with those of indigenous people and varied greatly throughout Africa just as tribal customs and beliefs varied greatly in Africa and among Africans as well. The Christian conversion of African slaves was not typically something they freely chose to undertake because they were not free to refuse without risking grave consequences. Conversion in this case represented an extension of racist oppression in that slaves were denied the right to openly practice their indigenous beliefs and were compelled to accept the faith of those who dominated them and who controlled every other aspect of their lives in ways that their descendants still struggle to overcome. Despite the extreme limitations placed on the Africans who were brought to the United States in bondage, their descendants eventually integrated aspects of Christian faith and principles into some of their indigenous practices.[8] In doing so they developed a theology of liberation in ways that represent a hallmark of their capacity to use the best elements of whatever was available to them to move their struggle forward. Liberation theology helped sustain African slaves and their descendants in the midst of hundreds of years of social oppression and became an important part of the civil rights movement. The belief in a higher power and connection to a force larger than themselves that would not abandon them in their struggles with the evils of racism cannot be underestimated as an important source of resilience for many African Americans throughout U.S. history. Not all Christian churches supported slavery or the legacy of racism that was to follow. Many people from White denominations colluded with slaves to help them escape plantations and actively fought against racist practices. That African Americans could employ Christian theology and Christian religious institutions to advance their liberation despite its use as a tool of racism illustrates their capacity to interpret doctrine in ways that support liberation and social justice rather than the status quo of social domination.[9] This clearly illustrates the capacity for African Americans and other people to use religious doctrine and scripture selectively in ways that are personally affirming and support social justice rather than the status quo of social pathology reflected in hierarchies of social dominance and subordination.

Despite their participation in Christian faiths, African American women are found among Muslims, Buddhists, Jews, agnostics, atheists, and other groups. However, it is fair to say that most African American women are affiliated with Christian denominations. For some, regular attendance at formal worship services and active participation in church is an integral part of their lives. For others, their spirituality does not at all involve formal worship or membership in any religious institution or collective. Rather, theirs is of a more personal and individualistic nature. On an individual level, religious/spiritual participation can be used to enhance the quality of one's life and can offer the community of a congregation as a potential source of both giving and getting tangible as well as spiritual emotional support.[10]

Historically, Black churches have often functioned as small business entities like local corporations that depended on members who had a range of organizational, creative, and leadership skills. Hence, some of these congregations have also offered African American women the opportunity to provide organizational leadership in ways that were denied them in a racially segregated and sexist world. Depending on the time and the congregations themselves, Black women might serve on boards of trustees, as successful fundraisers, and in other positions that were responsible for maintaining the fiscal integrity of these organizations. Many prominent African American women artists (for example,

Aretha Franklin, Sarah Vaughan, Kathleen Battle, Jessye Norman, Whitney Houston, and others) began shaping their talents in church choirs or as church organists under the guidance and with the support of church members who had musical training or knowledge. In fashion shows or other artistic productions, African American women found an outlet for their creative talents that they could not routinely exercise in the White world, where they were always compared unfavorably to White women. Indeed, Black women have often been considered the backbone of the Black church. However, congregations within every denomination vary and can also be as sexist as the dominant culture, such as those who refuse to allow women in the pulpit as ministers or church pastors and insist on limiting them to more traditional gender roles.[11]

Religious and spiritual beliefs can be used in repressive ways to reinforce defensive styles that preclude emotional growth and to rationalize self-destructive behaviors. Religious institutions in African American communities have often been sources of homophobia, sexual repression, and misogyny.[12] Among African American women, religious doctrine is sometimes used to support what Cheryl Thompson[13] calls moral masochism. Moral masochism may be understood as a constellation of selfless behaviors that receive strong cultural support but establish dangerous patterns of self-neglect reflected in Black women's tendency to feel compelled to care for others to the point of the depletion and neglect of their own needs. The use of religious beliefs to support such behaviors often goes unexplored in psychotherapies with such clients unless the client raises it as a conflict or the therapist views the client's religious participation as a problem. The understanding of this material in each client's life, particularly concerning the ways that religious faith may be a resource or alternatively a part of a maladaptive defensive constellation, is important.

ALL ARE GOD'S CHILDREN

I was born and raised in northern New Jersey in a large extended family that included three younger siblings. My elders were born and raised in the Deep South during a pernicious period of American apartheid and overt racism. Most of them left the South during the great Black migration to northern cities to escape the more brutal and overt racism that was characteristic of the South at that time and its accompanying dangers and limitations for education, employment, and life in general. Both sides of my family had lifelong histories of regularly attending and participating in church. My mother was raised Methodist AME (African Methodist Episcopal) and my father Baptist; however, my mother joined my father's church after their marriage. Both my parents and their surviving siblings continue their active participation in the same local Baptist church and have for more than sixty years. As children, we were expected to attend and participate. Attendance was mandatory; the level of participation was negotiable. While I was not eager to spend Sunday mornings in Sunday school and Sunday afternoons in church, I usually obliged. Refusing altogether was not an option until I was in my mid-teens. Sunday school was preferable because at least it seemed you could have something to say rather than just listen to sermons where only the minister got a chance to talk. I agreed to be baptized at thirteen but had little spiritual enthusiasm. I failed to see how the practice made me any closer to God, and no one could quite explain it to my satisfaction. I accepted that this was one of those ritualistic rites of passage that I knew I was expected to submit to. I thought it would be easier if I went along with the agenda rather than resisting. When I expressed my intention to cease routine church attendance, my parents acquiesced. By then, however, I was informed about church practices firsthand and I suspect that was all they had wanted in the first place. Despite their insistence on church involvement during our formative years, we were given the clear message that church attendance did not divide the world into good people and bad people. Everything that could take place among human beings, good and bad, outside of church, took place within church as well. Congregations were composed of human beings where organizing around the sacred did not make all behavior in that context "sacred." The minister who served our congregation for the longest period of my life was respected and viewed as a good man but a man with all of the limitations of human beings. In many African American communities, the church minister is viewed as a celebrity of sorts. Historically, church ministers were among the few members of the community who were literate and more knowledgeable about those matters requiring literacy. Hence, they were often sought after for advice. Members might also have to accept the minister's interpretations of biblical scriptures because they could not read them for themselves. In many parts of the world, religious fundamentalism can exploit illiteracy and lay claim to scriptural support of many actions that do not have that support at all. If people are illiterate, they have no way of making those judgments for themselves. Clearly people in positions of power represented by clergy can use that power to serve or to exploit; historically, they have done both. Our parents taught us that our minister was not God's emissary on earth nor was he considered superior to any of us in any way. Neither he nor anyone else stood between us and our relationship with God should we choose to have one.

The way we were raised would not have produced the kind of children who would simply go along with anyone's doctrine without question. We were given perhaps unusual license to express doubts and to question anything; religious ideas, scripture, and church practices were no exception. Overtly sexist practices in the church were attributed to social convention rather than per God's instructions, and were not supported in our household. Women, we were taught, were just as capable as men and had the right to seek opportunities to express their talents and abilities, and to be fairly compensated for their work. We were encouraged to harbor a kind of irreverence to any notion of infallibility among some people as opposed to others or to the incontrovertibility of church doctrine and rules. We were taught that rules both religious and secular existed to guide our actions but they were never a substitute for thinking. Our parents' guidance was that no rule or doctrine should be followed blindly, that blind faith was dangerous. It could lead people to do things that were harmful to others as well as themselves by avoiding the responsibility of thinking about the consequences of their behavior. While faith might inspire, faith alone would not always be sufficient to get the job done; hence, we were told to pray but also "move your feet." Faith, we were taught, does not require that you don't use your brain and your senses, as they too come from God. There was never a sense that rules had to exist outside of some use that served a greater good; since they could be used for good or bad, thinking about them was always important.

Whatever I have learned that is positive about being Christian came from observing the conduct of family, church, and community members and family lore about elders. Much of that lore was organized around social justice themes that involved caring about the misfortune of others and doing something about it whenever possible. It also included an explicit ethic to view doctrine as doctrine, not as words that fell from God's lips to someone's ear, who then wrote down that communication in exact measure. Doctrine was viewed as a creation of people in the leadership of religious institutions that could serve many purposes and had its place. However, knowing all the rules and practicing them perfectly meant little if the spiritual substance of charity and generosity was missing. My siblings and I were raised in ways that I can now view as clearly progressive for their time.

Like Martin Luther King, Jr., our minister, William Bailey, was educated at Boston University and espoused a theology of social justice. He often said that his role was not to "preach" but to minister to the congregation and more. His vision for the congregation and himself alike was that both he and the church existed to minister and serve the broader community with the aim of charity and social justice for all. He would often say that Jesus fought for the humanity of Christians when they were scorned outsiders and that it was the duty of Christians to do the same for those suffering a similar fate in the present. Organizing parishioners around challenging or supporting political decisions that would affect our city was an active part of his ministry.

Rev. Bailey called for donations for civil rights workers, members who wished to join the March on Washington, or perhaps simply a family who had lost their home to fire or misfortune. Collecting food and clothing for families who were firebombed for their involvement in voter registration in the South or who were simply convenient targets for Ku Klux Klan violence also were familiar pleas from his pulpit. While he used biblical references in his sermons, the emphasis was not on doctrine but on spirit. Treating other people with a generosity of spirit, particularly those who would be considered the least and most rejected of us, was the core feature of his message about how people who called themselves Christians were supposed to behave. Rev. Bailey's message was powerful because he lived that vision. His was a ministry of service not notoriety. He was a familiar figure in the community, a small, dark-skinned, unpretentious man with no fancy clothing, no car, or any of the trappings of wealth or materialism so often found among contemporary church leaders. You would see him walking around town or taking the bus here and there throughout the week to be sure that no church member who had been too ill to attend services went without a visit from him. He was known to arrange for jobs for many of the church's young people as well as members who had fallen on hard times. He also actively encouraged academic achievement among church youth.

Rev. Bailey's was a theology that most closely represents what Cornel West refers to as prophetic as opposed to Constantinian Christianity.[14] West ascribes the roots of prophetic Christianity to Jewish traditions that declare that those who lose sight of the poor and the most vulnerable in society insult their maker, while those who fight to lift up the poor exalt their maker. In West's paradigm, evil is not viewed as an alien or objectified "other" but is in our own indifference to the suffering and pain of one another. The challenge of being Christian or Christ-like in spirit, in this context, is to always be concerned about evil as it is manifested in unwarranted suffering and pain, to have compassion and care for those who are discarded, ill treated, most excluded, and most vulnerable among us, and still manage to find joy in your own life. Constantinian Christianity embraces the market; the acquisition of power, wealth, and size, the core of which represents materialism.[15] The most powerful messages I recall about the meaning of being a Christian were reflected in the expression of prophetic traditions within my family, first and foremost from my parents, but also in our minister and many members of our church, and in neighbors who had little themselves but were enormously generous in spirit during my childhood and whenever our family suffered some trial. However, among the most powerful influences was that of the simple but eloquent and gently lived wisdom of my maternal grandmother, Flora Roberson.

My grandmother was born in the early part of the nineteenth century into a harshly brutal world. I was always amazed that her experiences of early loss and hardship had not damaged her enormous capacity to be generous, kind, and filled with joy about what she had rather than misery about what she lost—and her losses were profound. Among them was a husband, five children, and many beloved siblings who predeceased her. There are many family stories about my grandmother's tenacity. She clearly saw herself and her progeny as children of God, meaning that they did not deserve to be exploited or ill treated because they were Black or for any other reason. She was known to confront White people who attempted to cheat her or her children out of their wages in ways that were quite extraordinary and dangerous at that time. There are also many stories about her kindness and generosity in what she considered a natural extension of her Christian spirit. Those stories never cease to have a powerful effect. During the Great Depression, when most people did not have jobs, many men were forced to leave their families and roam from place to place in attempts to find work. They were often relegated to begging for food at the doors of strangers. My mother and her siblings recall that many times, these poor souls appeared at their back door asking for just a piece of bread or any food they could spare. Whenever this happened, they say that my grandmother would go into the kitchen and scrape together a sandwich, a small portion of their evening meal, or whatever she could spare. She turned no one away. Her neighbors always admonished her for doing this and often expressed contempt for grown men begging for supper. The neighbors would assail her for giving a stranger food when she, a widow, working as a seamstress or whatever she could do to earn money, still had seven of her twelve children living at home. This, they felt, was wasting food that her children should have. Grandma responded to their admonishments with a cherished parable about Jesus showing up at someone's door, hungry and asking for food, but being mistaken for a common beggar and turned away. Would you want to be the person who does that, she would ask. She would say that you never know who may appear at your door in need of help whom you might one day need to ask for help. She also believed that Jesus would be found among the needy, not the mighty, and that having compassion for those who were in dire straits was a basic expression of both her faith and her humanity. She was known to say that as little as you may have, there is always someone who has even less; if you are a real Christian, you will feel compelled to be concerned about their plight just as you are about your own. Grandma also spoke from her heart as a mother who had other children out in the world where she could not be with them to help if they were sick or troubled. She expressed the hope that if they were in need, perhaps some stranger would give them a meal or assistance. How, she reasoned, could she hope for that if she were not willing to do the same? After all, a beggar was also someone's child who had fallen on hard times and who did not have his mother to look after him. Grandma reasoned that her children would not starve because of what little she gave away, but that what seemed like very little to her might make a considerable difference to beggars who had nothing. I am sure that she was influenced by her experiences growing up in the vicious social context of the Deep South as a motherless child herself by the time she was only 7 years old. Her own mother was just thirty-eight years old when she died from complications of both childbirth and the neglectful absence of medical care that was routine for Black people at that time. Many people died of ailments that could have been success-fully treated, but White doctors would not treat them and Black doc-tors were scarce. For three days she sat at her mother's bedside knowing that there was no help to found for her, watching her die and becoming motherless as a young child. Grandma would often say that people were cruel to motherless children, perhaps sensing their heightened vulnerability, and that meant you had to learn to stand up for yourself. Despite the grimness of her reality, she did not become bitter and closed off emotionally. Despite the hardship that began so early in her life, she was not consumed with her own losses. Nor did it diminish her capacity to feel for others who suf-fered while finding joy in her own life. Her faith and her sense of being spiritually connected to something larger than herself clearly helped her transcend many experiences that could have distorted her spirit and her capacity to reach out in ways that became so character-istic of who she was.

Despite her kindness and her generosity, my grandmother made a distinction between the spiritual essence of her faith, the institution of the church, and the fallibility of church leaders. She refused to be silent about one of the abusive practices that occur in Black churches as well as in the broader society when those practices were directed at her children. At that time, church ministers were seen as celebrities and were powerful men in poor southern African American communities. People looked up to them; some even idealized them. Some members of the clergy abused that celebrity by sexually exploiting young women in their congregations. How to address these occurrences continues to be fraught with ambivalence among church congregations and in our communities. Some of that ambivalence can be attributed to the fear that it would be used by racist Whites to support their damaging nega-tive sexual stereotypes of Black men as dangerous to the community. Those stereotypes could also be used to rationalize lynching and other forms of racial violence and further stigmatize African Americans as a whole. Another source of ambivalence was also rooted in the realistic fear that Black men in the custody of the criminal justice system would receive far worse treatment than White men accused of similar crimes. Of course, many women who were the objects of unwanted attention not only thought they would not be believed but that *they* would become objects of the community's rage for tarnishing the image of one of its leaders. Such fears were not then and are not now completely unwarranted and are often fueled by the misogyny and patriarchal interpretations of doctrine. Many members of our communities remain silent about these problems and further traumatize the women who are victims. Not my grandmother. This she could not tolerate. My mother and her older sisters informed her that they were on the receiving end of unwanted attention and sexual overtures by their minister. They were all underage at the time and this particular minister was known for this behavior. Despite his reputation, there was conspicuous silence about it in the church. My grandmother went to the church and directly confronted the minister in question. She warned him that if he ever touched one of her daughters, he could not count on her to be silent. She said that she would tell everyone and confront him publicly in front of the church congregation if need be. If he did not wish to be the focus of a very public scandal (not to mention her wrath or the pistol she sometimes carried), she warned, he had best leave her daughters alone. He never bothered them again.

PROFESSIONAL PRACTICE, MENTAL FLEXIBILITY, AND OPTIMAL MENTAL HEALTH

One of the hallmarks of good mental health is the ability to be mentally flexible and to develop a wide range of responses or repertoire of solutions to problems. It also includes the acceptance of imperfection, a tolerance for ambiguity and uncertainty about oneself and the world, an ability to both tolerate and view conflict as an opportunity for growth, a capacity for connection to other people, a capacity to be open to additional information about the world, ourselves, and others, in forms that we may not expect, and the ability to step outside of our own dilemmas and see ourselves and the world through the eyes of others. Spiritual and religious beliefs can assist people in accepting the reality of their own flaws and the imperfections of others. Belief can also enhance an individual's capacity to forgive themselves and others for those imperfections while taking responsibility for their actions and the consequences. It can support the development of alliances and connections across conflict. Cone observes that the search for religious faith often represents a search for meaning among those who have few resources, little power, and who are going against the odds, those for whom hope is critical.[16] Feeling connected to a power or reality that is larger than oneself can help people who are distressed to transcend their oppression and resist being defined by it.

The history of slavery, racial apartheid, social marginalization, and their psychological sequelae African Americans challenge the ability of African Americans to be mentally healthy people. It is noteworthy that perhaps most have managed to do so. Frustrated attempts to cope with these traumas often result in unhealthy manifestations of adjustment reflected in less-than-optimal physical and mental health. Many marginalized people internalize the negative depictions of themselves and come to believe that they deserve ill treatment. Some of these individuals may use religious scripture or doctrine to support their deep-seated sense of unworthiness in ways that are unwarranted. Booth observes that those who grew up in dysfunctional households may have been taught that they must blindly accept authority, including religious authority, making them even more vulnerable to exploitation.[17]

For many people who have experienced personal and social trauma, uncertainty is frightening and leaves them intolerant of the ambiguity that is an inevitable part of our lives. They may develop a perfectionist rigidity that requires a level of control over the environment that is not only unrealistic but interferes with the exercise of mental flexibility. Their rigidity may be expressed in religiosity and a tendency to be judgmental and rejecting of people or ideas that do not fit within their narrow frame of reference. Their judgments may be expressed in abusive behavior couched in religious doctrine.[18] Such behavior is less likely to foster connections in relationships and more likely to cause estrangement and social isolation. The more uncompromising, controlling, and judgmental people become, the more they alienate others in what may be desperate and ironic attempts to conceal their fragility and desperate need to connect. The more zealous a person is, the more they may be defending against their own uncertainty about what they believe. It may well be *themselves* they are trying to convince. As a result, they can justify viewing people who disagree with them as bad, evil, or inferior. The danger is that when people are seen this way, it not only justifies distancing them, but once at a distance, it can seem permissible to harm them and still feel righteous about one's faith-based imperative to harm. Booth observes that this can be seen in the hate speech used by people who advocate social bigotry and use biblical scripture to uphold their views.[19] This practice can be observed in historical atrocities against Native Americans, slavery, the Holocaust, Nazi views of mentally ill or disabled persons as defective and expendable, anti-Semitism, the Ku Klux Klan's reign of terror, and in the heterosexist rhetoric of the religious right. It is important to understand how Christianity and virtually any other religion can be used to support the selective abuse of people who are unpopular, make others uncomfortable, or can be exploited for their labor or property without their consent or adequate compensation. Every group in human history that has practiced social domination or genocide against another group did so out of values that were couched in religious beliefs or convictions. In many instances, such behavior was deemed part of religious mandates and often enjoyed popular support. In these cases, individuals or groups, often dominant group members whose behavior is abusive, have used religious doctrine to ease their conscience about the real nature of what they are doing and its destructive consequences.

Healthy religious practice and belief involves the kind of engagement in which one arrives at belief as a function of questioning and living with the tension that comes from ironclad certainty being nonexistent. Blind faith is not true faith; faith is that which persists in the presence of doubt and the absence of fact. Faith is not required when all of the facts are in; rather it is faith that helps people maintain hope in the absence of fact. Spiritual belief and faith can be used to promote good mental health just as they can be used to promote or support dysfunctional and destructive behavior.

The core of my identity as a Christian is not governed by formal religious doctrine, church attendance, or the formal trappings of religion. Rather it is firmly rooted in a spiritual and political sense of the importance of social justice and the liberation of the oppressed through personal and institutional actions in the prophetic tradition. It was most heavily influenced by my relationships with those who often have had little but themselves, and who demonstrated these principles by example, and particularly the powerful example of my grandmother's life and deeds. It compels me to use my voice and my privileged access to raise the concerns of those who are denied that access. Religious belief has influenced my practice to the degree that I have witnessed its power at sustaining people who were forced to bear what seemed unbearable. However, I have also witnessed its power to reinforce hate, deep-seated unworthiness, and the rationalization of abusive behavior. Like any other tool, its benefit and value are determined by the way it is used.

I have attempted to explore the role of religion and spirituality in the lives of African American women with particular attention to the adaptive and constructive as well as the destructive use of religious belief. The Black church has been a potent source of support in African American communities and in the lives of African Americans. The liberation theology of the Black church was a leading force in the progressive movement for civil rights and liberties for African Americans; however, religious belief, like any other belief, can be used in the service of character pathology and psychological defenses that may not best serve people or their communities. It can also be used to support the dominant cultural status quo of power and the exploitation of vulnerable groups. Religious practice and belief can be used in the place of other addictive behaviors to separate and polarize rather than bring transcendent communion within families and to members of Black communities, particularly in times of conflict or when fear is rampant.

It is important to discern the difference between religious and spiritual belief as resources for optimal mental health versus the misuse of belief in the defensive service of avoiding internal conflicts managing personal anxiety, and developing healthier ways of engaging the world.

NOTES

1. Lincoln and Mamiya, 2001.
2. Cone and Wilmore, 1991.
3. Cone and Wilmore, 1991.
4. Burlein, 2002.
5. Ibid.
6. Lincoln and Mamiya, 2001.
7. Wilmore, 1999.
8. Cone and Wilmore, 1991.
9. Wilmore, 1998.
10. Lincoln and Mamiya, 2001.
11. McBride, 2005.
12. West, 1999.
13. Thompson, 2000.
14. West, 1999.
15. Ibid.
16. Cone and Wilmore, 1991.
17. Booth, 1991.
18. Ibid.
19. Ibid.

BIBLIOGRAPHY

Booth, Leo. *When God Becomes a Drug*. New York: G. P. Putnam and Sons, 1991.
Burlein, Ann. *Lift High the Cross: Where White Supremacy and the Christian Right Converge*. Durham, NC: Duke University Press, 2002.
Comstock, Gary D. *A Whosoever Church: Welcoming Lesbians and Gay Men into African American Congregations*. Louisville, KY: Westminster John Knox Press, 2001.
Cone, James H., and Gayraud S. Wilmore. *Black Theology: A Documentary History, Volume I: 1966–1979*. New York: Orbis Press, 1991.
Lincoln, C. Eric, and Lawrence Mamiya. *The Black Church in the African American Experience*. Durham, NC: Duke University Press, 2001.
McBride, J. Lebron. *Living Faithfully with Disappointment in the Church*. New York: The Haworth Pastoral Press, 2005.
Thompson, Cheryl. "African American Women and Moral Masochism: When There Is Too Much of a Good Thing." In Jackson, L. and B. Greene, eds. *Psychotherapy with African American Women: Psychodynamic Perspectives and Clinical Applications*. New York: Guilford Press, 2000.
West, Cornel. *The Cornel West Reader*. New York: Basic Civitas Books, 1999.
Wilmore, Gayraud S. *Black Religion and Black Radicalism: An Interpretation of the Religious History of African Americans*. 3rd ed. New York: Orbis Books, 1998.

Chapter 14

Colors of the Invisible: Sufi Healing

Janet Pfunder

*To pray is to throw yourself in this transfiguring arch of light which spans
from what goes by to what is about to happen. It is to melt in it in order to
lodge one's infinite light in the fragile little cradle of individual existence.*

—*Clarice Lispector*[1]

The Sufi path of ecstasy, longing, and surrender was vital to my cellular and psychospiritual survival in the context of an annihilating relationship with my mother.

IN THE GARDEN: A SUFI WORKSHOP

Walking through the Brooklyn Botanical Gardens was lovely, on the way to a Sufi workshop one bright Sunday morning in autumn. My eyes contentedly traced the shapes of trees, the colors of chrysanthemums, and the perfect lawns as we found our way to the partial replica of the Ryoanji Temple. We did a few simple practices together for about two hours. We sat cross-legged in the dark shade of a wooden porch, overlooking a rock garden full of sunlight. We practiced slow breathing combined with sequences of gentle arm and torso movements. We chanted "Ya Shafi" inwardly, then rested softly. After resting, we gently clapped a series of varied rhythms in unison. We inhaled through our open eyes, taking in the beauty of the scene before us, then exhaled through our open eyes toward infinity, continuing on through many repetitions. We rested again in the stillness. A calm and quiet mood enveloped us.

I was taken by surprise as we retraced our steps after the workshop. The gardens, already so lovely before, were now beyond gorgeous. In a magnification of aliveness, I felt myself aware of every curve of every branch and conscious of every leaf poised on its stem. Every particle of my body and being was fluid, continuous with the air, and the entire expanse was saturated with the energies of light, color, and movement. Choreography transformed kaleidoscopically with each slow-motion, weightless step, with every effortless breath. The brightness of sunlight was intensified and seemed to speak wordlessly to me, almost as if from behind it. The light was more than sunlight.

Before the workshop I had been looking "at" the landscape, as if it were somehow "over there." I was walking through space, space with a view. It was an uplifting experience of gazing, something to be grateful for, most certainly, but I was nevertheless separate from what I was seeing. Other dimensions were still to be awakened.

In the very same gardens, after the Sufi practices, I was graced with an experience that has been with me since as a particularly vivid and radiant reminder of the beauty of a reality we repeatedly and habitually forget. The Sufis think of humans as forgetful creatures, in need of structured practices to assist them in remembering reality. Sufi practices include slow movement, breathing, chanting, fasting, drumming, dancing, meditation, and whirling. Music is a presence during much of the work. Extended immersion expands our capacity to embody subtle vibrations. We detoxify the psyche-soma, refining the senses to acclimate the nervous system to a different frequency. Our practices keep us ready and open to receiving *baraka* (grace) when it comes.

My teacher once said, "Healing happens when the cells are in a state of ecstasy." The spiritual fire of "the work" burns away encrusted layers of conditioning, numbing, and scarring. Laughter erupts in moments of freedom. Stillness yields to movement, and movement invites tranquility. Active practices are followed by resting deeply. Intentionality becomes exquisite, spontaneous surrender, which arrives as a gift. The heart's longing is fulfilled in extended moments of falling in love with a transfigured space of light and breathing in an oasis of music and motion.

GRAY RAIN FALLING

Dream: *I am sitting at my bedroom window with great sadness, looking out to the sidewalk below, where my mother's coffin lies alone and forgotten in the rain. Across the street stands a large red brick church. My mother's coffin looks so small and desolate against the massive edifice of the church as the gray rain falls down upon it.*

This dream occurred when I was young, around the age of seven. It seems to me a portrait of my mother's hidden depression and my feelings of grief and concern for her private loneliness and for the impossibility I felt of really reaching her.

Her outer personality was organized to project anything but vulnerability. She prided herself on being tough, strong, and stoic. She was

tall and powerful, and liked to take action. She had worked as a legal secretary after college, and had passionately wanted to be a lawyer herself.
She was always arguing a case, and she liked to win every argument. After presenting her evidence (often of my shortcomings) she would point
her finger at me and conclude, "That proves it!" I sometimes felt like I
was in a courtroom when I was with her. Although she told me "The
day you were born was the greatest day of my life," she also felt confined and constricted being a mother and homemaker. She once said,
"You don't have to get married and have children. It's not all that great."
When she later wanted to go back to school and work, she was stymied
by both her husband and father and she gave up her dreams.

RED DRESS BURNING

When I was a teenager, I had a favorite dress in a beautiful red
color, a soft cotton fabric that I loved. It was a shirtdress that fell down
to the knees or a little below, with a wide matching red belt. I wore it
often, too often for my mother's taste, and so often that it became a bit
frayed at the hem and cuffs, long before I grew tired of it and was
ready to give it up. The fraying didn't bother me at all. My mother
and I had screaming fights about this dress. She insisted that I throw it
away. I refused.

Arriving home from school one day, I saw my mother over by the
rubbish barrel at the edge of the backyard. It was quite common then
for people to have large metal barrels filled partly with sand for burning trash. She stood by the barrel with a stick, poking at something
burning, absorbed in her task, never looking up. She seemed to be
muttering to herself.

This memory trace is strangely crafted, all of it in slow motion and
totally silent, a distillation of a scene that must have had at least some
ambient sound and mostly certainly did not happen slowly. In my
memory, I walk as if in slow-motion toward my mother as she stands
without looking up, her stick in the rubbish barrel. As I approach, I see
that she is pushing the last fragments of my beloved red dress into the
flames. As I write these sentences, I am struck by a profoundly lonely
feeling in the figure of my mother, standing there, not looking up at
me. Lonely and stoic and desperate, off in her own world. There is a
kind of spooky feeling, too, about her standing there, not looking at
me, stirring with her stick. It is a strange, weird, bizarre quality. The
memory abruptly stops there.

DEADLY ESCALATIONS

She burned the red dress at the very moment that she would have
known I'd be arriving home from school. She had to show me the act,

like a mini "shock-and-awe" campaign. She displayed her willingness to escalate and her need to win. Looking through a certain lens, now, I experience it as an attempt to cremate my red, erotic, and fiery teenage female body and to subdue the creative flame of my very being.

My mother seemed driven to fight to the death. There were many, many such escalations over the years. In the middle of yet another heated argument, when I refused her demand, she screamed the stunning sentence that would echo in me viscerally for years: "I wish my womb had never held you."

ON MY OWN

My earliest response to my mother was resistance and protest. But matching her rage with my rage was useless. She was unable to even hesitate in her escalations. I had to get away and create a new world for myself.

Everything about my life, when it was separate from her life, was intensely upsetting for her. When I went away to college, she turned her full force against me. I was quite vulnerable to her even though I was trying to break away. I was devastated after our encounters, broken down and in need of recuperation. After a visit, it usually took me three full days to feel like myself again.

Finding solace and strength through new friendships and new ways of thinking, I still felt like an emotional vagabond, in need of a home I never had. "You're living on MY property, young lady!" she pointed out when I was twelve. I can vividly remember precisely where we were standing when she said that. The only thing about me that pleased her was my academic achievement. My mind itself was experienced by her as a direct personal threat.

When I was twenty-five, I received an offer to work as a private secretary to Ravi Shankar. Attending his live concerts for the next year induced very positive altered states and sparked the long-forgotten artistic expression that I had exhibited in early childhood. I became a painter, living in a loft in the SoHo neighborhood in New York City. I went to my first yoga class, and had an amazing vision during my first deep relaxation. Then the women's movement brought me together with other women artists. I joined a group called Feminists in the Arts and we founded the Women's Inter-Art Center, putting on exhibitions and performances. In addition to painting, I made Super-8 films and gave poetry readings.

I also became a psychotherapist. Learning to cope with my relationship with my mother had been like boot camp. At some point I discovered that if I gave her my pure and rapt attention for long periods of time, without discussion or comment, she would feel much better. I remember one time in particular when I listened to her for hours in the late evening. In the morning she really was, for a time, a changed person. I was onto something important.

My mother wasn't pleased with anything about the way my life was unfolding. She told me with exasperation, "When my friends ask me what you're doing since you graduated from Harvard, I have to tell them you're an artist and a psychotherapist!" Underneath her contempt was an obvious need for me to feel sorry for her and empathize with her plight. After all, she had only this terribly disappointing report to offer to her curious friends.

I learned to edit my speech around her. I stopped revealing or telling her anything of importance about myself, my life, my friends, or my interests. This self-stifling censorship was born of necessity, but became an internal habit around others as well. I worried about what I should or should not say, and whether I should or should not have said what I had already said.

THE BLUE TENT

I slept and painted in my round blue studio tent for many summers at Sufi camp, high up in the mountains. My tent rested on a bed of pine needles in the middle of a circular cathedral of trees, down the hill and across the meadow from where the workshops took place. Many of my favorite paintings were created there. I was doing the Sufi work for hours each day, living in a secluded and beautiful setting with a community of other Sufis, and was free to seek solitude or companionship as I chose. The Sufi work was concentrated, and free time was ample.

I loved painting in my tent and sleeping there, too. At night the fabric of the tent would move with the slightest of breezes, and often the moon would shine between the branches to dance in patterns over my head. Energy gathered in the workshops would expand into ecstatic appreciation of the landscape and the moods of the sky. One afternoon we drummed as a group for about three hours, and toward the end I had an experience of synesthesia. The sound of the drumming translated directly into vivid colors in my brain. The synesthesia experience initiated a significant shift in my style of painting. Another aspect of Sufi camp was that my dreams were vivid and intensely positive for several weeks after arriving.

Dream: *I'm with a beautiful woman who is also a horse with huge wings, and she is starting up a mountain. I reach out my arms and she slows down enough for me to catch up and put my arms around her back as she flies and gallops, ascending the mountainside. She is beautiful and strong, with suntanned skin. I can feel her breasts and the strong rippling muscles in her torso.*

The Sufi work, particularly in the extended setting of the summer camps, gave me access to powerful sources of energy that exactly matched what I needed as a wounded daughter. With my mother, personal power issues brought conflict, pain, and weakened conditions to us both. In the Sufi realm, powerful energies could carry, support, and lift me. In this dream, I was encountering a generous and confident form of embodied female power.

A GOLDEN COMMUNION

Before my mother's death, during the years of her illness, I took many trips to see her. This was a big change after several decades of only occasional visits. Our relationship was different by that time. I was stronger, and she was more open, which made for a better balance. Also, my Sufi life had prepared me to be quietly present, more attuned to what was needed.

One afternoon we had a new kind of experience together. I was assisting her with physical therapy exercises after a surgery. We read the instructions together, and I helped her through one round. Then we did them together. They were pleasurable, and gently activating, and doing them together was fun. But they also felt mechanical to me.

I suggested, without elaborating, that we add breathing to the movements, and she agreed. We inhaled slowly with lifting motions, and exhaled slowly with descending motions. The breathing added a relaxed flowing quality, as one movement eased into the next. Soon we were swimming together, as the room itself became part of our sea of moving and breathing. Our breathing together brought us into connection with the space itself. I experienced us as two beings in a larger energy field, which cradled us both.

My mother lay on the bed, resting quietly, and I spontaneously began guiding her in a golden light meditation, using visualization. She displayed no resistance, even though I had not explained it. She seemed quite content to close her eyes and "see" golden light. Ever so delicately we expanded the golden light throughout and around her body. Then she lay still and silent for quite a while. She seemed to be in a peaceful state.

When she eventually opened her eyes, she looked over to me and said, "That was great!" Her face was smooth and radiant. Her look had a new and distinctive quality that felt similar to what one sees on the faces of people in the middle of a Sufi workshop. I had never seen her quite like this before. I like to think that all the different parts of her energy had been synchronized and unified, and that her subtle surrender had initiated a healing state of ecstasy. I like to think that she found some moments of relief and comfort. I like to think we had our first Sufi workshop together.

BLACK AND BLUE

The Sufi work is not always easy. Transformation is an ongoing process, at times even a torment and a terrible ordeal.

The first evening of a long workshop with my teacher, after several months of separation, surprised me. A long period of slow movements, while sitting cross-legged, was followed by an interlude of resting in the softness of breathing. Later we were guided in standing movements, then asked to close our eyes. "Let the music move you." Within just a few minutes I felt myself indeed moved by the music into spiraling undulations, my heart palpably opening, and had a feeling like falling in love, as the music continued on and on as if forever into the night. An upwelling of vitality was flooding my limbs, the dancing more and more a song of joy. Resting, every part of my body felt enlivened beyond anything in recent memory.

Two weeks later, I was sobbing in the corner as the whole group danced with awakened passion. I had fasted from even water that day, for some reason, perhaps because I felt strong enough to try it after so many continuous days in the workshop. Then suddenly a brief interaction with my teacher, a micro-moment, had unleashed torrents of intense sorrow which turned to bitterness as my tears continued during my journey home that evening.

As an act of pure will, I did return to the workshop the next day. I didn't care anymore. I was not putting anything into the practices. I felt only hopelessness and a crushed, imploding crater of exhausted brokenhearted emptiness torturing my chest. When a time for resting came, after some movement, I focused all my awareness into that horrible sensation in my chest, and gave up. I fell into a vibrant dreaming.

Dream: *I am suspended over the smooth surface of a lake in the sunlight, hovering just above and behind a canoe in which two lovely women from another century are riding. They are clothed in long White dresses and are holding parasols. The back of the canoe glides gently from side to side. Each slow gliding movement is an intense ecstasy for me. The two women, although facing toward the front of the canoe, seem in some subtle way to be aware of my presence just above and behind them. We float effortlessly across the silky surface of the waters.*

I awoke to the blessed absence of that terrible devastation I had been feeling. It was gone. My dream had restored my life. And although I was still very tired, I felt a sweet contentment. Later, I mused to myself that this cycle of hitting the wall, catastrophic failure, and utterly giving up was part of the teaching for me. I had gone to zero, to a place of not caring, which meant no effort, just a showing up, and then a giving up. The Sufis say, "Die before you die." One meaning is that if we are able to soften our identifications and grasping in the now, if we learn to dissolve and melt and become transparent, our living will be more expansive. For many of us, this stripping away doesn't happen until we approach our physical death, or have a major crisis. This particular interval of surrender came to me in the aftermath of an extreme emotional storm. I really felt that I was "finished" when I lay down and gave up. Blessed relief was given to me, unbidden, by the mysterious and vivid dream of the two women in a boat.

CONCLUSION

Dream: *I'm with my family at a suburban house with lots of yellow sunlight and a positive feeling of daily life. My father is driving my mother and sisters and me in a big car. He is very centered and purposeful, taking us somewhere. We drive up through a steep, winding wooded area, steadily up and around, arriving at a large flat open area full of people and other cars. At the end of the space is a large open doorway. A big heavy man wearing a suit is helping people through the doorway into a large body of water. Somehow I know that we are on our way to a beautiful island for a summer vacation. My father jumps into the water. He is floating. His face is happy and blissful. Our yellow suitcase is also floating in the water. Some people begin walking on the water. Many people are on their way. My sisters have gone ahead. I'm near the door waiting for my mother. She arrives at the door and begins acting like an irate customer in a city hotel, asking angry questions about luggage, full of panic, being very rude to the man at the door. I gently urge her out into the water. "Come on ... come on...." We move out into the water together. We are together in the water and the sunshine. We are happy and on our way.*

FURTHER COMMENTS

My family was not religious. Although affiliated with a Protestant congregational church in a small town in New England, we attended only for baptisms, Easter, and Christmas Eve. My strongest memories of these occasional visits are the magnificence of Bach's music and the beauty of the light coming through clear windows into an unadorned room, rather than anything that was said in sermons. Sunday school memories are few, among them an image from family photos of me with my sister, posing and smiling for the camera with our new Bibles, dressed in our Sunday best. I have only one memory of being a leader as a teenager in the church youth group. I delivered a sermon one Sunday about "Jesus as the Light," which no one seemed to understand, and which I refused to let anyone revise.

My truest childhood spirituality had to do with the awe I felt when multitudes of birds gathered in the elm tree in our backyard every fall on their way south, and when the iris bloomed. The smell of roses and peonies and the brilliant sunlight were messengers of goodness. Seeing newborn kittens at their mother's breast was a real miracle. And I dreamed one night of a benevolent being of light flashing to me momentarily in the sky.

The struggles with my environment included an early experience in the medical system, when I was given general anesthesia (ether) at age four, by violent force and with no explanation. I believed, as I was spiraling down, that I had been murdered. There was also the ongoing annihilating power struggle with my mother that I described earlier.

There also was the larger cultural/political context. I felt alien, but without a way to think about it until I went to college and found politically conscious, artistic, and humorous friends. My otherwise-loving father was into the "Better Dead Than Red" slogan popular at that time, and included me in this context in a very literal way, to my deep surprise.

In terms of ethnic identity, my paternal grandmother's family was of English origin, and my paternal grandfather had come from Hamburg, Germany, as an orphan at the age of five, becoming a self-educated inventor. My father did not go to college. When he finished high school during the Great Depression, his family needed him to work. My mother's parents were of English origin. My maternal grandfather grew up without high school, and went into the business of growing tobacco. My father eventually went to work for him. We lived separately from the tobacco farm. My first summer job at age fourteen was there, a job which depleted my energy.

My mother graduated from college and wanted to become a lawyer, as I wrote earlier. Her ambitions for herself were thwarted, and transmuted themselves into ambitions for her children that included a hurtful desire for our upward mobility in terms of class, with a lot of fighting with me about how I should look, dress, behave, and think. Our family world, on my mother's terms, became a psychic prison, stultifying and terrifying, because of the intense and stormy states that were unleashed when her aspirations weren't fulfilled. She seemed to worship at the altar of some phantom, longed-for materialistic success, and this ersatz seeking was killing the spirit of our family.

My Sufi instructor teaches the way of spirituality, not religion. Sufism is like the heart of religion. My teacher grew up in an Arab country, has lived in the United States for five decades, and travels to many countries to teach. In Sufi workshops, I meet people from around the world and with various religious backgrounds. As I have hoped to convey in this piece, the Sufi practices of meditative movement, chanting, drumming, whirling, and dancing usher me into ecstatic states of being that resonate profoundly with my childhood experiences of sacredness.

For me, there has also been a kind of cultural liberation, which shows itself in seemingly small moments. One time, during a Sufi workshop in December, I went outside for a brief walk during a break. I saw some beautifully colored lights, and stopped to look at them. Only after quite a while did I realize they were Christmas lights. I felt so happy to have "forgotten" the very commercialized holiday, with its long history of family disasters and social pressures to buy and spend, in order to "remember" something else.

Another time, just after a workshop I was teaching, as some of us sat down to dinner, and before I began to converse in words, I noticed an area of lovely shapes and colors on the tablecloth. I marveled at the liquidity and shine. Only slowly did the visuals coalesce into the clear shape of a soup ladle reflecting the colors and lights of the room. Once again, I smiled with private contentment at this gap in the familiar. Rigid habit is the core of our internalized oppression, and it stifles creativity. Meditation and spiritual practice soften those rigidities. One is graced with the gift of surprise and the rich unfolding of life.

The Sufi work has been crucial for my very survival as a woman, especially regarding my heartbreaking relationship with my mother. The pain of my mother has been my biggest challenge, both as a person and as a woman. The women's movement gave me empowering connections with other professional women artists. My work and studies as a psychotherapist began simultaneously with my Sufi practice, and Sufi has been a powerful implicit influence on my work in sessions.[2] My Sufi life changed my way of painting, toward lyrical abstraction and flow. And, paradoxically, the nonverbal experiences in my Sufi work also liberated my verbal life. The Sufi path, which awakens the spiritual heart, nurtured a gradually improving communication with my mother over the years, and kept open the possibility of healing communion when the time was right. I am grateful that these golden moments with her occurred. Writing this has rewoven those moments more deeply into the complex fabric of our history together.

NOTES

1. Lispector, 1989, p. x.
2. Pfunder, 2005.

BIBLIOGRAPHY

El Saffar, Ruth. *Rapture Encaged: The Suppression of the Feminine in Western Culture.* London and New York: Routledge, 1994.

Harris, Adrienne. *Gender as Soft Assembly.* Hillsdale, NJ: The Analytic Press, 2005.

Helminski, Camille Adams. *Women of Sufism: A Hidden Treasure.* Boston and London: Shambhala, 2003.

Lispector, Clarice. *The Stream of Life.* Trans. Elizabeth Lowe and Earl Fitz. Minneapolis: University of Minnesota Press, 1989.

Murray, Tamsin. *Inside the Time: A Sufi Path.* vols. 1, 2, 3. Torreon, NM: Rhythmic River Publications, 2006.

Ozelsel, Michaela. *Forty Days: The Diary of a Traditional Solitary Sufi Retreat.* Brattleboro, VT: Threshold Books, 1996.

Pfunder, Janet. "Sufi Meditations on Psychotherapy," In Marcella Bakur Weiner, Paul C. Cooper, and Claude Barbre, eds. *Psychotherapy and Religion: Many Paths, One Journey.* New York: Jason Aronson, 2005.

Reinhertz, Shakina. *Women Called to the Path of Rumi: The Way of the Whirling Dervish.* Prescott, AZ: Hohm Press, 2001.

Tweedie, Irina. *Daughter of Fire: A Diary of a Spiritual Training with a Sufi Master.* Nevada City, CA: Blue Dolphin Publishing, Inc., 1986.

Chapter 15

Journeying in Twilight: Agnosticism and Spirituality

Mary Anne Siderits

In my mind's eye, there is a bookmark I received as a teenager. I still see vividly the red and black of the inscription attributed to the French writer Paul Claudel: "God writes straight with crooked lines." Decades later, I ran across Paul Elie's concluding comment in his work on the pilgrimage of four twentieth-century writers: "The clear lines of any orthodoxy are made crooked by our experience, are complicated by our lives. Believer and unbeliever are in the same predicament, thrown back onto themselves in complex circumstances, looking for a sign."[1] Elie's "crooked" spins from the page to rest beside the long-lost bookmark in the corner of my mind where Claudel's message retains its freshness. If there is a God, could the approach to that God be along paths made crooked by agnostic doubt? This chapter concerns the journey along such crooked lines, a path complicated by the attempt to integrate scientific and religious proclivities. The emotions of an unsure spiritual wayfarer are not easy to articulate, so I am including fragments of poems I have written at various points in my journey. These bits of verse may convey the depth of feeling better than academically sterilized descriptions could ever do. (For purposes of later reference, I am identifying them with Roman numerals.)

I.
*Here, where / the ripely tinted glass / makes even of noonday / a twilight sacrifice, /
we listen to the priest / whose shy-voiced urge to fellowship warms marble /
and the chill-veined saints / that brood upon our rite. /
And bidden handclasp / at the father-prayer, / our fingers strangely halt, /*

we try to touch, / to touch and not disturb / the rhythm of the other self. /
(For human sweat / what commerce with a God / living in cold towers of the mind?) /
We know each other/by the creak of bones, / the unanointed gesture, /
and the half-formed phrase. / Our light carves shadows as it falls, /
and we are bound to live / always before the epiphany.

The great Spanish mystic, John of the Cross, knew well those "cold towers of the mind." He spoke of the "dark night of the soul" in portraying the felt loss of a previously profound emotional connection with God.[2] (My sense of loss may be less acute—a gradual settling into twilight—but, unlike John, I must deal with doubt regarding the very existence of the God in whom I once so ardently believed. And again unlike John, who described his predicament retrospectively, I am still trying to get my bearings along my twilit road.)

Of course, I can represent only one of many possible agnostic experiences. Too often agnosticism is viewed simplistically, without due consideration for its rainbow of departures from theism, or variations in its chronicity. Indeed, Hecht recommends altogether abandoning the terms "believer," "atheist," and "agnostic," and, in the interest of clarity and historical stability, substituting the "divisions" she describes.[3] While Hecht's categories do not seem mutually exclusive and none is a perfect fit, three of them resonate with me: the "meaning and science spiritualist, who interprets the universe as having some force that unites life and gives it meaning," the "perplexed, who identifies him- or herself as personally unresolved" and the "'one of many' religionist, who believes all religions ... relate to a thinking, creative force."[4]

Hopeful of some of the outcomes espoused by the believer and fearful of the meaninglessness accepted by the atheist, while lacking the convictions of either, I find it difficult to articulate the content of my spiritual experience, but it does have several facets that appear in relatively recent attempts to describe contemporary notions of spirituality.[5] 1) Its focus is on a connection with something that transcends commonplace reality while recognizing that movement toward that target is asymptotic, since in its fullness that target may be unknowable. 2) It is an individual quest, substantially independent of institutionalized religion (although not necessarily inimical to it). 3) It does not exclude the possibility of participation in religious services, but with less reliance on doctrine than on a sense of community with fellow worshippers. 4) Mentorship—but not indoctrination—is essential to this quest. 5) Private contemplation and meditation help achieve a sense of the sacred (where "sacred" connotes whatever involves reverence).

This is the orientation of those persons whom Roof has described as "highly active seekers," those who have become particularly numerous during the years in which the baby boomers reached maturity.[6] Those years overlapped with most of my adult years, and I share with these "highly active seekers" an individualized spirituality that has more in common with the history of mysticism than it does with institutionalized religion. However, I also share with the members of my profession a commitment to the scientific understanding of the human predicament.

The realization that I am a child of my time has almost inevitably led me to wonder what might have been the complexion of my spirituality had I lived a century earlier. Would I have been secure within the sacred walls of my religious tradition? Or would feminist issues have claimed my attention even then, and would that have resulted in some contact with the ideas of the great mothers of feminism? Hecht and Gaylor have given us portraits of these early freethinkers.[7] Many of them appear to be atheist, an ideological commitment compatible with the coeval status of science—a confident materialism and a faith that the scientific horizon was unlimited. I do not share their optimistic atheism (to borrow a term used by Ferguson in a different context.[8] Nevertheless, I do admire the courage of these women in challenging the stereotype of females as unreflective keepers of the faith. As Kern has noted, "Much was made of women's passionate religiosity in this era"; to act otherwise was "to place [oneself] in a category populated mostly by men."[9]

Among these freethinking women, Elizabeth Cady Stanton is worth a closer look as a possible prototype of the "active seeker" of later decades. While a cursory glance at her might suggest that she was antireligious, a careful examination of her life and writings indicates that her rejection of religion was confined to two principal areas: 1) what one might call the darker, more terrifying aspects of traditional religion with its punitive image of the deity, as she had encountered it from childhood[10]; and 2) those aspects of creeds and catechisms that degraded women's creation and destiny.[11] Both types of grievance motivated her work on *The Woman's Bible*, in which offensive scriptural passages were expurgated. A woman of her century, she embraced the science of the times as she came to know it, acquainting herself with Charles Darwin's writing and reflecting its influence in her own writing and oral presentations. She identified with the positivist philosophy of Auguste Comte and its faith in the eventual scientific discovery of immutable laws undergirding the universe. She also identified with the Comtean substitution of a "religion of humanity" for traditional religion. Even after experiencing some disenchantment with Comte, Stanton described such a religion in her own terms as one "in which men and women will worship what they see of the divine in each other; the virtues, the beatitudes, the possibilities ascribed to Deity reflected in mortal beings...."[12] Yet at another point she was attracted by the ideas of the theosophists—a group whose beliefs had a decidedly mystical tinge.[13] It is not clear exactly where her spiritual interests lay, but in the closing lines of her introduction to *The Woman's Bible* she writes of "our ideal great first cause, 'the Spirit of all Good,' that set the universe of matter and mind in motion, and by immutable law holds the land, the sea, the planets, revolving round the great centre of light and heat ... the glory of creation forever and ever."[14] What does this composite portrait suggest? Stanton was an agnostic, quite possibly, but not an atheist—rather, an active seeker whose notion of the ultimate object was in continued development. One can readily imagine her moving smoothly into the spiritual climate of the century that followed her death.

II.

Closely prized, a mote of fallen snow / becomes a most articulate web /
whose fine-veined vanishing assaults the hope / that we can hold a mystery, / to test /
its clockwork secrets till a safer world / emerges, where truths are simply limned /
and nature's convolutions are unfurled / in patterns that hard passions cannot dim. /
Not only children reach for Christmas stars / to bring some contract from a universe /
where threats of emptiness stretch lifetimes far, /
and in those soundless nights no small flame stirs.

One may easily feel lost in a universe whose ultimate source is unknown and perhaps unknowable. We wish to find our place in the chain of being so beautifully inscribed on a letter to a character in Wilder's *Our Town*: "... the Earth, the Solar System, the Universe, the Mind of God."[15] Living in the twenty-first century and attuned to the advances of knowledge, we also wish for an understanding of the human predicament enriched by scientific findings. Our search is complicated by the recognition that people often believe something simply because they want to believe it; we become fearful of falling prey to our own yearnings. At the same time, we know the psychological power of an intuitive grasp of the mysterious—the sense of connectedness with what lies beyond the self, a feeling people experience during prayer or meditation. Both the scientific and the intuitive make claims on our consciousness, often pulling us in different directions. Experiencing this cognitive tension, we may be tempted to emphasize one or the other of the apparently dissonant possibilities. In other words, one might develop what Hecht has characterized as "tone-deafness"—on the one hand, "to the idea of evidence" and, on the other hand, "to the *feeling* that there is a higher power."[16] As an agnostic seeker, I have chosen to do otherwise, namely, to remain responsive to the disparate urging.

One more complication: We are such things as stars are made of, but we are also living, sentient beings. Therefore, we must enter the domains of both physics and biology—both data-driven sciences. But wait. Several writers over the past decades have perceived an interesting difference in the perspectives of these two sciences. Davies, for example, cites the remarks of psychologist Harold Morowitz: "What has happened is that biologists, who once postulated a privileged role for the human mind in nature's hierarchy, have been moving relentlessly toward the hard-core materialism that characterized nineteenth-century physics. At the same time, physicists, faced with compelling experimental evidence, have been moving away from strictly mechanical models of the universe to a view that sees the mind as playing an integral role in all physical events."[17]

Panek gives us another view of these shifting perspectives. He notes that nineteenth-century scientists were able to restrict their investigations to a world cloaked in the mechanical tidiness of Newtonian physics. Moreover, "... if you (even unconsciously) assumed that you were describing a universe that was nothing but motion and matter, restricting your investigations to increasingly close studies of matter in motion wouldn't merely suffice—it would tend to reinforce the mechanistic view."[18] The life sciences may have clung longer to the positivist view because these fields have allowed them a modus operandi wherein the rules of Newtonian physics still apply. Thus, among life scientists one may more easily find hard-bitten atheists like Dawkins[19] who might fit Hecht's description of the "science secularist, who thinks the universe is a natural phenomenon and that religion adds more bad than good."[20]

By contrast, Panek demonstrates that, at the start of the twentieth century, those who dealt with the universe had to contend with invisible subject matter that—even with highly refined optical aids—was beyond the scope of the direct sensory evidence to which nineteenth-century positivists had urged that science be confined. Of course, there is no implication that the scientist entering what Panek calls "the invisible century" had abandoned the search for evidence—only that it was complex mathematical evidence that would be used to shape the initially grand speculative leaps required by a universe whose consideration demanded that one go beyond the direct perception of matter in motion. Trafficking with such a universe left even some prominent scientists (for example, Davies) speaking in terms of "The Mind of God."[21]

The ventures of the new physicists into the minute and the colossal have taken them beyond the reaches of the biological world—and its customary probes—into a realm where space and time are warped and waltz in ways beyond my paltry imagination. Kitty Ferguson became my contemporary lay guide through the intricacies of this strange world—a world where there can be events without history; a mathematical proof of truth beyond the scope of mathematics; a blur of possibilities where predictability is not entirely banished but is the exceptional visitor.[22] Breathless, I try to keep up with the parade of strange vocabulary and equally odd conceptions that strain the comprehension of the unsophisticated.

Where does that leave me? With a sense of gratitude that I live in a time when the most ambitious scientific journeys have a terminus more congenial to my questioning mentality than the mix of matter and mechanics that marked the work of earlier physicists. At the very least, contemporary physics points to a basic energizing principle, even an underlying intelligence, and while it is not equivalent to the notion of a personal God, neither is it incompatible with it.

> *III.*
> *I hear the faintest echo of/ the Christmas choristers (my onetime self /*
> *that years could never crystallize); / their untouched voices seem to show /*
> *the very fragile anonymity / of unscarred snow. Unvisited / by passion or by*
> *pain, they sing /*
> *of birth accomplished without both. And for / a while I could believe that we /*
> *crave gentleness and come with care / to the tender places in each other's lives, /*
> *that in such love are moments fixed, / our brush with immortality.*

Biologist Ursula Goodenough is a nontheist who regularly attends her local Presbyterian church, participating in the ritual and singing in the choir. This might seem like a contradiction. However, Goodenough's quest has been essentially spiritual, culminating in the conviction that, even without the deep belief in the supernatural experienced by most of her fellow congregants, she can share their religious emotions while experiencing what she calls "religious naturalism" (what others might call "natural spirituality"). This is a joy in the repeated emergence of new life, the uniqueness of individual existence, the wonder of evolution and biodiversity, the transforming power of meditation, inherent and unrehearsed maternal altruism, the possibility of earthly love, and the realization of values and ideals.

Goodenough is also profoundly moved by what we might consider the perquisites of worshipping with other spiritually focused individuals. "Those of us who find a religious home feel deep affinity with those who have moved through with us and before us, congregating, including, supporting. We offer and receive sympathy and affection. The musicians sing their hushed responses or chant their solemn rhythms and we breathe together, sense our consciousnesses heal."[23]

Note the importance of two things here: 1) human connectedness and 2) the response to sacred music. Quite clearly Goodenough's reactions are those of what Hecht would label a "ritualist, who thinks the universe is a natural phenomenon and we should celebrate our humanity in the ritual and allegory of traditional religion."[24] Hecht's description of the melding of fellowship and sacred music is clearly in terms related to the emotion of awe—an important component in the religious response that has influenced a long line of American naturalists.[25]

Goodenough's resolution of her nontheistic and religious inclinations, as she portrayed it in 1998, was to articulate a "covenant with mystery"[26]—reverence for "the whole enterprise of planetary existence, the whole and all of its myriad parts as they catalyze and secrete and replicate and mutate and evolve."[27] In this spirit, she enunciates what she calls a "credo of continuation."[28] "For me, the existence of all this complexity and awareness and intent and beauty, and my ability to apprehend it, serves as the ultimate meaning and the ultimate value."[29]

I have recognized some of the feelings associated with Goodenough's "credo of continuation" in a setting that is neither the great outdoors nor a biological laboratory—that is, in my regular visits to the aviary in the nursing home where my husband has been struggling with the aftereffects of a surgical incident. Watching the birds has been progressive: At first it was just flashes of feather, whorls of color, and diagonal ballets along several planes. After I had watched for awhile, the sensory plethora resolved itself into patterns, with the emergence of distinct "bird-alities" (as I dubbed the individuality of the little creatures). Gradually I experienced a thoroughly surprising serenity—one I associate with connectedness—as I lost myself in the avian panoply. Yet there was more. I began to feel a genuine love for these small beings, and I realized that it was Maslow's "B-love," the variety of loving that occurs when the emphasis is not on what each of the parties can do for the other.[30] One simply appreciates the other's existence—contemplating the unfolding of the other's life, without interference.

I have said that I recognize in myself some of the feelings associated with Goodenough's credo, but I have another set of feelings quite foreign to her religious naturalism that finds its ultimate and complete satisfaction in the contemplation of nature. Looking at the birds, my mind's eye was tempted to envision some hypothetical supreme being (a rather stilted label for the divine, but one that seems peculiarly fitting in the wake of latter-day physics). If there is a God—and if God is self-limiting (an inescapable theological condition for me, given the problem of human suffering)—could it be that God regards us with B-love while creating and supporting, but not ordinarily interfering with, our world?

That thought is somewhat satisfying at least for awhile, but it can bring me to the less comforting side of seeking God in nature. I appreciate Johnson's observation that "the message of the 'hidden God' in nature can be so annoyingly ambiguous as to drive a thinking person to a kind of spiritual madness."[31] Johnson pairs this observation with one of my favorite passages from Pascal's *Pensees*:

> Nature offers me nothing that is not a source of doubt and anxiety. If I saw nothing in it which was a sign of the Divinity, I should answer in the negative; if I saw everywhere the signs of a Creator, I should live at peace in the faith. But, seeing too much for denial and too little for certainty, I am in a state which inspires pity and in which I have wished a

hundred times that, if there is a God who preserves it, it should reveal him unequivocally, and that, if the signs it offers are illusory, it should obliterate them completely; that it should tell all or nothing so that I should know what attitude I ought to adopt.[32]

It is not spiritual madness that I experience, though, but a deep disappointment that can be quieted only by prolonged meditation. As in the case of many contemporary "seekers," meditation has become an integral part of my spiritual journey—but only in the wake of a singular personal experience that, with some hesitation, I label mystical.

IV.
There are nights so pure they pare the mind / and leave it thick with stars and loose /
the bars that keep the outside out. / One can lose one's self in such a night /
when silence moves with its own weight. / The shepherd breathes the rhythm of
his fold /
and trails his shifting center like a lamb / among the crags ... /
There are not many who are ready / to receive the wonderful, whose eyes can rest /
until all membranes disappear, / and a star shakes the solemnity of their brains /
with a fine percussion, or a rose's / wandering roads throb with their own blood. /
The shepherd is like that, / lying so gently on the night / that no sound loses
shape, /
and it is as if he saw the sea / (or his own life) from some height /
where he only longs for what already is.

Goodenough remembers an episode of sheer terror she had while looking at the stars during a Colorado camping trip soon after she had heard about the universe in physics class.[33] The bleak nihilism that overcame her during her early forays into the infinite and infinitesimal eventually yielded to her covenant with mystery, and she could let the enormity of unseen galaxies wash over her.

Richard Dawkins recalls himself more happily, "under the stars, dazzled by Orion, Cassiopeia, and Ursa Major, tearful with the unheard music of the Milky Way, heady with the night scents of frangipani and trumpet flowers in an African garden."[34] The reader is led to surmise that this self-styled "quasi-mystical response to nature and the universe" was a thoroughly positive one of the sort that Dawkins elsewhere describes as touching "the nerve-endings of transcendent wonder."[35]

Stars blazing in the Colorado sky and the African garden were what I, too, was contemplating one summer night when I was several years short of adulthood. The setting was a homelier one—sky-watching while sitting on the porch—and the stars washed by city lights were undoubtedly less brilliant than those that sparkle in the memories of Goodenough and Dawkins. A sense of beauty and enormity was also part of the experience, but there was something more that I can call only a sense of profound *connectedness to* something larger than myself. It enveloped my unaware and unsophisticated self. It would be years before I could place it in the context of mysticism.

Carmody and Carmody contend that the starting point of the path to mysticism is usually just such an experience, to which they assign two components: 1) a sense of being transported in response to beauty or pain; and 2) at least a partial conversion to the proposition that "reality is much more than what it was before this happened to you."[36] Prime components, indeed, but there is no mention of the sense of connectedness with the larger reality—and it was the profound connectedness that distinguished this single and singular experience in my life from other moving responses to the beauties of art and nature, to the intellectual thrusts of astrophysicists, or to the experience of watching small birds.

Goodenough may be aware of a similar mystical gradient when she distinguishes between the sense of cosmic mystery and "immanence," defining the latter as a "particularly intense form of self-awareness and Enlightenment: a detachment from self-awareness so that all else can penetrate."[37] In considering immanence, she asks, "Is this God? Is this Perfection of Understanding?"[38] She is quick to answer, "As a nontheist, I find I can only think about these experiences as wondrous mental phenomena"—truly wondrous, though, because they become "a part of my self that I most treasure and value, the part that most deeply celebrates the fact that I am alive, the part that sustains me through discouragement and loss."[39]

The questions that Goodenough raises are my questions, too. In pursuing them I enter the corridors of neuroscience. There I am struck by the work of Andrew Newberg and his colleagues and their exploration of the neurological substrate of some of the more unusual dimensions of religious experience.[40] These are some of the very phenomena that William James discussed in his landmark work on the varieties of religious experience.[41] A century after James's Gifford lectures, scientists are able to name organic correlates of mystical experience. The bottom line (but by no means the last word) is that human beings seem to be wired for transcendental experiences of connectedness. Newberg and his colleagues do not go beyond their data, but neither are they facile reductionists. The object of the connectedness is beyond the grasp of their scientific apparatus. Is it, after all, as Goodenough might have it, some aspect of the human mind that is ordinarily inaccessible when humans go about their mundane activities? Or is it what physicist Davies would call "mind"—a sustaining universal intelligence? And if the latter, is it—as many traditional faiths would suppose—a personal God? To answer any of those questions requires a leap of faith. I am capable only of a smaller leap—in the direction of hope.

V.

... And then there are the birds, their movements like a fugue, /
its pattern set by silent walls they did not raise. /
Rarely do they break the rhythm of their days. / Only, at one point of the floor, purblinded by
a ledge whose solid height is greater than their own, /
do they spin mad circles with their futile wings /
until they lift themselves to see beyond the glass. /
It is enough. They turn once more to weave a nest. /
We watch and try to learn their ways.

A year ago I would not have thought that a flock of birds could be the source of spiritual insight or that my verse at Christmas would reflect the predicament of a zebra finch we had come to love. We called him "the master builder" because of the industry and artistry he applied to creating a series of carefully woven nests in the domed baskets that hang from the roof of the aviary. He provided more nests than his mate could possibly need, each woven with discernment. We were charmed by his apparently continual critique of his efforts, as he darted into an unfinished construction to place yet another wisp of straw and then return outside, the nest material still in his beak as he essayed placement from a different angle. This tiny avian architect seemed happily occupied in his daily routine. But one day his behavior was quite different. While standing close to the glass at one side of the aviary, but on a level with its wooden frame, he beat his wings in evident distress—like a prisoner trying to escape. It took awhile for us to realize that the crucial variable was not the confining residence but his inability to see beyond it.

It also took some time to realize that there is a similarity to the human predicament. One can easily feel trapped in one's own skin in an incomprehensible universe "where threats of emptiness stretch lifetimes far" (poem II). After all is said and done, after hearing the scientific voices to which I chose to listen, I still bump up against the unknowable. Fight as I may against it, I face the realization that we are, indeed, "always before the epiphany" (poem I). Unable to alter the existential predicament, I find a saving inspiration in the situation of the small birds (poem V), that is, I identify with their reduced frustration, with the return of their customary serenity when they are able to glimpse something of a larger world. For me the glimpses come in meditation, in the contemplation of art, and in appreciation of the human pursuit of ethical behavior. In this connection, I am charmed by Polkinghorne's position on the transcendental significance of aesthetic and moral insights,[42] beautifully enunciated in sentences such as these:

"Aesthetic experience and ethical intuitions are not just psychological or social constructs.... Although atheism might seem simpler conceptually [than theism], it treats beauty and morals and worship as some form of cultural or social brute facts, which accords ill with the seriousness with which these experiences touch us as persons."[43] As a depiction of human yearning and of the direction in which humans move in encountering the mystical, Polkinghorne's sentiments are compelling but still leave one trapped within what are essentially belief systems.

Indeed, Newberg wonders whether entrapment within belief systems is an inevitable part of the existential predicament. Yet he is able to sound some notes of optimism: "The more we push science and spirituality to their limits, the better chance we have to answer the 'ultimate question.'"[44] Also: "It is in the nature of our brain to search for its deepest truths, and although we may never grasp truth in its entirety, it is our right and our biological heritage to try."[45]

Now how am I to push science and spirituality to their limits within the context of my life? At this point it seems to require of me something akin to Pascal's famous "wager"[46]—which in my estimation involves my conducting my life on the assumption that there might indeed be a transcendental being with which some connection is possible. In contrast to Pascal's own use of his wager, the notion of a punitive God is not brought into a consideration of the stakes. Nor is it a matter of feigning belief in God (as Dawkins would have it in his appraisal of Pascal)[47] but, rather of "living one's life on an assumption (in the face of uncertainty)"[48]—which is what Dawkins himself has done in what I view as his leap into atheistic optimism. Mine is a different optimism—the optimism of the hopeful agnostic seeker.

Having made my wager, I plod on. It is twilight still, but there is enough light for one to move.

NOTES

1. Elie, *The Life You Save May Be Your Own*, 472.
2. Saint John of the Cross, *Collected Works*, 358.
3. Hecht, *Doubt*, 485.
4. Ibid., 485.
5. For example, Hill et al., "Conceptualizing Religion and Spirituality."
6. Roof, *Generation of Seekers*, 79–83.
7. Hecht, *Doubt*; Gaylor, *Women without Superstition*.
8. Ferguson, *Fire in the Equations*, 281.
9. Kern, *Mrs. Stanton's Bible*, 46.
10. Stanton, "Memory of My Own Sufferings," 172.
11. Stanton, "Christian Church and Women," 113.
12. Stanton, "Worship of God in Man," 158.
13. Kern, *Mrs. Stanton's Bible*, 93–94.
14. Stanton, "Introduction of the Women's Bible,"168.
15. Wilder, *Our Town*, 45.
16. Hecht, *Doubt*, xi.

17. Davies, *God and the New Physics*, 8, 72; 210–211.
18. Panek, *Invisible Century*, 170.
19. Dawkins, *The God Delusion*.
20. Hecht, *Doubt*, 485.
21. Davies, *God and the New Physics*.
22. Ferguson, *Fire in the Equations*.
23. Goodenough, *Sacred Depths*, 73.
24. Hecht, *Doubt*, 485.
25. Helson, "Strength of Wonder," 137.
26. Goodenough, *Sacred Depths*, 167.
27. Ibid., 170.
28. Ibid., 170.
29. Ibid., 171.
30. Maslow, *Farther Reaches*, 142–144.
31. Johnson, *Finding God*, 53.
32. Pascal, *Pascal's Pensees*, 110.
33. Goodenough, *Sacred Depths*, 9–10.
34. Dawkins, *The God Delusion*, 11.
35. Ibid., 12.
36. Carmody and Carmody, *Mysticism*, 293.
37. Goodenough, *Sacred Depths*, 101.
38. Ibid., 101.
39. Ibid., 102–103.
40. Newberg et al, *Why God Won't*; Newberg and Waldman, *Why We Believe*.
41. James, *Varieties of Religious Experience*.
42. Polkinghorne, *Faith of a Physicist*, 69–70.
43. Ibid., 70.
44. Newberg and Waldman, *Why We Believe*, 279.
45. Ibid., 245.
46. Pascal, *Pascal Pensees*, 201–204.
47. Dawkins, *The God Delusion*, 103–105.
48. Ibid., 51.

BIBLIOGRAPHY

Carmody, Denise Lardner, and John Tully Carmody. *Mysticism: Holiness East and West*. New York: Oxford University Press, 1996.

Davies, Paul. *God and the New Physics*. New York: Simon & Schuster, 1983.

Dawkins, Richard. *The God Delusion*. Boston: Houghton Mifflin, 2006.

Elie, Paul. *The Life You Save May Be Your Own*. New York: Farrar, Straus, and Giroux, 2003.

Ferguson, Kitty. *The Fire in the Equations: Science, Religion, and the Search for God*. 2nd ed. Philadelphia: Templeton Foundation Press, 2004.

Gaylor, Annie Laurie, ed. *Women without Superstition: "No Gods—No Masters": The Collected Writings of Women Freethinkers of the Nineteenth and Twentieth Centuries*. Madison, WI: Freedom from Religion Foundation, 1997.

Goodenough, Ursula. *The Sacred Depths of Nature*. New York: Oxford University Press, 1998.

Hecht, Jennifer M. *Doubt: A History*. San Francisco: HarperOne, 2004.

Helson, Ravenna. "Rachel Carson: The Strength of Wonder." In Eileen A. Gavin, Aphrodite Clamar, and Mary Anne Siderits, eds. *Women of Vision: Their Psychology, Circumstances, and Success*. New York: Springer Publishing, 2007.

Hill, Peter C., Kenneth I. Pargament, Ralph W. Hood, Jr., Michael E. McCullough, James P. Swyers, David B. Larson, and Brian J. Zinnbauer. "Conceptualizing Religion and Spirituality: Points of Commonality, Points of Departure." *Journal for the Theory of Social Behavior* 30 (2000): 51–77.

James, William. *The Varieties of Religious Experience*. New York: Simon & Schuster, 1997. (Original work published 1902.)

Johnson, Timothy. *Finding God in the Questions: A Personal Journey*. Downers Grove, IL: InterVarsity Press, 2004.

Kern, Kathi. *Mrs. Stanton's Bible*. New York: Cornell University Press, 2001.

Maslow, Abraham H. *The Farther Reaches of Human Nature*. New York: Viking, 1971.

Newberg, Andrew, Eugene D'Aquili, and Vince Rause. *Why God Won't Go Away: Brain Science and the Biology of Belief*. New York: Ballantine Books, 2001.

Newberg, Andrew, and Mark Robert Waldman. *Why We Believe What We Believe*. New York: Free Press, 2006.

Panek, Richard. *The Invisible Century: Einstein, Freud, and the Search for Hidden Universes*. New York: Viking, 2004.

Pascal, Blaise. *Pascal's Pensees* (Martin Turnell, trans.). New York: Harper & Brothers, 1962. (Original work published 1670.)

Polkinghorne, John. *The Faith of a Physicist: Reflections of a Bottom-up Thinker*. Minneapolis: Fortress Press, 1996.

Roof, W. C. *A Generation of Seekers: The Spiritual Journey of the Baby Boom Generation*. San Francisco: Harper, 1993.

Saint John of the Cross. *The Collected Works of Saint John of the Cross* (Rev. ed.) (Kieran Kavanaugh and Otilio Rodriguez, trans.). Washington, DC: Institute of Carmelite Studies, 1991. (Original work published 1578–1591.)

Stanton, Elizabeth Cady. "The Christian Church and Women." In Annie Laurie Gaylor, ed. *Women without Superstition: "No Gods—No Masters": The Collected Writings of Women Freethinkers of the Nineteenth and Twentieth Centuries*. Madison, WI: Freedom from Religion Foundation, 1997. (Original work published 1888.)

———. "Introduction of *The Woman's Bible*." In Annie Laurie Gaylor, ed., *Women without Superstition: "No Gods—No Masters": The Collected Writings of Women Freethinkers of the Nineteenth and Twentieth Centuries*. Madison, WI: Freedom from Religion Foundation, 1997. (Original work published 1895.)

———. "Memory of My Own Sufferings." In Annie Laurie Gaylor, ed. *Women without Superstition: "No Gods—No Masters": The Collected Writings of Women Freethinkers of the Nineteenth and Twentieth Centuries*. Madison, WI: Freedom from Religion Foundation, 1997. (Original work published 1898.)

———. "Worship of God in Man." In Annie Laurie Gaylor, ed. *Women without Superstition: "No Gods—No Masters": The Collected Writings of Women Freethinkers of the Nineteenth and Twentieth Centuries*. Madison, WI: Freedom from Religion Foundation, 1997. (Original work published 1892.)

Wilder, Thorton. "Our Town." In Thorton Wilder, *Three Plays: Our Town, The Skin of Our Teeth, The Matchmaker*. San Bernardino, CA: Borgo Press, 1985. (Original work published 1938.)

Chapter 16

A Quiet Soul Listens to Her: Women, Spirituality, and Psychology

Mary Banks Gregerson

Let us be silent—so we may hear the whisper of the gods.
—Ralph Waldo Emerson, "Friendship," 1841

A quiet soul dwells within me. It was not always so. From this solitude, God leads my life. Moments when God lifts me to Her bidding transcend ordinary consciousness. This is my reward for shedding the controls. It is not easy. Listening for direction requires quieting, believing, discerning, trusting, launching, and flowing.

My "her"story of spirituality, femaleness, and psychology combines Eastern, Western, and Native American spiritual traditions with scientific and humanistic knowledge of gender and psychology. A worldwide zeitgeist, or "holding environment," supports such women/soul/ psychology fusion. Brief analyses of three pairings of women, psychology, and spirituality underline the qualitatively distinct nature of this trio apart from the pairings, as illustrated in my life.

This fusion is not a quantitative sum of the three dimensions, but rather a qualitatively distinct dimension. My personal "her"story cannot be quantified. Science need turn to anthropological methods such as qualitative analysis. This chapter starts with my spiritual "her"story, moves to the presence of spirituality in my psychology work, and concludes with future visions where femaleness, spirituality, and psychology intersect in my work and in my life.

MY PERSONAL "HER"STORY

A quiet soul breathes inside my inner being. This serenity dawned in my mid-twenties. It has not always been that way. As an undergraduate I began dancing with the Sufis. That's when the quiet started. Since then, the welcome silence fills me from within. From this solitary center, my life responds to God.

To pare away the noise I have traveled an eleven-year exodus through Eastern religions and Native American traditions to a twenty-year homecoming to Christianity to cultivate a cohesive ethos that "speaks" with one voice. Judeo-Christianity, Taoism, Confucism, Zen Buddhism, Yoga, and Aikido underpins much of this chapter. This combination works for me.

Moments when God lifts me to her bidding transcend ordinary consciousness. That is my reward for shedding the controls. It is not easy.

LISTENING

Listening requires quieting, believing, discerning, trusting, launching, and flowing. The first three steps derive from a cognitive behavioral therapeutic approach called "focusing."[1] The last three steps comprise the action part of listening.

Focusing rests upon an intuitive "felt sense" to choose between possible-hypotheses testing. This felt-sense phenomenon is a psychophysiological relaxation and release. As a focuser, I have experienced internally the shift and "truth" when felt sense detects a spot on hypothesis. As a clinician, a client's shining eyes and perceptible relaxation inevitably reveal a felt sense "hit."

Listening, though, does not stop with felt-sense insight. Action is required. It's almost a process of action steps: quieting, believing, discerning, trusting, launching, and flowing.

While the first three steps follow focusing, the last three rest upon the humanistic/phenomenological tradition in psychology and human relations.[2] Carl Rogers coined the term "unconditional positive regard" for the deep sense of self-respect as well as mutual respect between people that is the foundation of personal and interpersonal mental health[3]; in listening, this step is trusting. Fritz Perls identified the actualized moments when the focused energy mobilizes all parts into a holistic synthesis called "gestalt"[4]; in listening, this step is launching. Barry Stevens articulated the Eastern—mostly Taoist—notion of effortless oneness, or flow, with the universe when congruence exists between internal and external environments[5]; in listening, flow depicts this final end-state of listening. Each individual step also has specific action components.

> *Quietness* requires relaxation, calmness, and centeredness.
> Conviction, or *belief*, is simply an act of decision.
> *Discernment* requires choosing between messages.
> *Trust* derives from communion with those around to bolster faith.

Launching requires centralization and focus that results in motion starting.

Flowing requires surviving and thriving within the current of life.

The moment between discernment and communion is when internal contemplation tipples into external motion. For exquisiteness and elegance, that moment requires stillness within for a most efficient commotion trajectory without. None of this stillness is passive.

Lao-tzu termed this active inactivity *wu-wei*.[6] Such an Eastern concept, at first blush, runs directly counter to the Western notion of value in action. Yet quieting, believing, discerning, and trusting require immense activity to maintain this stillness. Then communing, launching, and flowing, on the other hand, minimize the exertion required for this activity.

Across many cultures, theories, and cosmologies, this internal calm exists for the best external being.[7] This transcendence theoreticians call mysticism,[8] autonomous self,[9] ecstasy,[10] peak or oceanic experience,[11] *kensho* or *satori*,[12] and authentic self.[13] Whatever the name, the universe and I are one during those times.

When do they occur? At the oddest moments. For instance, when tenure was not granted to me as an assistant professor, I was "at one with the universe." Who would have thought *that* would be a spiritual experience? Yet, while hearing the news I breathed deeply, took a step back, and intoned to myself, "Lord, if not this, then something better. Take me where you want me now." Instead of an anticipated awkward moment, I literally bowed to this administrative messenger bearing what he thought was bad news. When speaking of this cleft with others in prospective academic departments, an echoing refrain from the faculty was incredulity at my sanguinity, or adjustment, as the psychologists called it.

My faith is strong, my belief deep.

I understood then, and now, all these trappings to be just that, corporeal accouterments artificially imbued with meaning to color the time between birth and death. These counted steps have little to do with spiritual value, with doing God's work. As a matter of fact, if you have given your life to God, then look for foiling on the secular plane.

MY PROFESSIONAL "HER"STORY

This transcendence above the corporeal trappings pervades the clinical work that I conduct. I typically couch the phrasings used within the nomenclature and belief system of my clients.[14] I teach them to "rise above" a difficult situation.

This transcendence perspective permits "meta-change."[15] This "meta" level underpins much of transpersonal psychology.[16] It also "unsticks" clients mired in conflicted situations on interpersonal and personal levels.

Although I indigenously use spiritual dimensions in my clinical work, I have yet to imbue my theoretical work with notions of spirituality. The ineffability of spirituality trips me up every time. For more than thirty years my conceptual model of health, disease, and wellness called synchronous systems[17] provided a conceptual framework for literature reviews,[18] empirical work,[19] public policy papers,[20] and, now, indirectly in this professional/personal chapter on spirituality, women, and psychology.

The definitive article has yet to be written on how spirituality imbues the conceptual model per se. This is the challenge of the future. With God's help and direction, this final pièce de résistance will someday be composed.

THE HOLDING ENVIRONMENT

Contemplation of our world today consists of the social, political, and professional context, called also the contemporary zeitgeist, or "holding environment."[21] My own life that combines being female with the profession of psychology and a core of spirituality illustrates the personal willpower necessary for cohesion.

Before launching on this odyssey, a note is warranted about the choice of the word "spirituality." Spirituality means a "living, breathing presence"[22] that essentially seeks a union between a transcendent entity and an inner sanctity.

SPIRITUALITY AND RELIGION

A caveat is warranted concerning the preference for the concept of spirituality over religiosity in this chapter. These concepts differ fundamentally. Spirituality refers to the inner experience of the sacred. Religion refers to the rites, texts, rituals, and formalized structure for those practicing a doctrine. Discussion of these two separate concepts has peppered the arts and sciences.

In a 2002 Center for Women and Spirituality discussion "Spirituality and Psychology: Connections and Intersections" at St. Catherine's College in St. Paul, Minnnesota, four faculty discussed distinctly different yet compatible views.[23] At the outset, professor of psychology David Schmit noted that "... spirituality ... [is] when religious feeling spreads out beyond the churches."[24] Professors of Theology Catherine Michaud and Ed Sellner joined and the latter semifacetiously added that "... religion is for people who are afraid of hell and spirituality is for those who have already been there."[25] Mary McLeod, director of the Counseling Center, offered that "sometimes religion seems to be the container and spirituality the content."[26] What emerged in this conversation[27] is that the form, that is, religion, should not be confused with the substance, that is, spirituality.

McLeod called religion the cultural/community "holding environment."[28] This holding environment is observable. On the other hand, inner experience and nonobservables compose spirituality. Psychology, too, has both observables and nonobservables.

Ethics form a bridge between the seen and unseen. Distinguished theologian Richard Gula noted that "morality is the public face of spirituality."[29] Contemporary morality turns from episodic or situational ethics toward virtue ethics. In virtue ethics, the living between big decisions determines being—that inner place that guides action. This internal gyroscope, if consistent and constant, gives "stability to character and momentum to daily living"[30]:

Who we are affects what we do. What we do, affects what we will become.... Morality grows out of the call to respond to those who come our way.

This ethics of virtue model moves from a legalistic one to a relational one. Instead of a focus on "individual acts and sins to avoid" (legalistic), the relational model emphasizes "what standing in right relation to the other demands."[31] An emphasis on the relational is essentially a female dimension. So, much of modern ethics emanates from the feminine. This context of contemporary relational ethics illuminates the "her"story that follows.

For this chapter, emphasis is on spirituality rather than religion. Religious doctrine per se only will imbue articulation to the often-ineffable spirituality. This delimit becomes important especially when considering spirituality and psychology.

"HER"STORY

"Her"storical analysis examines over the years the compatibility of women, spirituality, and psychology. Besides a combination of the three, each pairing has a special "her"story coloring that helps fill in that final amalgam. Women and spirituality, women and psychology, and psychology and spirituality "her"storically wove in and out of communion with each other over time, creating ironic checkered pasts as pairs.

A "her"storical glance at these pairs illustrates how remarkable the achievement is of any foundation for the trio. The question to ask while reading this paper is: Does the contemporary holistic combination of what's holy, what's female, and what's psychology produce a Venn diagram qualitatively different from the addition of the individual aspects and intersecting pairs? In other words, do we have something entirely different today?

WOMEN AND SPIRITUALITY

"Women and spirituality" resurges within different cultures today around the world. Eastern and Western traditions spill into each other. Almost a global homogenization is occurring.

Refreshing wit infuses parts of this resurgence, even in an evil holding environment. In the United States, the 1990 film *Burning Times* in the *Women and Spirituality* series documented the fifteenth- through seventeenth-century persecution of women who were midwifes and healers but thought to be witches.[32] In India, K. Srilata[33] has written *The Other Half of the Coconut: Women Writing Self-Respect History*, and V. Ramaswamy[34] has written *Walking Naked—Women, Society, Spirituality in South India*. These metaphors are not to trivialize the situation. Rather, such humor defiantly refuses to be cowed even in the face of death and destruction. The spirit thrives whether or not the world persecutes.

Women around the world now have centers for women and spirituality, programs of study, and series in various media outlets. Yet, I would propose that the very quality of this new movement differs fundamentally from what was before. It is as if women and spirituality took a giant leap forward rather than baby steps in a spiritual "Mother, may I?" game. Why?

How did the world move, though, from burning witches and heretics such as Joan of Arc to permitting the droll boldness of modern media mavens? What made the holding environment receptive, almost nurturing, rather than expulsive or destructive? Of what use and purpose does women's participation in spirituality serve the heretofore-oppressive male? While we celebrate the permissiveness, we should also look for the tail of the scorpion. Was Karl Marx right when he said, "Religion is the sigh of the oppressed creature, the heart of a heartless world, just as it is the spirit of a spiritless situation. It is the opium of the people."[35]

Such jaded wariness and suspicion belies the positive energy emanating from the new women and spirituality movement. This very volume and this chapter ("A Quiet Soul Listens to Her") speaks from the center of this change. Still, the functionality of this new social force may be revealed in progress found in the other two pairings, which will be examined next.

WOMEN AND PSYCHOLOGY

Women were invisible in psychology for many years. Only after the Society of Experimental Psychology's founder Edward Titchener died in 1929 was Margaret Floy Washburn admitted.[36] What began as a tremulous appearance has now become a veritable roar for the presence of women in psychology.

In 1987, a banner year occurred for women in psychology. Scarborough and Furumoto[37] wrote about the neglected first generation of women in psychology. The Web site "Women's Intellectual Contributions to the Study of the Mind" lists anthropologists, psychologists, psychoanalysts, and sociologist/social workers; more than 100 women psychologists and psychoanalysts comprise the list of recognized leaders.[38]

In 2005, Lips[39] published *A New Psychology of Women: Gender, Culture, and Ethnicity*, which featured a global, multicultural psychology of women. The contemporary narrative approach used in *A New Psychology of Women* echoes the style of this particular chapter and other parts of *WomanSoul*. Women within psychology embraced new methods and new concepts, as this narrative indicates.

One innovation concerned individual differences. Rosi Braidotti,[40] an Italian scholar located in the Netherlands, spearheaded novel ways of defining individual differences. A new legacy of affirmation, inspiration, and equality replaced the European heritage of exclusion, persecution, and murder. Particular individuality rather than conformity would rule the day. Today differences are celebrated, not eschewed.

Besides the rising presence of women professionals in psychology, women's cultural, social, and gender issues have garnered attention. Women's studies programs have spread throughout regions of the United States as well as internationally. Up-to-date information emanates from Germany, France, Canada, Australia, New Zealand, United Kingdom, South Africa, Scotland, Ireland, Switzerland, Indonesia, Sweden, the Netherlands, Iceland, Croatia, Austria, Italy, Russia, and Turkey.[41]

This global renaissance of women's concerns, viewpoints, and approaches shows signs of endurance and growth. A major emphasis in all these programs is individual differences and gender within culture. Issues for women in psychology are here to stay. Psychology has gained another face—female joins male today.

PSYCHOLOGY AND SPIRITUALITY

A detailed examination of the spawning and intertwining of psychology and spirituality is beyond the scope of this chapter. Early mention extends to ancient times. Psychologist David Schmit delineated for these two dimensions three Great Awakenings, that is, "when religious feelings spread out beyond the churches" as spirituality surged coincidentally with psychology[42]:

1) Study of the Soul, nineteenth century as psychology appeared
2) Study of Behaviors, mid-nineteenth-century scientific psychology reductionism eschewed non-observables

3) Study of Enlightenment, late nineteenth century, when psychology opened the inner doors of perception

Each awakening brought different dimensions of psychology. The second awakening brought sole reliance on observable content based on animal models, and then moved swiftly away from spirituality and mentation. Schmit proffered that "psychology lost its soul and then lost its mind."[43] Psychology chose measurable physical reductionism.

Within psychology, certain movements rebelled against this physical reductionism, which lead to the Study of Enlightenment. Most notably, Jung's[44] analytical psychology, Maslow's[45] humanistic psychology, and transpersonal psychology[46] offered the basic premise that religion was central to the psyche. These models eschewed reductionistic animal models while touting an essentially unique, human-centered approach. Just as abstract thought is believed to be reserved exclusively for humans, perhaps spirituality is, too.

Yet, many naturalistic religions embrace animal figures prominently. Most notably, many Native American traditions feature dreams with animal guides.[47] Shamans and medicine men observed what animals ate to identify natural remedies.[48] Thus, the physicality of animal nature can harmonize with humanity rather than be at odds with it if the belief system supports that synchronization.

Mental health can affect spiritual health. Theologian Catherine Michaud[49] identified five components of mental health that influence the state of spirituality:

1) Treasuring oneself so there is no need to manage others' perceptions
2) Containing oneself and protecting oneself physically, psychologically, emotionally, intellectually, spiritually, and sexually
3) Owning one's own reality by honestly perceiving and knowing one's being and world as well as experiencing one's own vulnerability
4) Taking care of oneself so that one's needs are met legitimately
5) Being intimate with others is a key component of spirituality

Health research has found appositive correlation among religion, spirituality, and good health.[50] No causal direction has been established. The question still remains: Are those who are religious/spiritual healthier, or are the healthier more religious/spiritual?

With this spirituality and psychology question left up in the air, this chapter turns to how the three aspects—women, spirituality, and psychology—fit together. To emphasize the qualitative difference from these individual and pairs dimensions, a different exposition style turns from the professional/impersonal to the personal. This choice of departing from didactics into a narrative exposition style should further underline the qualitative proposition. That is, melding femaleness, psychology, and spirituality becomes systemic and qualitatively distinct rather than additive and quantitative.

If this qualitative proposition appears appropriate for female/spiritual/psychology, then new methods of investigation rather than quantitative scientific methods must be developed for this field. Perhaps what emerges "between the lines" becomes even more important than what is in the lines themselves. We must approach the task differently, not just more intensively.

My personal "her"story cannot be quantified. This chapter started with my spiritual "her"story, moved to the presence of this spirituality in my psychology work, and concluded with future visions of the intersection of femaleness, spirituality, and psychology in my work and in my life.

If it is possible, this oneness is becoming ever more unified. Maslow[51] calls this process self-actualization. As I age, I experience becoming even more "me." Listening with a quiet soul allows this emergence to dawn and to enlarge like the crescendo of a sunrise that never ends.

NOTES

1. Gendlin, 2003.
2. Maslow, 1962.
3. Rogers, 1980, 1995.
4. Perls, 1969.
5. Stevens, 1985.
6. Lao-tsu, Feng, and English, 1997.
7. Lu, Jung, and Wilhelm, 1975; Perry, 1976.
8. James, 1902/2007.
9. Jung and Wilhelm, 1954.
10. Laski, 1961.
11. Maslow, 1962.
12. Suzuki-Roshi, 1971/2006.
13. Lajoie and Shapiro, 1992.
14. Bandler, 1975; Grinder and Bandler, 1975; Watzlawick, 1974.
15. Walsh and Vaughan, 1993.
16. Lajoie and Shapiro, 1992; Walsh and Vaughan, 1993.
17. Jasnoski, 1984; Jasnoski and Schwartz, 1985; Jasnoski and Warner, 1991.
18. Jasnoski, 1984; Jasnoski and Schwartz, 1985; Jasnoski and Warner, 1991; Gregerson, 1998, 2000, 2002, 2003, 2004, and 2005.
19. Bell, Jasnoski, Kagan, and King, 1991; Bell, Jasnoski, Kagan, and King, 1990.
20. Jasnoski and Trobliger, 1994; Gregerson (Jasnoski), 1995; Gregerson (Jasnoski), 1995; Gregerson (Jasnoski), 1997a, b, c, and d; and Gregerson (Jasnoski), 2007a, b, and c.
21. Schmit, Sellner, Michaud, and McLeod, 2002.
22. See note 21, 5 above.
23. See note 21.

24. See note 21, 2 above.
25. See note 21, 7 above.
26. See note 21, 15 above.
27. See note 21.
28. See note 26.
29. Gula, 2007.
30. See note 29.
31. See note 29.
32. Read, 2006.
33. Srilata, 2003.
34. Ramaswamy, 1997.
35. Marx, Engels, and Jones, 1962/2002.
36. Russo and Denmark, 1987.
37. Scarborough and Furumoto, 1987.
38. Woolf, 2005.
39. Lips, 2005.
40. Waaldjik and Utrecht Coordination Team, 2006.
41. "Indonesian women's studies," 2007; Pankin, 2007.
42. See note 21.
43. See note 21, 3 above.
44. See note 9.
45. See note 11.
46. Tart, 1992.
47. Chicoke, 2001.
48. Lee, 1996.
49. See note 21.
50. Levin, Larson, and Puchalski, 1997; Matthews, McCullough, Larson, Koenig, Swyers, and Milano, 1998.
51. See note 11.

BIBLIOGRAPHY

Bandler, Richard. *The Structure of Magic: A Book about Language and Therapy.* Palo Alto, CA: Science and Behavior Books, 1975.

Bell, Iris R., Mary Banks Jasnoski, Jerome Kagan, and David S. King. "Depression and Allergies: Survey of a Non-Clinical Population." *Psychotherapy and Psychosomatics* 55 (1991): 24–31.

Bell, Iris R., Mary Banks Jasnoski, Jerome Kagan, and David S. King. "Is Allergic Rhinitis in Young Adults with Extreme Shyness? A Preliminary Survey." *Psychosomatic Medicine* 52 (1990): 517–525.

Chicoke, Anthony J. *Secrets of Native American Herbal Remedies: Comprehensive Guide to Native American Tradition Using Herbs Mind/Body/Spirit Connection for Improving Health and Well-Being. (Healing Arts).* New York: Avery, 2001.

Gendlin, Eugene T. *Focusing. 25th Anniversary Edition.* New York: Rider Books, 2003.

Gregerson, Mary Banks. "Allergies: General." In Andrew Baum, Stanton Newman, John Weinman, Robert West, and Chris McManus, eds. *Cambridge*

Handbook of Psychology, Health, and Medicine. New York: Guilford Publications, 1997a.

———. "Allergies: General." In Susan Ayers, Andrew Baum, Chris McManus, and Stanton Newman, eds. *Cambridge Handbook of Psychology, Health, and Medicine*. 2nd ed. Cambridge, UK: Cambridge University Press, 2007a.

———. "Allergies to Drugs." In Andrew Baum, Stanton Newman, John Weinman, Robert West, and Chris McManus, eds. *Cambridge Handbook of Psychology, Health, and Medicine*. New York: Guilford Publications, 1997b.

———. "Allergies to Drugs." In Susan Ayers, Andrew Baum, Chris McManus, and Stanton Newman, eds. *Cambridge Handbook of Psychology, Health, and Medicine*. 2nd ed. Cambridge, UK: Cambridge University Press, 2007b.

———. "Allergies to Foods." In Andrew Baum, Stanton Newman, John Weinman, Robert West, and Chris McManus, eds. *Cambridge Handbook of Psychology, Health, and Medicine*. New York: Guilford Publications, 1997.

———. "Allergies to Foods." In Susan Ayers, Andrew Baum, Chris McManus, and Stanton Newman, eds. *Cambridge Handbook of Psychology, Health, and Medicine*. 2nd ed. Cambridge, UK: Cambridge University Press, 2007.

———. "Asthma as a Psychosomatic Illness: An Historical Perspective." In E. Sherwood Brown, ed. *"Asthma: Social and Psychological Factors and Psychosomatic Syndromes." Advances in Psychosomatic Medicine* 24 (2003): 16–41.

———. "A Role for Clinical Psychology in Health Care and Policy Concerning the Physical Environment." *Clinical Psychology in Medical Settings* 2 (2) (1995): 205–221.

———. "Environmental Stress." In Alan J. Christensen, René Martin, and Joshua Morrison Smyth, eds. *Encyclopedia of Health Psychology: Studies in Philosophy and Religion*. New York: Springer, 2004.

———. "Environmental Health Psychology Designs Ordinary Settings to Promote Mental and Physical Well-Being." *Northern Virginia Society of Clinical Psychology Newsletter*, 4 (Winter 2005): 14–16.

———. "Immunopsychological Panic Disorder: Behavioral and Genetic Implications." *Directions in Clinical Psychology* 5 (5) (1995): 1–20.

———. "It's Not About You: Designing Your Unique Lifestyle." *Northern Virginia Society of Clinical Psychology Newsletter* (Spring 2002): 4–7.

———. "Lactose and Food Intolerance." *Cambridge Handbook of Psychology, Health, and Medicine*. Andrew Baum, Stanton Newman, John Weinman, Robert West, and Chris McManus, eds. New York: Guilford Publications, 1997d.

———. "The Curious 2,000-Year Case of Asthma." *Psychosomatic Medicine* 62 (6) (2000): 816–827.

———. "Relaxation for Women." In Elaine A. Blechman and Kelly Brownell, eds. *Behavioral Medicine for Women: A Comprehensive Handbook*. New York: Guilford Publications, Inc., 1998.

Grinder, John, and Richard Bandler. *The Structure of Magic II: A Book about Communication and Change*. Palo Alto, CA: Science and Behavior Books, 1975.

Gula, Robert. *Morality Beyond the Commandments*. Talk presented at University of St. Mary's, Leavenworth, KS, October 16, 2007.

"Indonesian Women's Studies." Retrieved September 23, 2007. http://www.lib.berkeley.edu/SSEAL/SoutheastAsia/seaindon.html, 2007.

Irwin, Lee. *The Dream Seekers: Native American Visionary Traditions of the Great Plains (The Civilization of the American Indian Series, Vol. 213)*. Norman, OK: University of Oklahoma Press, 1996.

James, William. *Varieties of Religious Experience: A Study in Human Nature*. Charleston, SC: Bibliobazaar, 1902/2007.

Jasnoski, Mary Banks. "Ecosystemic Perspective in Clinical Psychology." In William A. O'Connor and Bernie Lubin, eds. *Clinical Applications of Ecosystems Theory*. New York: Wiley & Sons, 1984.

———. "The Physical Environment Affects Quality of Life Based upon Environmental Sensitivity." *Journal of Applied Developmental Psychology* 13 (2) (1992): 139–142.

Jasnoski, Mary Banks, Iris R. Bell, and Rolf Peterson. "What Connections Exist between Shyness, Hay Fever, Anxiety, Anxiety Sensitivity, and Panic Disorder." *Anxiety, Stress, and Coping* 7 (1994): 19–34.

Jasnoski, Mary Banks, and Gary E. Schwartz. "A Synchronous System Model for Health." *American Behavioral Scientist* 28 (4) (1985): 468–485.

Jasnoski, Mary Banks, and Robert W. Trobliger. "Psychoneuroimmunology and women." *Boletin: de la oficiana sanitaria Panamericana* 116 (3) (1994): 264–272.

Jasnoski, Mary Banks, and Rebecca Warner. "Graduate and Postgraduate Medical Education with the Synchronous Systems Model." *Behavioral Science* 36 (1991): 253–73.

Jung, Carl, and Joseph Campbell, ed. *The Portable Jung*. New York: Penguin (Non-Classics) Books, 1954.

Lajoie, D. H., and S. I. Shapiro. "Definitions of Transpersonal Psychology: The First Twenty-Three Years." *Journal of Transpersonal Psychology* 24 (1) (1992): 79–98.

Laski, Marghanita. *Ecstasy: A Study of Some Secular and Religious Experiences*. London: Crescent Press, 1961.

Lao Tsu (Author), Gia-Fu Feng (Translator), and Jane English. *Tao Te Ching (The Way of Life) 25th Anniversary Edition*. New York: Vintage Press, 1997.

Levin, Jeffrey S., David B. Larson, and Christina M. Puchalski. "Religion and Spirituality in Medicine: Research and Education." *Journal of the American Medical Association* 278 (9) (1997): 792–793.

Lips, Hilary M. A *New Psychology of Women: Gender, Culture, and Ethnicity*. New York: McGraw-Hill, 2005.

Lu, Tung-Pin, Carl Jung, and Richard Wilhelm (Translator). *The Secret of the Golden Flower: A Chinese Book of Life*. Bushmills, County Antrim, Ireland: Causeway Books, 1975.

Marx, Karl, Friederich Engels, and Gareth Steadman Jones. *The Communist Manifesto. New Edition*. New York: Penguin Classics, 1962, 2002.

Maslow, Abraham H. "Lessons from Peak Experiences." *Journal of Humanistic Psychology* 2 (1962): 9–18.

Matthews, Dale A., Michale E. McCullough, David B. Larson, Harold G. Koenig, James P. Swyers, and Mary Greenwold Milano. "Religious Commitment and Health Status: A Review of the Research and Implications for Family Medicine." *Archives of Family Medicine* 7 (2) (1998): 118–124.

Pankin, Mary Faith. "Archival Sites for Women's Studies." Retrieved August 8, 2007. Washington, DC: George Washington University. http://libr.org/wss/wsslinks/archwss.htm, 2007.

Perls, Fritz. *In and Out the Garbage Pail.* Boulder, CO: Real People Press, 1969.

Perry, John Weir. *Roots of Renewal in Myth and Madness.* New York: Jossey-Bass, 1976.

Ramaswamy, Vijaya. *Walking Naked—Women, Society, Spirituality in South India.* Shimla, India: Indian Institute for Advanced Study, 1997.

Read, Donna. *Women and Spirituality Series: Part Two.* DVD. Santa Monica, CA: Direct Cinema Ltd., Inc., 2006.

Rogers, Carl R. *On Becoming.* New York: Delta, 1980.

———. *On Becoming Partners.* New York: Mariner Books/Houghton Mifflin, 1995.

Russo, Nancy Felipe, and Florence L. Denmark. "Contributions of Women to Psychology." *Annual Review of Psychology* 38 (1987): 279–298.

Scarborough, Elizabeth, and Laurel Furumoto. *Untold Lives: The First Generation of American Women Psychologists.* New York: Columbia University Press, 1987.

Schmit, David, Ed Sellner, Catherine Michaud, and MaryAnn McLeod. *Spirituality and Psychology: Connections and Intersections.* Retrieved September 17, 2007. An interdisciplinary conversation at The College of St. Catherine, St. Paul, MN, 2002.

Srilata, K. *The Other Half of the Coconut: Women Writing Self-Respect History.* New Dehli, India: Kali for Women, 2003.

Stevens, Barry. *Don't Push the River.* Berkeley, CA: Ten Speed Press, 1985.

Suzuki-Roshi, Shunryu. *Zen Mind, Beginner's Mind.* Berkeley, CA: Shambalaya Books, 1971/2006.

Tart, Charles T. *Transpersonal Psychologies: Perspectives on the Mind from Seven Great Spiritual Traditions.* New York: HarperCollins, 1992.

Waaldjik, Berteke, and the Utrecht Coordination Team. "Rosi Braidotti and the Making of European Women's Studies." *Athena* 7 (2006): 1–3.

Walsh, Roger, and Frances Vaughan. "On Transpersonal Definitions." *Journal of Transpersonal Psychology* 25 (2) (1993): 125–182.

Watzlawick, Paul. *Change: Principles of Problem Formation and Problem Resolution.* New York: W. W. Norton, 1974.

Woolf, Linda M. "Women's Intellectual Contributions to the Study of Mind and Society." Webster University. Retrieved November 20, 2007. http://www.webster.edu/~woolflm/women.html, 2005.

PART IV

Applications to Mental Health Practice

Chapter 17

Hindu Indian Spirituality, Female Identity, and Psychoanalytic Psychotherapy

Pratyusha Tummala-Narra

The search for a core sense of self lies at the heart of spirituality and psychoanalytic thought, both of which have guided my understanding of human nature. In this chapter, I explore how my training as a psychoanalytically oriented psychologist coexists with my Hindu spirituality despite some important conceptual differences between these two perspectives. The ways in which feminism and multicultural psychology have informed my spiritual life and my clinical practice will be explored with a psychotherapy case study.

PSYCHODYNAMIC TRAINING, RELIGION, AND SPIRITUALITY

Sigmund Freud, in his paper, "The Future of an Illusion," described religion as an "illusion," and as "the universal obsessional neurosis of humanity."[1] Freud connected religion with the Oedipus complex, likening the father-child relationship to an individual's fantasies of God images. There have been considerable changes in the ways in which religion and spirituality are conceptualized by psychoanalysts since Freud's early writings. For example, object relations theory, first developed in the 1950s and 1960s, and later expanded in the 1970s and 1980s, brought forth new psychoanalytic conceptualizations of spirituality that emphasized the individual's relationship with God as paralleling the development of relationships with significant others, such as parents or siblings.[2, 3] Relational psychoanalysis, a more recent

development in psychoanalytic theory, deemphasized Freud's applica-
tion of a universal sense of reality to understanding human behavior,
and instead emphasized a more personal sense of reality.[4–6] Ogden
described the relationship between the client and the therapist as
involving an "analytic third," where the subjectivity of the therapist
and that of the client interplays through unconscious communication.[7]
Relational psychoanalysts underscore the ways in which the therapist
as observer and the client as the observed are interdependent in creating the therapeutic relationship and, ultimately, the type of self-inquiry
that is therapeutically beneficial.

Religion and spirituality have been controversial topics within psychoanalysis and more broadly in the field of psychology, partly
because of their conceptualization in psychoanalytic history, and also
because of the growing emphasis on scientific observation in psychological research and practice.[8, 9] The valuing of the objective, scientific
study of human behavior across different theoretical orientations in
psychology has more or less excluded an open discourse on religion
and spirituality. It is only in recent years, with the advent of relational
and postmodern perspectives in psychoanalysis, that several prominent
psychoanalysts have revealed in their writings their beliefs about the
centrality of spiritual life to the inner lives of their clients, and to their
own professional development.[10–12]

Training as a psychodynamic clinician, and more broadly as a clinical psychologist, prepared me to attend to the underlying aspects of
human behavior. My training opened up the world of understanding
wishes, defenses, dreams, and conflicts, all of which I consider to be
central to identity and relationships. My training as a psychologist,
however, remained distant from another central part of my experience
that involved my race, ethnicity, and spiritual faith. I now realize that,
throughout my training and beyond, the topic of spirituality was and
continues to be silenced as a way of reifying a self-image involving scientific objectivity. In fact, I have been struck by the way in which I
have unconsciously and consciously spoken less about my spiritual
beliefs during my training years, possibly to manage the dissonance I
experienced when issues of spirituality were not invited into class discussions or clinical supervision. This challenge continued beyond graduate school when I began to develop my own theoretical and clinical
sensibility as a psychologist, with few models who integrated spirituality with psychotherapy.

FEMINIST INFLUENCES

Throughout my upbringing and training, feminist perspectives
informed my exploration of spirituality. The heavy emphasis on education and achievement for men and women in my family reinforced my

developing sense of feminism as an adolescent, as did my reading of feminist literature. In graduate school, my preoccupation with feminism seemed to contradict my emerging interest in psychoanalytic theories. These two perspectives eventually informed my spiritual development and my life as a psychologist.

Feminist perspectives posed major challenges to psychoanalytic theory and brought much-needed attention to power differences within religious institutions and interpretations and the hierarchical structure inherent in classical psychoanalytic techniques. Funderburk and Fukuyama suggested that the invisibility of women in social structures of religious institutions contributes to the "spiritual wounding of girls and women."[13] It is well noted that Freud's view of God involved a father representation.[14, 15] While Jung attempted to reintegrate feminine aspects of the God image, his notions of the archetypal feminine convey female inferiority. Gendered images of God have been challenged by feminist psychoanalysts such as Julia Kristeva, who suggested that a maternal core exists within the imagery of God, but that the maternal core has been transformed into the paternal symbolism of Christianity.[16, 17] Similar to other feminist psychoanalysts, Kristeva examined the psychological sources and meanings connected with the male image of God.

The masculine imagery of God coupled with the exclusion of women from power structures of religious institutions complicate the development of women's identifications with spirituality and religion. The highly imbalanced place of the masculine and the feminine in religious institutions across cultural and religious contexts is further juxtaposed against feminized aspects of spiritual beliefs and practices. For instance, the "soul" is often connected with the feminine whereas the "mind" is typically linked with the masculine.[18] Women, particularly mothers, are thought to play a critical role in passing on spiritual traditions and practices to younger generations.

This contradictory position of women in the realm of spirituality is evident across religions. For example, Hindu God imagery involves a fluidity of masculine and feminine images, not to mention a fluidity of human and animal forms, such as in the case of Ganesha, the elephant-headed God. These various forms are thought to represent different aspects of one God. Despite Hindu philosophical notions of God as assuming powerful feminine and masculine elements, religious rituals and practices often exclude women from power and/or connect women with destructive aspects of power. One illustration of this involves the taboo against Hindu women entering temples during their menstrual cycles. The common belief among many Hindus is that women are unclean or impure during this time. The obsession over women's purity and the fear of impure women is, of course, prevalent across many religious contexts, and is often promulgated through religious interpretations.

The subordinate position of women associated with male reactivity to the potential for female power in religious epistemology has important implications for women's perceived and actual roles in society. Daly, in reference to Judeo-Christian traditions, stated, "If God in 'his' heaven is a father ruling 'his' people, then it is in the 'nature' of things . . . that society be male-dominated." She noted how societal images, derived from traditional religious interpretations, and values are projected into beliefs that justify social infrastructure, and such beliefs develop an "unchangeable independent existence and validity."[19] These beliefs often become connected with women's sense of purpose and meaning in relation to the world.

THE INFLUENCE OF MULTICULTURAL PSYCHOLOGY

While Western views of feminism have played an important role in addressing power differences within religious structures, they tend to value Western individualism and the image of God as White. As a Hindu Indian American woman, I have felt less connected to this particular construction of God and spiritual life. In their analysis of self-images of Hindu women in Orissa, India, Menon and Shweder described the tendency of some feminist scholars to depict Hindu women as passive victims and blame the Hindu religion for the subordination of women.[20] They also noted that the image of the Hindu woman as a passive victim is sharply contrasted with the image of the Western or Westernized woman as educated, cosmopolitan, autonomous, and having control over her body. Similarly, in the United States, some White feminists have depicted women of color in devalued images. This lack of attunement to the complex interaction of racism, sexism, classism, and homophobia in the lives of ethnic minorities has raised a significant lack of trust of White feminism, similar to the mistrust of psychoanalytic therapies, by many ethnic-minority women who face experiences of multiple forms of oppression.[21]

Misapprehension about spiritual meanings for ethnic-minority women can influence how clinicians appraise mental health, pathology, and spiritually based explanations for the etiology, course, and treatment of psychological distress. This is particularly important because of the centrality of spirituality in the lives of many ethnic-minority women. Numerous clinical case reports and empirical studies have documented holistic views of health and the significance of prayer in engendering hope in the lives of American Indian, African American, Hispanic American, and Asian American women.[22, 23]

It is clear from Freud's example and from that of contemporary psychoanalysts who have written on the subject of religion that sociopolitical realities can contribute significantly to individual approaches to spirituality. An individual's spiritual life involves a dynamic process of change during his or her life, as well as across interaction with different sociocultural contexts. One example of this process is evident in the experience of immigrants. Immigration evokes various types of anxiety related to leaving one's country of origin to a new, unknown cultural environment, and involves a multitude of trajectories with respect to acculturation. Immigrants may experience either a strengthening or a weakening of their identifications with their religious communities or some vacillation from one perspective to another. For some immigrants, moving to a new country presents challenges in establishing connections with a religious community because the physical realities (that is, the lack of proximity to a religious institution or community) preclude the possibility of forming these bonds. Others may experience ambivalence about recreating a religious community that resembles one in the country of origin.

Tarakeshawar, Pargament, and Mahoney reported, in their study of religious practices among Hindu Indian immigrants in the United States, that those who are less acculturated are likely to be more involved in religious practices.[24] They suggested that religious practices in this group may be motivated by stress and isolation. These findings underscore the relationship between spirituality and the individual's need for belonging to a larger community that extends beyond immediate family, especially when faced with profound change of physical and cultural environments and/or life transitions.

Religious life is often connected with cultural life in that many Hindus view God as manifested in various different forms, implicating complex relationships among the God representations, sometimes harmonious and other times conflicting. This view of God is connected with broader Indian social values of interdependence on family and community. It is not surprising then that most Hindu Indians view Hindu religious practices and their broader cultural identifications as inseparable. An individual's connection with his/her ethnic and religious community can be highly varied. The religious community can be a strong source of collective resilience providing a sense of purpose and connection.[25] In other instances, intense relationships with religious communities and/or religious authorities can contribute to the creation of ethnic-religious identities often tied to political tensions across groups of people.[26]

SPIRITUALITY AND HINDU WOMEN

While spirituality and religion are linked closely for many Hindu women, spiritual beliefs and traditions specific to the female experience can also be differentiated from organized Hindu religious doctrine and structures that formed in the post-Vedic era following foreign invasion of the Indian subcontinent. Many Hindu women view spiritual faith as central to feminine identity and the experience of personal power. The Vedic period of Hinduism (1,500–500 BCE) is still one of the most influential in the beliefs of many Hindus today. Hindu mythological stories of goddesses from this era provide important feminine images that are internalized by Hindu women. Goddess images that stem from the early Vedic period reflect women's ideals of strength, power, devotion, intelligence, and nurturance. The emphasis on feminine power, or shakti, is evident in the belief that the soul is both feminine and masculine. A physical symbol of spiritual strength and power is the bindi worn by many Hindu women on their foreheads, although in more recent times, the bindi is worn also for decorative purposes.

The early Vedic Hindu emphasis on women's strength and devotion continues to pervade the inner lives of Hindu women. Many Hindu girls, including myself, grow up listening to stories about warrior queens and princesses who at times hold powerful and other times powerless positions in the course of important events. For example, in the epic Ramayana, Sita is described to have great spiritual power equaled only by her husband, Rama. Sita and Rama are thought to be incarnations of the goddess Lakshmi and the god Vishnu, respectively. In the course of the epic, Sita is abducted by Ravana, a demon king. Her abduction is thought to initiate a long battle between Rama and Ravana as Rama seeks to save Sita. Sita's virtues of fidelity and loyalty to her husband are extolled by both Hindu men and women in contemporary society. In a related vein, women in epics, such as Kunti in the epic Mahabarata, are praised for their spiritual devotion. Kunti, the widowed mother of the five Pandava princes, is thought to have achieved spiritual grace through her prayer and devotion to the god Krishna. Her sons are later protected by Krishna in a great war that ensues against their cousins over ownership of their kingdom. This notion of female devotion to God is significant to the lives of many Hindu women who view God as a protective force both for their own safety and well-being and that of their families.

In contemporary Hindu communities across the Indian diaspora, women are actively involved in spiritual practices such as prayer and meditation. Girls are taught that prayer will provide inner strength as well as material success. There has also been a resurgence among Hindu reformists and female gurus or teachers of earlier Vedic philosophy that provides access to spirituality across gender and class. In the United States, there are numerous Hindu spiritual centers where women participate in teaching Hindu spirituality and create spiritual communities for themselves and their families.

MY HINDU SPIRITUALITY

One aspect of my spiritual life has involved both socialization into Hindu culture and life, including traditions I mentioned earlier. The other, perhaps more central part of my spiritual life has involved a personal search for meaning and purpose, including a deeper understanding of physical and mental suffering, peace, and social justice. I consider all of these to be relevant to spirituality, and interestingly, these issues are also of interest to the field of psychology.

My view of spirituality is connected with my exposure to the Hindu religion in my family and the Hindu community in India and the United States. As a child in India, I woke up to the daily Hindu prayers conducted in Sanskrit by my great-grandfather. I then heard Muslim prayers in Urdu from a neighboring mosque, and then attended a Christian grammar school. My experiences with different spiritual traditions of my friends, classmates, and neighbors continued after I came to the United States as an immigrant. These experiences were the backdrop to my understanding of Hinduism and my own relationship with God.

Like many Hindus, I grew up with a belief in one God that is expressed in different forms. God ("Brahman") is thought to be a timeless and formless entity that is worshipped in many forms. The goal of a purposeful life for Hindus centers on the realization of the true nature of the self. Hindus also believe that different spiritual paths can lead to self-realization. These paths include the path of devotion to God (bhakti yoga), the path of right action or selfless service (karma yoga), the path of meditation (raja yoga), and the path of spiritual knowledge (jnana yoga).

While there are many ways in which Hindus attempt to integrate this philosophy into their lives, I was raised with an emphasis on prayer (bhakti yoga) and service to others (karma yoga). As a child, I participated in prayer rituals taught by my parents, and as an adult, I continue to pray, and have become more interested in the philosophical underpinnings of Hinduism and its relationship to the spiritual and psychological dimensions of my life. I've experienced a deepening of my faith in God, and attempt to integrate my conception of Hinduism into daily life with my family. My exploration of religious scriptures, particularly the Bhagavad Gita, has informed my understanding of psychological conflicts, and perhaps even more poignantly opened the possibility for a spiritual dimension in my role as a therapist. At the same time, I have struggled with decontextualized interpretations of Hindu scriptures that involve a diminution of women.

While I had not been exposed to this aspect of the Hindu scriptures while growing up, the complicated position of women in Hindu culture has been evident to me in my adulthood. It is clear that Hindu concepts such as dharma (sense of duty) have been interpreted by men and women within a patriarchal religious structure. I continue to pursue my own inquiry into my experience as a Hindu, and, ironically, it may be that the flexibility that is inherent in Hindu philosophy with respect to pathways to self-realization has contributed to my ability to tolerate the confusing nature of women's positions in Hindu life. Interestingly, this perspective may have influenced the way in which I have approached the complicated relationship between psychoanalysis and sociocultural realities, and more broadly my bicultural identifications with psychoanalytic and multicultural psychology. Psychoanalytic inquiry challenges therapists to tolerate the unknown in our clients' mental lives in an attempt to find meaningful insights into the true nature of the self. It is at this juncture that I have found common ground for my Hindu spirituality and psychoanalytic perspectives.

SPIRITUALITY, HINDU WOMEN, AND PSYCHOANALYTIC PSYCHOTHERAPY: THE CASE OF KAVITA

The ways in which I attempt to integrate spirituality into the context of psychoanalytic psychotherapy are illustrated in the following case vignette.

Kavita is a twenty-three-year-old Indian American woman who sought psychotherapy on her own initiative to help cope with stress and anxiety related to her performance in medical school. In her initial session, she reported feeling anxious about failing even though she completed her program requirements quite successfully. She stated that she had never felt this anxious before, and connected her anxiety with family conflicts.

Kavita grew up in a middle-class neighborhood with her parents and older sister. She reported that she had a close relationship with her sister whom she described as the "good one" in the family who followed a "straight" path both socially and academically. She described her parents as loving, strict, and deeply religious. Her parents were actively involved in teaching Hindu philosophy at their local temple and were invested in their daughters' learning this philosophy. At the same time, she explained, they were sort of like rebels in the community, because they had two girls who knew just as much about Vedanta (Hindu scriptures) as many of the uncles (older men in the community). Kavita felt strongly identified with her Hindu Indian community, but at times was deeply disconnected from the community while growing up. While in high school, she recalled feeling sexually attracted to other girls. She was silent about her feelings for several subsequent years. When she attended college, she became involved in relationships with women, and in her third year, decided to come out to her family. She stated that her parents expressed feeling confused, and that they didn't really believe that she is a lesbian. Kavita's sister was apparently supportive of her and was able to accept her sexuality.

I worked with Kavita in weekly individual psychotherapy for more than two years. When I met Kavita, her sister was engaged to be married to an Indian man, and her family was preoccupied with organizing a traditional Hindu wedding. About a year prior to this, Kavita had disclosed to her parents her relationship with an Indian American woman. Her parents, while acknowledging the presence of this relationship in Kavita's life, told her that they were not ready to meet her partner. Kavita struggled with her feelings of disappointment with her parents' response and her feelings of failure in her personal life following some difficult interactions with her partner. She described her partner as someone who is "Indian by birth but not by heart," referring to her partner's strong identifications with White feminism. Kavita mentioned that her partner also had a Western view of relationships that centered on the self instead of commitment to one's family.

Kavita's distance from her parents and partner were compounded by her feelings of alienation from her religious community. Kavita stated in a session during our fifth month of working together, "I can't stand it that I have to pretend like I'm not gay when I'm around my parents. I miss them. I even miss the temple ... but I can't do anything about it until they can accept this about me." I asked her why she thought she couldn't tell anyone about being a lesbian. She replied, "I don't want to hurt my parents, maybe ... or maybe I don't want to feel like more people are ashamed of me or look at me in a different way. They don't even talk about sex in the community. How are they going to talk about homosexuality?" Kavita's response resonated with my own experience of discussing taboo topics in the Indian community and with my own questioning of the patriarchal ideologies of some Hindu traditions. I wanted to protect her from the potential reality that she may indeed feel further isolated, and I also wanted her to reconnect with friends, family, and God. I remember that in these moments I prayed for her safety and for her growing capacity to take the emotional risks necessary for a more complete engagement with significant people in her life. Our work involved considering the various trajectories involved with coming out to her community, and what this would mean with respect to her relationship with God.

At times, Kavita indicated how angry she felt toward God, who in her mind was masculine. In our discussions about her male image of God, she stated, "I know I should think of God as being male and female, I'm just so used to it. I mean in Hinduism, Gods are male and female ... But I have a hard time thinking of a woman God." I found this point in the treatment to be a critical one in that Kavita began to question her longstanding assumptions about both God and her position in the world. In other words, she began to wonder about the sources of these assumptions (that is, her religious community and her parents), and the possibility of forming different self-images and God images. Her ambivalence about women having real power and agency in the world, as reflected in her gendered God images, seemed to have mirrored her concept of herself, and possibly her view of me as a less-powerful female therapist.

I also believe that she experienced me, mostly on an unconscious level, as her parents and her partner at different times, symbolizing traditional and nontraditional Indian perspectives. She expressed her appreciation for being able to talk with me openly, and her ambivalence about my "challenging" her to think more about her own loving and aggressive feelings toward both God and people in her life. In one session, while describing her feelings of loss of her temple community, Kavita stated, "I probably sound like some kind of fanatic. I'm really not . . . I mean, you wouldn't expect someone like me to be so religious." I was aware of how both of us were concerned about being perceived as either "fanatic" or "atheist," both of which felt disconnected from our individual subjective experiences and our shared therapeutic space.

CONCLUSION

My work with Kavita represents some of the typical dilemmas with which both clients and therapists struggle when exploring spirituality and religious identifications. The inquiry into spirituality is often essential to people's lives in that it allows for an engagement with a core aspect of the self. I believe that prayer played a central role in my therapy with Kavita, although praying was never an explicit part of the psychotherapeutic relationship. We prayed in separate spaces, yet prayer remained a shared experience. In my work with Kavita, I felt the need to attend to my own spirituality, a sense of relief, perhaps for both of us, in being able to talk about God in psychotherapeutic work, and a deepening of trust in our therapeutic relationship. My psychoanalytic orientation was helpful in considering the ways in which my spiritual subjectivity interacted with that of my client, and in exploring spiritual growth and change, as evident in Kavita's reconsideration of her gendered images of God.

NOTES

1. Freud, 1927, 38.
2. Guntrip, 1956.
3. Rizutto, 1979.
4. Mitchell, 1993.
5. Sorensen, 1997.
6. Stolorow and Atwood, 1992.
7. Ogden, 1994.
8. Aron, 2004.
9. Simmonds, 2006.
10. Aron, 2004.
11. Rizzutto, 2004.

12. Roland, 2005.
13. Funderburk and Fukuyama, 2001, 10.
14. Akhtar and Parens, 2001.
15. Rao, 2005.
16. Jonte-Pace, 2001.
17. Kristeva, J., 1982.
18. Elkins, 1995.
19. Daly, 1994, 263.
20. Menon and Shweder, 1998.
21. Greene, 2004.
22. Adams, 2000.
23. Musgrave, Allen, and Allen, 2002.
24. Tarakeshawar, Pargament, and Mahoney, 2003.
25. Tummala-Narra, 2007.
26. Fayek, 2004.

BIBLIOGRAPHY

Adams, J. M. "Individual and Group Psychotherapy with African American Women." In L. C. Jackson and B. Greene, *Psychotherapy with African American Women: Innovations in Psychodynamic Perspectives and Practice*. New York: Guilford Press, 2001.

Akhtar, S., and H. Parens. *Does God Help? Developmental and Clinical Aspects of Religious Belief*. Northvale, NJ: Jason Aronson, 2001.

Aron, L. "God's Influence on My Psychoanalytic Vision and Values." *Psychoanalytic Psychology* 21 (3) (2004): 442–451.

Daly, M. "After the Death of God the Father: Women's Liberation and the Transformation of Christian Consciousness." In M. Schneir (ed.), *Feminism in Our Time: The Essential Writings, World War II to the Present*. New York: Vintage Books, 1994.

Elkins, D. N. "Psychotherapy and Spirituality: Toward a Theory of the Soul." *Journal of Humanistic Psychology* 35 (2): (1995) 78–98.

Fayek, A. "Islam and Its Effect on My Practice of Psychoanalysis." *Psychoanalytic Psychology* 21 (3) (2004): 452–457.

Freud, S. "The Future of an Illusion." *The Standard Edition of the Complete Psychological Works of Sigmund Freud* 21 3–66. London: Hogarth Press, 1927.

Funderburk, J. R., and M. A. Fukuyama. "Feminism, Multiculturalism, and Spirituality: Convergent and Divergent Forces in Psychotherapy." *Women and Therapy* 24 (3/4) (2001): 1–18.

Greene, B. "African American Lesbians and Other Culturally Diverse People in Psychodynamic Psychotherapies: Useful Paradigms or Oxymoron?" In J. M. Glassgold and S. Iasenza, eds. *Lesbians, Feminism, and Psychoanalysis: The Second Wave*, pp. 57–77. Binghamton, NY: Harrington Park Press, 2004.

Guntrip, H. *Psychotherapy and Religion*. New York: Harper and Brothers Publishers, 1957.

Jonte-Pace, D. "Analysts, Critics, and Inclusivists: Feminist Voices in the Psychology of Religion." In D. Jonte-Pace and W. B. Parsons, eds. *Religion and Psychology: Mapping the Terrain*, pp. 129–146. New York: Routledge, 2001.

Kristeva, J. *Powers of Horror: An Essay on Abjection*. New York: Columbia University Press, 1982.

Menon, U., and R. A. Shweder. "The Return of the 'White Man's Burden': The Moral Discourse of Anthropology and the Domestic Life of Hindu Women." In R. A. Shweder, *Welcome to Middle Age!* Chicago: The University of Chicago Press, 1998.

Mitchell, S. A. *Hope and Dread in Psychoanalysis*. New York: Basic Books, 1993.

Musgrave, C. F., C. E. Allen, and G. J. Allen. "Spirituality and Health for Women of Color." *American Journal of Public Health* 92 (4) (2002): 557–560.

Ogden, T. H. "The Analytic Third: Working with Intersubjective Clinical Facts." *International Journal of Psychoanalysis* 75 (1994): 3–19.

Parsons, W. B. "Themes and Debates in the Psychology-Comparitivist Dialogue." In D. Jonte-Pace and W. B. Parsons, eds. *Religion and Psychology: Mapping the Terrain*. New York: Routledge, 2001.

Rao, D. G. "Manifestations of God in India: A transference pantheon." In S. Akhtar, ed. *Freud along the Ganges: Psychoanalytic Reflections on the People and Culture of India*. New York: Other Press, 2005.

Rizzuto, A. M. *The Birth of the Living God*. Chicago: University of Chicago Press, 1979.

———. "Roman Catholic Background and Psychoanalysis." *Psychoanalytic Psychology* 21 (3) (2004): 436–441.

Roland, A. *Cultural Pluralism and Psychoanalysis: The Asian and North American Experience*. New York: Routledge, 1996.

———. "The Spiritual Self in Psychoanalytic Therapy." In M. B. Weiner, P. C. Cooper, and C. Barbre, eds. *Psychotherapy and Religion: Many Paths, One Journey*. New York: Jason Aronson, 2005.

Rubin, J. B. "Psychoanalysis is self-centered." In C. Spezzano and G. J. Gargiulo, eds. *Soul on the Couch: Spirituality, Religion, and Morality in Contemporary Psychoanalysis*. Hillsdale, NJ: The Analytic Press, 1997.

Simmonds, J. G. "The Oceanic Feeling and a Sea Change." *Psychoanalytic Psychology* 23 (1) (2006): 128–142.

Sorensen, R. L. "Transcendence and Intersubjectivity: The Patient's Experience of the Analyst's Spirituality." In C. Spezzano and G. J. Gargiulo, eds. *Soul on the Couch: Spirituality, Religion, and Morality in Contemporary Psychoanalysis*. Hillsdale, NJ: The Analytic Press, 1997.

Stolorow, R., and G. Atwood. *Contexts of Being*. Hillsdale, NJ: The Analytic Press, 1992.

Stone, C. "Opening Psychoanalytic Space to the Spiritual." *Psychoanalytic Review* 92 (3) (2005): 417–430.

Tarakeshwar, N., K. I. Pargament, and A. Mahoney. "Measures of Hindu Pathways: Development and Preliminary Evidence of Reliability and Validity." *Cultural Diversity and Ethnic Minority Psychology* 9 (4) (2003): 316–332.

Thoresen, C. E., A. H. S. Harris, and D. Oman. "Spirituality, Religion, and Health: Evidence, Issues, and Concerns." In T. G. Plante and A. C. Sherman, eds. *Faith and Healing: Psychological Perspectives*. New York: Guilford Press, 2001.

Tummala-Narra, P. "Conceptualizing Trauma and Resilience across Diverse Contexts: A Multicultural Perspective." *Journal of Aggression, Maltreatment, and Trauma* 14 (1/2) (2007): 33–53.

Chapter 18

Spiritual Awareness in Life and Psychotherapy

Lisa Miller

My oldest daughter stands a head above most children in her nursery-school class. I encourage her to embrace her height with delight and to integrate her body with her powerful gentle soul, through her nickname "Swan." When on occasion her stature fields comment, I whisper closely in her ear, "Leah is an elegant Swan."

Getting Swan out the house in the morning has been most inelegant. On a recent morning Swan and I were late for school one too many times. I ruminatively focused on being prompt primarily out of my anxiety to respect and not irritate her teacher. Clapping my hands, I urged, "Let's go. Let's go. Let's go. We're late again." Swan stayed in one place. "You need to help Mommy." I explained again. Swan slowly rose and gracefully glides across the room, "I am helping. I am coming, Mommy." Swan slowly sweeps and spreads her arms, as if we had all the time in the world.

"I will help you put on your socks," I assert as I bend over her limp foot. Swan is unhappy with the position of her socks. She takes off the sock I have just put on her foot. I wiggle a shoe onto her limp foot, as she laughs uproariously at the game. I am angry. I carry Swan to the car, dump Swan in her seat, race to her school, and, in an aggravated manner, I escort Swan only halfway to her classroom.

Then I pause to look over my shoulder as Swan approaches the classroom door. This time she is not gliding. She seems out of sorts, moving awkwardly; her foot turns inward, she seems hurt. She is a wounded Swan. I feel sick to my stomach. The school door (left open only for her) closes. I stand in the schoolyard feeling that I have hurt my daughter.

Still feeling horrible, sick to my stomach, I drive to find coffee. This particular morning I feel a sense of being directed across a bridge that I do not usually take. There I see the excruciatingly painful confirmation of my actions. Smack in the middle of the road, for the first time ever (after eight years of living in the area), is a mangled mass of white feathers. A large white swan is rigid and disfigured—she has been killed. The swan is folded over itself, awkwardly—distorted from her beauty.

I knew it. I hit Swan like a truck this morning. I pray for healing for Leah and for forgiveness. I walk the banks of the river praying some more. I ask the creator to help heal Leah. I ask for guidance in how to better mother my daughter.

With Swan at the forefront of my mind, I enter the library to attempt to set to work. I feel guided away from my desk to an Italian book of fifteenth- through seventeenth-century art on display. I open the book immediately to a page displaying a painting of a beautiful nude woman gently embracing a glad swan. The swan loves to play and delights as the woman rubs her long neck. The swan, long and lean, is joyful and intermingled with the image of femininity. A cherubic figure (or small child) smiles joyfully upon the embrace between the gentle feminine woman and swan.

I feel grateful and guided. My daughter Swan is gentle, glad, and sensual. I sometimes move through the world as a truck, pushing her. She needs an embrace by the feminine, a joyful, glad, and delightful playfulness, from me. I now have direction.

The image of the classic Italian painting is emblazoned on my consciousness. The next day I attempt to adopt a Swan-like approach to preparing for school. We get ready for school in an entirely different way. Swan likes to dance while she dresses. I dance with her a moment, and make jokes about her wiggling as I attempt to put on her socks. The next day, not surprisingly, we are back to being tardy and rushed. However, the dynamic is far better because I am less truck-like. I remain aware of the playfulness, gentle vulnerability, and gladness in Swan. Swan moves the only way she can—namely, she expresses in each physical motion her inner nature. In preparing for school I still use hurry-up words. However, the *spirit* behind my words is different as I urge her to comply with putting on her socks. She walks in late but not demoralized. Swan is delighted to join her class.

As a mother, my goal is to evolve into a person who supports my child in her endowed nature, on her journey through life. If I can do it, Swan will have radically facilitated my own development. We seem to get just the children we need to evolve. Swan has reawakened my own feminine nature.

MOTHERHOOD AND SPIRITUAL AWARENESS PSYCHOTHERAPY

Everyday motherhood powerfully influences my cosmology, and more specifically has plunged me into an intensive awareness of a relational spirituality, a sense of an ongoing connection with the universe. A relational spirituality includes a sense of dialogue and a personal relationship with the creator—the individual interacting each day respectfully and mindfully with the loving guiding universe based upon the view that the universe is in us, through us, and around us.

Personal experience, including that shared through work with clients, had led me to understand the human journey as a path of spiritual evolution in which parenting is a rare gift of love and growth. We are not alone in the ultimate challenge of parenting. As perhaps shown in the events around Swan, we have constant guidance and support through the living, guiding universe. This guidance, in my view, expresses the loving, guiding creator. Our living dialogue with the universe is replete with synchronicities, awareness through prayer, understanding through dreams, and sacred moments of clarity, epiphany, and inspiration. Expressed through vivid and varied messengers, the help of the creator surrounds us at every moment.

In my experience, the greatest gift I could offer a psychotherapy client is awareness and support in the development of this sacred dialogue with the universe. The client's vision, challenges, and goals will naturally come forward through this perspective. Dialogue with the universe has a powerful life of its own.

Unfortunately, until recently, a relative minority of psychological settings offered discussion of the sacred theater in which we live our daily lives. In contrast to listening to the universe, some schools of psychotherapy have implicitly worked from a stance that humans act upon an inert universe, where meaning is constructed within atomistic consciousness. Recently, in response to the limitations of these treatment models, some psychotherapists have been forging new treatment models. An elegant compendium of spiritually oriented treatment models was recently published by Sperry and Shafranske.[1] As a companion to their book on spiritual strategies for counseling and psychotherapy, Richards and Bergin[2] built a casebook with contributions from a broad and practical range of spiritually inspired psychotherapists.

Concomitant with this movement in psychotherapy, spirituality and religion increasingly are researched within mainstream psychology from the perspective of being central to health and well-being, interwoven with emotion and cognition, and part of human development. (For an overview, see *Handbook of the Psychology of Religion and Spirituality* by Paloutzian and Park; on spirituality in youth specifically, see *The Handbook of Spiritual Development in Childhood and Adolescence* by

Roehlkepartain and colleagues).[3, 4] As the notion that spirituality is central to our lived experience and constitution is studied more, over time (perhaps much time) psychology may come to see humans as foremost spiritual beings. In a landmark study, perhaps opening up this direction, Kendler and colleagues,[5] using a twin study design, found that a personal sense of connection to the creator is about 30 percent attributed to broad heritability, such that (biological reductionism aside) a personal connection to the universe is part of our inherent constitution.

Training new psychotherapists to be in touch with their own spiritual experience will allow the field to expand beyond its current limitations. By way of training new psychotherapists, I support my graduate students in the process of spiritual awareness through spiritual awareness pedagogy.[6] In teaching kind and emotionally sensitive healers, it is clear that spiritual attunement may be in our nature, but often it has been ignored or denied in academia as well as in the personal relationships surrounding our development. Students shared that parents sometimes have been too uncomfortable to welcome discussion about spiritual matters. Teachers often remain silent on the topic—through omission of attention and support. Our inchoate spiritual awareness may be muted or relegated from our inner, daily-lived experience.

What has naturally emerged in my work with clients is a process of spiritual awareness psychotherapy (SAP). Clients often come to treatment unconfident about the validity of their own lived spiritual experience. SAP starts by validating the hunch, surprise, or whisper of spirituality the client feels and reports. In this sense, I see the initial process of SAP as giving dignity and honor to our birthright.

Through developing ownership and certainty about lived spiritual experience, the client augments an innate capacity to listening to the universe, hearing guidance and meaning, and interacting with the universe. In the middle phase of SAP, as the client begins to see the living nature of the universe and shares personal lived accounts, the therapist can share awe, which supports the momentum of the work. Ultimately, in the final phase of SAP, the clarity of a fundamental spiritual reality comes to the fore, and the client considers a life built upon relying on the spiritual as a foundation.

As a psychotherapist, I certainly do not claim to be a spiritual expert. I cringe at the thought of such an attitude. My greatest contribution to a client is to support what the client already knows, inchoately, of her spiritual path. This knowledge, while her birthright, usually is occluded by secular-materialist socialization and (for more affluent clients) years of academic training from within an exclusively secular ontology. In that sense, I am a witness to the transformative presence of the universe in each person's life, and the increased receptivity and spirituality of the client. As the client builds a living dialogue with the universe, a process gains momentum that redirects and elevates the lived experience of the client toward far deeper meaning.

Among my esteemed colleagues in this meaningful volume on women's spirituality, I pause to consider the extent to which spiritual awareness as a governing principle, as a lead part in life and psychotherapy, might be particularly feminine. Certainly a feminine psychology has been built around the primacy of the relational. Using this lens or paradigm of femininity, a relational spirituality, on which spiritual awareness is built, might be viewed as feminine. In terms of method of inquiry, it may be feminine to overtly consider parenthood as a valid source of academic knowledge from which to draw theory or practice. Also by way of method, the use of the first person, the explicit "I," in academic social scientific writing has been reclaimed in the past decade primarily through a feminine review of scientific methodology. Perhaps most significantly, in understanding the forces of the universe, there exist thousands of years of cross-cultural human traditions regarding the feminine as receptive, in balance to the instrumental, at the psychological level and beyond to the mythical or mystical realm. That SAP relies on a respect for receiving and balancing the life of the universe with personal autonomy may be quite a feminine contribution.

TECHNIQUE AND MAP OF SPIRITUAL AWARENESS PYSCHOTHERAPY

Spiritual awareness allows the universe more fully to inform our choices and hoist us along our journey toward growth and healing. The goal of treatment is to help untangle our errors housed at the ego level, and simultaneously to move forward toward our calling by listening to the loving, guiding universe. Working from this perspective, I view myself as therapist, as witness in the spiritual journey of my clients (for more specific techniques and an expanded conceptual framework, please see the *Spiritual Awareness Psychotherapy* DVD.[7]) A stance of collaborators on the road of life mitigates a sense of asymmetry with client, allows for transparency, and makes the therapist, as part of the client-therapist relationship, subject to the wonders and transformative power of the universe.

Broadly speaking, rather than a secular-materialist frame, SAP adapts a fundamentally spiritual frame for treatment that permits discussion of spiritual beliefs. In other words, rather than view the human journey as one of meaning-maker upon an inert or random universe, SAP holds that the universe is alive, divine, and guiding us as individuals and as a collective toward growth and spiritual evolution. The work of treatment is to become *aware* and ultimately to dialogue with the universe so that we each might garner the lessons to journey our spiritual path. The spiritual reality is viewed as most fundamental to the human experience and human existence. Our psychological experience is viewed as an index of our spiritual struggles, challenges, opportunities, and derailments. Spiritual truths govern our healing, growth, new directions, and also may elucidate the source of illness.

UNDERSTANDING RELATIONSHIPS IN SAP

Within the perspective of SAP we express the creator, and our paths cross for a crucial reason in our spiritual development. The purposefulness and absolute meaning of relationships might be highlighted by five central views in SAP around the sacredness of our relationships.

1) All relationships are divine. We are expressions of the creator. We come together in relationships, a gift of the creator. This gift is one given in love and is a guided process. Just as we are created by the divine, so too our meetings through relationships are an expression of the creator.

2) Relationships are sacred vehicles for spiritual evolution and reveal spiritual truths. Our work in relationships allows us to evolve spiritually. We learn love, compassion, forgiveness, justice, and many spiritual truths through loving each other in relationship. Relationships are as central to our spiritual growth as other forms of spiritual work, such as individual or private contemplation and retreat.

3) Relationships are made, including the challenges and hardships. In this sense, every relationship counts, as the spiritual clock is always running. The people who come into our lives are just right to help us grow, and we are just right to help them grow. This does not mean that it will be easy to get along; some relationships can be extremely full of challenges. Nobody we pass on the street, with whom we share a bus ride, marry, debate at work, or love, crosses our path without transforming us, nor do they appear accidentally. The right people come at the right time. All relationships transform us.

4) Times of relational transformation—parenthood, the birth of a child, the death of a spouse—carry specific and universal opportunities for spiritual evolution. There is a form of ego dissolution associated with each passage that initiates us into a new chapter of spiritual development. Ignoring the call to transform in each of these passages causes suffering. Depression and unrest can be associated with the release of the previous way of living. New sensibilities and unexplored psycho-spiritual territory come forward with the advent of each developmental passage.

5) Spiritual awareness heightens around the edges of life—namely birth and death and the proximity to these events. Clarity on our fundamentally spiritual nature emerges, giving us access to the prominence of spiritual reality.

SPIRITUAL AWARENESS PSYCHOTHERAPY WITH CHILDREN AND FAMILIES

In contrast to work with adults, which (once past the immediate precipitant of depression) often focuses on personal development, individuation, or actualization, most children and families seek treatment to resolve disruptive and painful crises. SAP is particularly helpful for families in crisis. Trapped in patterns of familial functioning, families benefit enormously from the redirection found through spiritual guidance.

Spiritual guidance, of course, does not come directly through the therapist but through attunement with the universe. The therapist being far from omniscient cannot possibly fashion a *prior* treatment plan or envision what the best outcome for a family. Beyond matters of physical and emotional safety, the crisis, most fundamentally, is a spiritual opportunity for everyone in the room, including the psychotherapist. As therapists, we can start the regenerative process by allowing and acknowledging the guiding spiritual presence that has sustained the family in the past, that precipitated the crisis, and note such a great presence in bringing the family in search of healing through treatment. From the initial session of treatment, it can be acknowledged that the family in crisis may find a new and better direction than previously imagined. A letting go of the previous expectations for the family may host a deeper, more satisfying situation.

The healing process can be introduced as an act of sacred creation for the family, in that a new family life can be born through crisis. As in any psychotherapy, narrative accounts of positive family transformation and evolution through crisis generally resonate more than statements around cosmology. The sacred universe does the work, if we pay attention to the guidance and host the presence. In the sacred theater, the cues are loud if we listen. Central in supporting families in SAP are three spiritual perspectives about the relationship of parent and child.

1) *The child is the spiritual teacher for the family.* The child is the truth speaker, the exemplar of compassion, and a guide through conflict.

2) The parent is the spiritual ambassador for the child on behalf of the creator. We can show the child around our world, with an eye toward teaching our best-learned spiritual lessons. As merely an ambassador, the parent holds the awesome responsibility to support and cultivate the child's inherent spiritual nature. *The spiritual call of parents is to support* their *children* on *their own sacred paths, which will ultimately sustain the parent's own spiritual path.*

3) *Parenting is an ultimate spiritual absolute* such as charity, mercy, or devotion or any other spiritual absolute, which is sustained and for which guidance is offered by the universe. The parent as a spiritual ambassador holds the responsibility to support and help cultivate the child's inherent spiritual experience.

The child's spiritual presence brings illumination to the family in many forms. I share anecdotes of the child as truth speaker, spiritual barometer, healer, and non-egocentric peacemaker. I then explore, from the perspective of a parent, ways in which help and guidance from the universe can sustain our calling and duty as spiritual ambassadors.

THE CHILD AS TRUTH SPEAKER

One night as I was tucking Swan into bed, I kissed her and warmly said, "You are Mama's special daughter. You are my sweet, kind daughter." A voice from deep inside her responded slowly and deliberately, "You borrow me." The child is a teacher, as an emanation of the creator. The parent is guardian or spiritual ambassador showing the child the ways of humanity and the earth.

When a parent feels in need of spiritual direction, or clarification, the child may be the informant. The parent has the blessing of baring witness. By way of example, I share a story of an annunciation of a blessing through my youngest child, Lila.

For a several days, I had been thinking about my grandmother's sister, my Great-Aunt Fran, who had died about ten years before. As a child, I had spent considerable time with Great-Aunt Fran (who I called Aunt Fran). She had an uplifting energy, and a joyous, nearly laughing quality. She delighted in having a niece. Aunt Fran always looked pretty and fashionable, with scarves and necklaces wrapped around her neck. Her memory was coming to me right around the time I sensed that my daughters (then ages three and four) were entering a strong phase of archetypal identification with feminine beauty, symbolized through Aphrodite, or in their daily currency through Disney princesses. To mother my daughters, I sensed that I needed to encourage their own sense of beauty. After several days of reflection, but not speaking of my experience, I suddenly had the feeling that I needed to pay attention to Lila. Rather than giving her the usual space to play with her sister, I loitered within proximity.

A great gift from the creator then came through to us. Lila grabbed her brother's walkie-talkie and starting speaking loudly. "Hello, it's your Aunt Frannie (the name my aunt had used with family). Aunt Frannie is here." Lila continued, "I'm here to watch you. I'll stay here." I had never told Lila about my wonderful deceased aunt.

The child, being intimately connected with the universe, provides through her actions guidance for the family. Healing and revelation for each member of the family, as well as the family as a unit, come from adults listening to and integrating the raw message from the child. The message is targeted and crucial to the wellness and evolution of each person in the family.

Truly baring witness to the child prompts parents towards psychospiritual evolution. This corollary view of the child in family treatment suggests that the entire family must grow in order for the child to develop freely. I share here some of the ways in which the child, as teacher, has redirected treatment and brought healing to the family.

THE CHILD AS SPIRITUAL BAROMETER

Much suffering in families comes from the psycho-spiritual disruption of dishonesty between parents, or from the parents to the children. Dishonesty usually attempts to cover over a disavowal of a psycho-spiritual truth in the family. This abrogation of truth is held by the child.

The case of Nina vividly illustrates the child as a literal embodiment of parental deceit. Nina is a nine-year-old girl who presented for treatment rifled with extreme anxiety. Her symptoms were so acute that her body seemed stiff and hard and her posture was guarded. She barely spoke in school and had stifled social manner. Nina's eyes, however, revealed an active, intelligent mind, present in the moment. At times, it looked as if Nina were about to communicate, but then her mouth froze.

As usual in a case involving a child, the first diagnostic questions concern the conditions in which Nina lived. Nina shared that she lived with her mother and father, who had been married for about ten years, in an upper Manhattan area of New York City, where her father worked in a restaurant. I then spoke individually with her mother to discover that each year her father left the family for several months to travel to Egypt, where he secretly had a second wife and several children. Other than Nina's mother, the two families reportedly knew nothing of each other. Nina's mother insisted that I not disclose this information to Nina.

The next session, I asked Nina to draw a picture of her family. She drew herself, her mother, a space, and then her father. Then, in the bottom corner of the page, she drew some small figures. When asked who they were, she explained, "That's my father's other family in Egypt." This was not surprising. The child in her actions was already speaking the truth, including the fact that she had been silenced in her birthright of the child as truth-speaker.

The child, understood through her actions as well as her words, is always truthful. She has not severed her mind or her body from the immediacy of reality. While all people (including adults) are emanations from creation, the child has not yet lived in such a way as to distance herself from the innate connection to the presence of the creator. Nina had not converged on just any lie or problem within the family—Nina was silently screaming the way back to living truthfully.

The treatment was clearly not going to be about "telling" Nina the adult secret. Nina was telling the adults about the degradation of her mother, acts of deceit by her father, and a violation of the absolute value of family. Sadly, in this case the parents did not want to listen to their daughter. The parents rigidly sustained the life pattern they had established, and were not willing to respond to Nina's call. She could be affirmed only by the psychotherapist as not being crazy or socially odd, but as connected to a truth about love and disappointment around her father's love. Nina's experience of reality, the psycho-spiritual index of the ultimate reality, needed to be supported.

The child, an embodiment of truth, can redirect parents who are willing to hear. When parents are committed to healing, the child's message catalyzes the treatment. The case of eight-year-old Augusta radically differs from that of Nina because of the receptivity of her parents, Sara and Jordan, to change.

Sara was shocked upon learning of her husband's four-year extra-marital affair with a mutual friend. So hurt was she that she considered divorce, but expressed fear at the prospect of providing for their two young children. Underneath her sorrow, it seemed that much of her desire to stay actually resonated from an enduring love for her husband, despite the deceit and pain. After a few weeks passed, Sara expressed feeling utter rage and confusion at moments, followed by a hope that the family might stay together and that she might be able to forgive Jordan. Sara would say, "I never stopped loving Jordan, I am just so hurt." This wavering state of ambivalence continued for several months. The couple was stuck.

Then during a session, Sara started to cry. She told me, "Augusta heard us arguing in the night. The next morning she looked very upset and came to my room. 'Mommy, I heard you say that Daddy had sex with someone else. But I know that you only have sex with someone you love. Does Daddy love somebody else, other than us?'" Augusta's comment reflected back to Sara exactly where she was stuck. She looked in my eyes with clarity, "I don't know what to say to Augusta." Sara's lingering unanswered question was: "Do you love this other woman? Do you not truly love me?" Sara had yet to viscerally feel an answer to the question from Jordan.

When Augusta's question was identified as marking the parental impasse, Jordan heard it and responded by showing Sara, and the children, his love through his actions. Jordan transformed. He grew as a spouse and father to meet the call. He radically modified his professional schedule to be home for breakfast, cooked pancakes for the family, and starting playing games and reading to the children. Sara and Augusta increasing felt convinced of Jordan's presence and love. The affair clearly had sparked a painful family crisis; the opportunity was seized to deepen the love within the family. The family, guided by the wake-up call, was strengthened from the crisis. They shifted from just living together in one house to living with a heightened sense of family.

THE CHILD AS HEALER

The child's connection to the universe fills her with a sense of strength and compassion that can help to heal the family. It is crucial that this natural endowment not be mistaken as grounds for "parenti-fying" the child, forcing the child into the ongoing role of emotional caretaker or flooding the child with information that is not necessary for her understanding of the current moment. Rather, I am suggesting that the child often is able to witness the truth about her pertinent im-mediate world, and to provide acceptance, healing love, and support for her family. In even the worst family situations, I am perpetually surprised by the strength and tenderness children exhibit around the suffering adults. The case of Iliana taught me a lesson on the fortitude of children and their capacity to heal.

Iliana was an eleven-year-old girl from a Latin American family. She lived with her mother and grandmother in a predominantly Latin neighborhood in upper Manhattan, a walk from the hospital where I was seeing patients. Her mother was in treatment for substance abuse, had enormous difficulty seeing beyond her own needs, and paid little attention to her daughter. Iliana's grandmother presented as highly guarded, and was extremely rigid and authoritarian as the primary parent of Iliana. Iliana seemed to be emotionally choking. She was required to come home immediately after school. Each day she entered the apartment, went into her room, and shut the door until dinner. She felt alienated and starved for affection by her emotionally cut-off grandmother. Yet, there was a strong spirit in Iliana, as she had brought herself to treatment and was seeking a way for the family to get better. She had not chosen to sneak around the harsh, restrictive rules and willy-nilly authoritarianism of her grandmother.

After some work, Iliana was able to identify that her grandmother was most rigid and stifling around Iliana's interaction with boys. Speaking to boys was considered wrong, dangerous, and promiscuous. When her school hosted an all-school dance, Iliana was the only girl in her class not permitted to attend. Iliana was extremely disappointed and asked her grandmother to reconsider. After a series of negotiations with her grandmother, and council from her extended family, she was allowed to attend the dance only if her older male cousin chaperoned. Iliana felt a stifling of her natural emerging interest in boys.

Iliana was enraged by the restrictions binding her life, mainly because the limitations around boys did not make sense to her. She had come to treatment for liberation, to lift her depression, and to make sense of her very confused relationship with her grandmother. After getting permission from the grandmother, I chose to share with Iliana that her grandmother might have strong feelings about dating young men because she had survived ongoing sexual abuse. Iliana's response was one of sadness, followed by a very strong sense of com-passion. She was not floored. Now everything made more sense. The confusion of her life came into perspective. Iliana could understand her grandmother's anxiety about her being with boys. Iliana's understanding and compassion impacted her grandmother. Iliana was much warmer toward Grandma. Grandma seemed somewhat less burdened, more understood, and ultimately softer to Iliana. Occasionally Grandma even started to give Iliana hugs. Iliana quickly felt a stronger love for her grandmother, and seemed significantly less depressed.

Grandma's unanswered suffering of many years was met by Iliana's compassion. The child's pure love of family is undaunted by social constructions such as shame or stigma. Children have a deep reservoir of healing love, a natural sense of acceptance of the people they love. For the burdened adult and the confused child, working in honesty in the moment allows the true love to flow.

THE CHILD'S NON-EGOCENTRIC PERSPECTIVE

Moments before the school day started, a rambunctious boy in Swan's class, who we shall call Bart, ran up to Swan to deliver an unprovoked, swift punch. Bart had come a long way out of his path, right as the classroom door started to open. His mother, focused on the needs of a new baby, came over afterward to urge "no hitting." Nearly the identical scenario played the next school day, and then again for several days after school. I first spoke to Bart's mother and then with the teacher urging her to watch the children and to address the no-hitting rule. I explained that I felt concerned that my daughter would not feel safe going to school or think that being hit was not viewed as a problem.

The scenario did not improve. Day after day, Bart waited with exquisite patience until the adults turned their heads, and then ran up to my daughter and punched her. I made clear to Swan that it was wrong for Bart to hit her. I repeatedly discussed the distressing situation with my spouse, who suggested that gentle Swan hit Bart back and shout, "Never hit me again!" I took my spouses' plan as a symbolic fantasy of our frustration, anger, and helpless feelings around the unmonitored actions of a three-year-old boy.

Then, one day, Swan worked it out by herself. Joyful Swan was in the backseat of our car, riding to school, excited for her new day. All of sudden, in a gentle voice, she explained, "Sweet little Bart, he's just a young boy, and I am teaching him not to hit." I was astonished by her perspective. I whipped my head around, "Yes, Swan, you are a kind teacher of love." Swan (who, after all, was the one being hit) had been the one to find clarity from a non-egocentric perspective. Closer to the truth of the creator, Swan did not sink into a tit-for-tat stance, but rather saw herself and the nature of her peers as fundamentally loving. Swan's non-egocentric perspective instructed me on how to understand some forms of aggression.

I had failed to solve the problem through an appeal to authority to Bart's parent and the teacher. Swan, in a stance of love, saw the boy as a growing soul. She saw herself as a teacher. Swan's understanding proved to hold more traction. Within a week of her insight, I spotted Bart running across the playground, right up to Swan, for a big hug.

THE UNIVERSE AS PARENTING GUIDE

The story of the sacrifice of Isaac has been deeply instructive to me around the imperative of faith in parenthood. Abraham fully gave the life of his only son over to G-d, trusting in the goodness and all power-fulness of G-d. I find it far easier to put faith ahead of fear for myself than for my children. As a mother, I often seek to loosen protective control of my children and turn over their well-being to the creator. In my heart, I believe it is the only way that my children can thrive.

Through this stance, I find the best parenting instruction comes from the universe. Through SAP with parents, I have the opportunity to en-courage clients to have faith in their spiritual sensibilities and trust their souls on this most important calling. The parenting approach that best supports a specific child, within a specific challenge, hardly seems formulaic. Allowing parents to be inspired by the direction of the crea-tor opens up limitless possibility for a family. Fashioning parenting support from a stance of spiritual awareness fosters a parenting con-sciousness more than a rigid parenting style that reflects the inter-mingled spiritual paths of parent and child.

SUPPORTING THE CHILD'S INNATE SPIRITUAL AWARENESS

SAP hosts the reigniting of awareness. However, some children are raised by parents, clergy, or community members to be aware of the vital spiritual reality that surrounds us. Parents can encourage children to listen to the universe, and to regard this relationship as the lead foot in their jour-ney. As ambassadors of the creator, parents are the guardians of the spirit-ual development in their children. This does not mean that parents need to hold answers or be great sages. The spiritual journey of the child gains support if the parent adapts a consciousness that welcomes, respects, and hosts the spiritual experience and inchoate spiritual growth of the child.

The chief assumption of spiritual awareness is that every bit of the universe resonates with being alive, loving, and guiding. This seems evident to the young child. The young child shows us through awe, play, and explanation of her experience that our natural surroundings are alive and feeling, and teaching. This is as inherent and natural to the child as the ability to smell or hear rhythm in music. By way of illustration, I share with you a story of Isaiah, my oldest child, who spent the first ten months of his life in a Russian orphanage.

Despite excellent care and commitment in the orphanage, the high ratio of children to providers precluded the feasibility of babies leaving the orphanage to go on walks or sit outside. Consequently, our son had never seen a world beyond the walls of the orphanage when suddenly we arrived one day to take him home. Isaiah appeared absolutely faithful and trusting when we scooped him up from his familiar walls to start the long journey back to the United States. Everything was thrilling: "Dah! Dah!" he joyously yelled through the airports of Europe on the way home. He was delighted by the fellow passengers on the flight, rather than scared or distrustful. He ate the food I fed to him, never fearing he would be poisoned. The vast world was his friend and was good.

Still Isaiah had seen nearly nothing of the outdoors. No trees, hills, or sunsets. At last, once home in our backyard, we set Isaiah by the banks of a river. The bright sun sparkled on the current. For the first time as a parent, I experienced that which I had read and inferred through science. Isaiah looked up from the river with an expression of spiritual awe. His face was purely numinous. Every day that followed that summer, for two months, Isaiah splashed on the near bank of the river. Then for the next three years, Isaiah played every day along the banks of the river. At age four years, he swam in the summer, dropped leaves and sticks in the autumn, and even played along the banks in a Connecticut February to test the ice.

Then one summer day by the river, Isaiah got a bee sting, which was surprising and confusing to him. He was truly shocked and confused that a bee would string him. I could sense in his retreat indoors that he was processing the event. After a few hours Isaiah and I took a walk outside, "Mommy, if a bee stings Buddha, what does Buddha do?" I had never taught Isaiah about the stories of Buddha. (He had seen only a sculpture of Buddha to learn his name.) I was unprepared to answer Isaiah's question, but sensed it might have been asked rhetorically. My little son, I thought, born with a soul so wise, if either of us knows, it would surely be you. "Isaiah, if a bee stings Buddha, what does Buddha do?" He nodded resolute, tranquil and sure, "Nothing. If a bee stings Buddha he does nothing." In his eyes was the sparkle present in his first look at the river.

Isaiah knew more about the bee and Buddha then did I, perhaps in general and certainly at the moment. I do not need to know answers to support the child's spiritual experience and wisdom. I just need to regard the child's lived spiritual reality as powerful, meaningful, and true. I can ask the child questions. I can say I do not know but that the matter is of utmost value. I can try to explore the question using my own inner spiritual connection to the universe.

NATURE AND SPIRITUALITY IN CHILDREN

A number of outdoor oriented "at risk youth" interventions tacitly support spiritual awareness through encouraging the child or teen to dialogue with nature. Programs held at nature centers, particularly preschools and after-school programs, support the child's awareness of the consciousness of animals and plants in nature.

Isaiah, like just about every child to have read the classic children's book *Make Way for Ducklings*, identifies with the baby ducks. When the duck family comes down the river each spring, we welcome the ducks as we would appreciate infants born to humans "welcome loving ducks, we love your new babies." All creations of nature are alive, yet naturally not all hold as central human well-being. If the geese (who leave enormous amounts of dung on the children's play area) come down the river, with fluffy babies, we say "we love you loving geese, and new babies. We respect that you need a home, but this area of land is where our children play." And when we call the exterminator to clear out a very dangerous wasps nest under the picnic bench, we prayed "we are sorry wasps, but we must protect the family. Dear God, we are sorry to have to hurt your baby wasps."

Several Native American tribes speak of all living beings in nature as "all my relations." It is clear to many Native Americans that animals and plants are emanations of the living, guiding universe, and teach and endow us with understanding. Stories and myths are told to children to teach them the wisdom of their natural relations, and to awaken their own like endowment. I once had a Cherokee graduate student, a wonderful teacher herself, who explained to our class, "When I get into a jam, I think what would the fox or the turtle do here." She went on to explain, "This is because as a child I heard many myths that taught me how these animals think and act." The child naturally seeks to be like a duck, goose, or wasp to understand these great powers and propensities within us. The child wants to explore her goose-likeness. Child's play is important spiritual work. Properly honored, child's play can fortify our spiritual path the rest of our lives.

CONCLUSION

Children naturally ignite my awe for creation. A child lives in the presence of the creator, offering adults and family a chance for healing and growth. Parenthood holds a sacred call to witness the child's spiritual wisdom and support the child's learning—while they are still very good at inductively and intuitively figuring out the ways of the universe. The wisdom of the child can be honored by listening.

Creation is present in the child. Creation guides us as parents. Spiritual awareness, as a sustained consciousness of dialogue with the universe, is all I have to share with my family and those families who give me the honor me of sharing their experience.

NOTES

1. Sperry and Shafranske, 2005.
2. Richards and Bergin, 2004.

3. Paloutzian and Park, 2005.
4. Roehlkepartain, Ebstyne, King, Wagener, and Benson, 2006.
5. Kendler, Gardner, and Prescott, 322–329.
6. Miller and Athan, 17–35.
7. Miller, 2005.

BIBLIOGRAPHY

Kendler, Kenneth S., Charles. O. Gardner, and Carol. A Prescott. "Religion, Psychopathology, and Substance Use and Abuse: A Multimeasure, Genetic-Epidemiological Study." *American Journal of Psychiatry* 154 (1997): 322–329.

Miller, Lisa. *Spiritual Awareness Psychotherapy*. DVD. Hosted by Jon Carlson. Washington, DC: American Psychological Association, 2005.

Miller, Lisa, and Aurelie Athan. "Spiritual Awareness Pedagogy." *International Journal of Children's Spirituality* 12 (2007): 17–35.

Paloutzian, Raymond F., and Crystal L. Park, eds. *Handbook of the Psychology of Religion and Spirituality*. New York: Guilford Press, 2005.

Richards, P. Scott, and Allen E. Bergin, eds. *Casebook for a Spiritual Strategy in Counseling and Psychotherapy*. Washington, DC: American Psychological Association, 2004.

Roehlkepartain, Eugene C., Pamela Ebstyne King, Linda Wagener, and Peter L. Benson, eds. *The Handbook of Spiritual Development in Childhood and Adolescence*. Thousand Oaks, CA: Sage Publications, 2006.

Sperry, Len, and Edward P. Shafranske, eds. *Spiritually Oriented Psychotherapy*. Washington, DC: American Psychological Association, 2005.

Chapter 19

Strange Attractors or Hand of God: A Spiritual Journey

Lee Richmond

"Spiritus," meaning to animate or to enliven, is the root of the word "spirituality." Spirituality comes from within. It is an awareness of the connection between that which is held dearest and best within the self to that which is believed to be the greatest in universe. It is a personal experience, usually associated with reverence and awe. Others have defined spirituality in many ways, and some connect it to religion. For me, however, there is a distinct difference between spirituality and religion. People may practice religion, but religion is a cultural phenomenon that is taught: its origin is outside of the person. It is associated to a greater or lesser degree with ritual. The defining characteristic of spirituality is connection; it is the recognition of that connection between the self and the all that animates, gives meaning, and enlivens.

Interested in what enlivens or animates women, two colleagues and I decided to ask them. We listened to their answers and their stories. The result was the book, *What Brings You to Life: Awakening Women's Spiritual Essence.*[1] In the process of hearing the stories of others, I began to ask myself about my own story and answer the question: "What is it that enlivens me, and what is my own spiritual essence?"

Common answers came quickly enough. My children and grandchildren bring me to life, as does my work as a professor and a counseling psychologist. Good theater, good music, and the seashore enliven me. But, there is more. The roots of my spirituality lay deeper than the things I choose to enjoy and those to which I resonate. I asked myself what personally attracts me to a theory called constructivism, a theory about how we come to know, and how I associate it with the social construction of career. I pondered my fascination with what is commonly called "the new science," which involves complexity theory and a calculus that I have never formally studied. Are there links, I wondered, between chaos theory, mystical theology, and existential psychology? And, why have I tried to apply what knowledge I have of these things to career development, even to the point of writing articles and books about them, when my original interests and college majors were English literature and history? How is it that these seemingly disparate things link to my spirituality and my personal career path. The answer lay in my story and in my love of story, a love that blossomed when I was very young.

I was born of second-generation immigrant Jewish parents whose own parents migrated from Eastern Europe shortly after the turn of the last century. My maternal grandfather, prior to his journey in steerage to America, had lived not far from the Freud house in a Jewish ghetto-ized section of Vienna. From his street corner he could see the horse-drawn carriages entering and exiting the Palais Esterházy, and it was there that he vowed that once in America, he would have such a surrey. Acquiring the surrey did not come easily, and by the time it eventually did arrive, it was a motorized Buick automobile. Entering the United States as a poor tailor, and marrying a Jewish peasant woman from Russia, he emerged from World War I a manufacturer of men's pants, having supplied the U.S. Army with more than few. He also founded a synagogue to which I was dutifully sent, to both Hebrew school and Saturday services for children.

It would be a lie if I said I enjoyed Hebrew school; in fact, I hated it! But I loved children's services on Saturdays. Every week a *rebbe* would come to tell us stories, and what wonderful stories they were! I did not know then that what I was hearing were adaptations of the Tevye stories of the now-famous Yiddish writer Shalom (Rabinovitch) Aleichem. I did not know that "Dos Vintishfinger" ("The Magic Ring"), "Fishke der Krumer" ("Fishke the Lame") and "Dos Kleyne Mentshele" ("The Little Man") were stories originally written by Mendele Mokher Sefarim, now called "the grandfather of Yiddish literature." I did not know that "Bontshe Shvayg" ("Bontche the Silent"), a story of a humble man who asked God only for a warm roll with butter every morning when he could have had anything in the world that he wanted, was a satire. Nor did I know the rebbe and the Litvak in "Oyb Nit Hekher" ("If Not Higher"), my favorite story of a sainted man and a fool, written by the great I. L. Peretz, was also satire.[2] A child, I took the tales as reality. I found a home in the *stetl* (a small townlet; a tiny village in Poland where Jews lived) of story, in the European pale of Jewish settlement, just as my grandparents, both maternal and paternal, had found new homes in America.

What is interesting to me now is that the entertaining stories I had heard so frequently, told to us children for entertainment, moral messages, development of conscience, and spiritual growth, were also tales of social construction. They portrayed Jewish community life and values with simplicity and honesty, but they also said that life is what you make of it. In simple language, they taught that we construct our world as we traverse it, and that *how* we construct our lives is important. This message became clear when I reached my teen years and began to create a different world for myself. It started when I began to question why each morning in prayer, I thanked God for making me as I am (female), when the boys in the family were thanking God for not making them women. It was then that I wondered why Jews were grateful that we were not like "the nations of the world." I missed the true intention of those words, and did not recognize that, in the Jewish mind, the words recalled one's Jewish existence is a life lived in covenant with God, a call to holiness, and an ethical way of treating one's fellow human beings. As a result of my misunderstanding, I began to see how my non-Jewish, public school classmates lived. They were, of course, people of the "nations of the world," and I found their ways not to be so bad.

As a teenager I became involved in social-justice activities, civil rights, and women's rights, and moved both within and without the Jewish community. I was no longer in Hebrew school, nor did I attend services for children on Saturday, but the stories had taken root and I carried them inside me to my new communities. One was made up of young people from a local Methodist church, who, like some Jewish kids in my high school, thought that the segregation then practiced in Baltimore was wrong. Along with a few other Jewish friends, I formed a club with some Methodist and Episcopalian kids. More than few adults were impressed with our ecumenism and with our stated purpose of doing community service. As a group we decided one day to do what we thought was a good work. We rented a room in a hall for a social function, and invited some local African American young people to join us. We wanted to integrate what was then a segregated hall. The owners of the room that we had rented were unaware of our plan. On the night of the party, the managers of the hall saw what was happening and called the police. We did not cease and go home. That night, almost fifty teens spent some time in jail. Outwardly, we wore our trip to the "clinker" like a badge of honor, but inside we were scared stiff. While behind bars, I heard some new stories about a guy named Jesus. According to the gentile kids, He, like us, did things to right the wrongs of his day. He even shared our incarceration experience. After hearing that story, I got interested in different faiths and decided to learn about them. The various religions blended so well for me that I began to see only similarities and not differences. However, the differences were made clear to me in college. Still an activist, I told my jailhouse story to a Christian friend and told her that I thought that by engaging in civil-rights struggles and feminist activism, young people were saving the world. Upon hearing this, my Christian friend told me that saving the world had already been accomplished. At that moment I saw some very real differences between the faith of my ancestors and that of my friend.

In college I began to study world religions in earnest, and both similarities and differences became more evident. The more I studied the more interested but more secular I became, yet my childhood stories continued to travel with me. I told them in the girls' Catholic high school where, upon graduation, I was employed to teach English and world history. To this day I am not certain that the good sisters who hired me trusted me to teach the history of the rise of Christianity, but I know that they trusted me less when the girls from the glee club quit the chorus and joined my folk music group. This occurred during the 1960s. The Age of Aquarius had dawned and sex and drugs had worked their way even into private religious schools. The girls began to confide their problems to me, the youngest teacher in the school, and I decided that it was in my best interest and theirs to get a master's degree in counseling. The effects of the Aquarian age served as a strange attractor that pulled me out of my routine as an English and history teacher and set me on a new trajectory, casting me into the world of psychology, with my PhD to come later.

I stayed at the Catholic school for only two years. During that time I learned that a thousand girls sinking to their knees in unity when a bell rang at noon was the norm. The Angelus bell was a call to prayer and not a warning as I first thought. I also learned that wearing strapless gowns to proms could get girls expelled. Vocational guidance meant helping girls decide which religious order to enter.

Elsewhere in the city there were serious problems involving racial tensions, even race riots. So, at the end of two years I packed my book bag and headed for where the action was: an inner-city middle school. By then I was a counselor and I thought that I could be of help. However, nothing I learned in graduate school prepared me for my inner-city experience. As luck, serendipity, happenstance, or the hand of God would have it, another strange attractor appeared. Through an experimental program with the Baltimore city public schools, the Pediatric Psychiatry Department of the Johns Hopkins University offered to train a handful of counselors to work with some really tough issues like those that the young people in "my" middle school had to handle. The attraction was the opportunity to acquire training. Despite long hours and double-time work, I grabbed it. From truly great teachers I learned about "doing therapy" with kids, and I wanted to know even more. A job opened up at a local community college. I could teach there and attend the University of Maryland. Since I could teach in the day and at night, and also attend graduate school in the day and night, I figured that I could work out a full-time schedule that would not be questioned. I was right. I could earn a PhD.

I taught psychology at the community college to first- and second-year students. While there, I designed a program for older women returning to college, then one for disabled people. My dissertation was a study of the lives of the women who came back to school. The program for the disabled, which was modeled on the one for women, exists to this day. As a result of these successes, I received several grants to design other programs that would be of community service and effect organizational change. I began to teach them part time at the continuing studies division of Hopkins, then called the Evening College. Soon I was offered a full-time position there. I took it on the condition that I could teach in their school-counseling program. My community college granted a year's leave of absence. I stayed at Hopkins for ten years, eventually directing their graduate program in school counseling and rising from assistant to full professor.

As program director, I was able to hire part-time faculty. One person that I hired to teach career development was a friend from my community college days. An unforgettable character, master teacher, and expert career counselor, Ray Ziegler died one night in the middle of the semester. I did not know it until someone called me the next morning asking me to teach Ray's course. When I asked why, he said, "Didn't you know? Ray died last night!" I was stunned. All that I could reply was that I already had a teacher. "Who?" the caller asked. "Me," I said. I could not think of giving my good friend's course to a chance caller, or anyone else for that matter. Such was my entry into the field of career counseling, one that I had never particularly liked. Was it the hand of God, serendipity, or a strange attraction that caused this change? I knew only that once again I was on a new trajectory that would affect the rest of my life.

I do not know whether I thought of the biblical story of Ruth at that time, but Ruth is a good metaphor for how I experienced my connection between myself and the universe. Like her, I was to enter a "land" where I had never been, learn a new discipline, and have no idea where it would take me. Ruth embraced her future out of love for Naomi, I out of respect for Ray, but what lay ahead for me was dark, and the connection with what had been before felt broken. I did not know at the time that I was embarking on the journey that would take me to the place where I am now.

Much has happened since then. My newfound practice of teaching career counseling led me to the National Career Development Association and the American Counseling Association. In later years I was to become president of each. Through my ties to professional associations, I met David Tiedeman,[3] whose interest was emergent process theory. Mark Savickas has written the following about Tiedeman in *Career*

Development Quarterly: "Tiedeman adopted the systems concept from physics, believing that self-organization reflects the inherent creativity of autonomous human beings adapting to changing environments. The self organization becomes increasingly complex as the whole organizes the parts."[4] David and his wife Anna introduced me to what is commonly called new science, complexity theory, and taught me of its usefulness in career counseling and career theory. It happened when I signed up to attend the 1982 Conference to Advance Career that the Tiedemans organized at the University of Southern California. Once again it was happenstance, a drawing of straws by Anna, a theorist in her own right, that made me her roommate for three days. During which time, unbeknownst to me, another new path was being set.

My relationship with David and Anna was my introduction to process theory (emergence), to complexity theory, and to the link between ideas from new science, postmodern philosophy, and career development. This link has been verified to me by personal experience and is at the base of my spiritual existence today. All things are connected in a purposeful universe.

Life-as-career is what Anna and David were teaching at the time. Many of their ideas were generated in a postmodern philosophy that says that people are self-organizing systems and can adapt to the conditions in which they find themselves, or change those conditions based on a perception of purpose. Purposeful action comes from within, and is executed as we respond to "signals" from the universe. All things are connected. Recognizing this connection, Anna and David had a saying: "Life Works."

As I thought about these things I recognized that how life works is more than happenstance. All things really are connected, and although the links are sometimes hard to see, we do get nudges from the universe to pull us in the direction of awareness. New science calls these nudges strange attractors. Religion would be more likely to dub them the hand of God. My spirituality existed solely in the recognition that these exist.

It has been the presence of strange attractors that has led me to edit and write books and inventories with Dr. Deborah Bloch[5] and Dr. Carole A. Rayburn.[6] Dr. Rayburn and I developed instruments to measure religion and spirituality and wrote articles about our findings to consult with the maintenance leadership development program for the U.S. Postal Service and to introduce a career development facilitator program in Japan. These are disparate activities, but linked in my life in a network that has connected everything. My recognition of this link is what has held my life together. I can connect these activities to a strand that defines me, to a life that continues to be created as I live it. I recognize that, as the strands are linked to me and define my life, my duty is to live in connection with all of life. The ability to change direction, pull together diverse activities, and open myself to new experiences is at the core of my spirituality. It was given to me as life was given to me, and I have the ability to bring energy to order when I acknowledge this.

Constructivism as a philosophy tells us that by reflecting upon experience, we construct our understanding of the world. Human beings are complex, adaptive systems that can respond to turbulent events sometimes called strange attractors. Many people have noted that strange attractors have jettisoned them on new pathways and links that have somehow emerged to connect all events in their lives. Jane Fonda is such a person. I have never met her, but I feel like I know her through her memoir, *My Life So Far*. She describes the myriad events that constitute her life: "Sometimes I feel as though I have a magnet on my skin and when I walk though the world, the relevant input that I need for my journey jumps out from the hurly-burly and speaks to me."[7] In simple English, Ms. Fonda has described how both physicists and mystics explain the workings of the universe.

The October 18, 2007, issue of *Newsweek* magazine had women as its theme. The cover story examined the issue of whether powerful women lead differently than men. The stories told are of CEOs, movie stars, sports figures, TV moguls, and political figures. Challenges, problem solving, and overcoming obstacles mark each woman's story, but what is more interesting is the underlying sense of connectedness and purpose in their lives. Maria Shriver wrote about her journey from public person in her own right to becoming California's First Lady. In speaking about her transformation from one to the other, she said: "I now understand that true power has little to do with what is written on your resume. It is about being true to yourself and finding your own path in the world ... through your life experiences and knowing who you are." She further stated: "I feel that I will always be a work in progress ... we have to give ourselves permission to grow, evolve, and change."[8] In Maria Shriver's case it was her husband's election to governor, the strange attractor, causing her to go on a new path. However, it is her own openness to change, her talents, and her willingness to recognize her connection to others that allows her to tell her story and express her feminine spirituality.

Shirley Franklin, mayor of Atlanta, wanted to be a ballerina as a child. She told *Newsweek* that she was surprised to find herself in politics, especially since she is shy. She called her journey from a private to a public life a spiritual one.[9] Once again, the fusion of very different activities resulted in a future that she did not foresee.

I could not know when I prepared to be a high school English and/or history teacher that I would later be a psychologist, nor could I anticipate a specialty in career development. If I had dreamed of becoming a college professor, I would not have included consulting for the postal service or working in Japan. I would not have imagined developing assessment instruments with Dr. Rayburn or being the grandmother of eleven children. Yet these are some of the things that have defined my life, have enlivened me, and become a part of my spiritual being.

A mark of feminine spirituality as related to women's career patterns is the ability and inclination to pull things together, turn inner work into outer work, and thus transform mystery into meaning. Powerful metaphors can be used to describe this process. Some compare the journeys of women, where career involves work, learning, leisure, and family, to biblical passages that describe the journey of the Israelites though the desert, or, reminiscent of Paul's sea voyages, fighting the shoals of discontent.

A rather mysterious and meaningful part of my personal path has been my involvement with Roman Catholicism. I have taught in Catholic high schools and colleges, been cared for in Catholic hospitals, been housed in convents, and befriended and nurtured a Roman Catholic nun. All of this may have been serendipitous happenstance, but there has been too much synchronicity or serendipity involved for me not to think that Roman Catholicism has been another strange attractor. I wonder if the hand of God was a part of at least some of it.

For example, as a new mother, married less than two years to a serviceman, I took my baby to Alaska to join my husband who was stationed there. In those days, it took twelve hours to travel from the East Coast to the West Coast and another few hours to get from Seattle to Juneau by seaplane. From Juneau, I had to take a puddle-jumper to Skagway, where my husband staffed the Alaska Communication System. The problem was that a blizzard had hit Juneau, and no planes could fly out after I landed.

I arrived in Juneau with only one bottle left for a three-month-old, bottle-fed infant. I was stranded, and at first did not know what to do. Luckily, I was able to get the last taxi out of the airport. I asked the driver to take me to a hospital, figuring I could get formula and a warm bed for my baby there. The cab driver told me that there were two hospitals in town, a military one and a Catholic one. Remembering the Jesus stories that I had been told, I thought the Catholic hospital would not turn away a young mother and her child. I asked to be taken to the Catholic hospital. The cab left me off at an old building with a statue in front. Behind the statue was a door with a bell. I rang it, and a woman in a long black dress and black-and-white headpiece answered the call. She must have seen both desperation and exhaustion in my face, for she invited me in and took the baby from my arms. She found food for both of us, a bed for me, and a bassinette for the infant. The blizzard lasted for five days. The sisters who ran the hospital asked nothing of me, and gave me rest and respite while it snowed. During that time, there was only one other person in the hospital, a wounded Native American. The nuns had plenty of time to answer my questions about their order and special mission. They also found time to care for and play with my child.

I learned that the sisters had come from Canada. They were the sisters of Sainte Anne de Beaupré. They told me they were named for Anne, the mother of Mary, and they told me about a shrine, known for healing, that existed in Beaupré, Quebec.[10] When the snow subsided on the fifth day, the sisters contacted a nurse pilot with a two-passenger plane that would transport my baby and me to Skagway. Years later, when I worked as a freelance writer, I wrote about the experience I had with the sisters of St. Anne. It was my first story published. Titled "Black and White Angels," it appeared in the *Annals of St. Anne de Beaupré*,[11] a small Catholic publication with a worldwide circulation. Although I never saw the sisters again, I visited the shrine years later, and in the interim received letters of thanks from people the world over for telling the story of the kindness of a handful of Catholic nuns who took in a wandering Jewish mother and her child.

It was the story of the nuns that started me on a publishing career, but that is not the point of the story. The point is the chain of events. Was it all chance, the blizzard, the virtually empty hospital, the sisters' stories, my discovery of the *Annals*, the publication of my story, and a later trip to the shrine to accompany a Catholic friend whose child was critically ill and who survived? Was my early encounter with the sisters of Saint Anne the catalyst that caused me to respond to the strange attractors that jettisoned me into Catholic higher education? And was all of this somehow also connected to other events of my life that I have related in this chapter? As my friend Ray Ziegler used to say, "There are connected strands like themes in one's life that sing the story of who one is and how one can best use the time one is given on earth."

Whether we call it universe process theory, complexity theory, chaos theory, or new science, all tell us that we are looking not at chance but at emergence and connection when we consider what causes things. Causality is not linear. Complex systems can produce simple things, and simple things can produce complex effects. This is complexity, non-linearity, the laws of which hold universally.[12]

In David Aaron's book *Seeing God: Ten Life-Changing Lessons of the Kabbalah*,[13] he tells many tales not unlike those that I heard in my youth from my rebbe. In a section entitled "Expect the Unexpected," Rabbi Aaron uses parable to illustrate how dangerous it can be to resist new ways of being and cling to old ideas. The story he tells is of a dove being harassed by a lion. Frightened, the dove prayed to God for help. The next morning the dove discovered that God had given her something new: wings!

When the dove saw the lion, she was no longer afraid. She trusted that God's gift would protect her and even taunted the lion into chasing her. Shortly after the chase began, the dove tripped over her wings and fell. The lion pounced on her and ate her. In heaven, the angry bird confronted God, for she believed God had deceived her. In response, God called the dove foolish. Her creator had given her wings with which to fly, and she had used them only to run.

Are there links, I wondered, between chaos theory, mystical theology, and existential psychology? And why have I tried to apply my knowledge of these things to career development, even to the point of writing articles and books, when my original interests were English literature and history? Perhaps because I have written my own history about how these seemingly disparate things somehow have become my spirituality and my personal career development. At least I alluded to an answer that lay in my story and in my love of story. It is a love that blossomed when I was very young.

NOTES

1. Eanes, Richmond, and Link, 1.
2. All stories mentioned can be found either under the title or the author's name.
3. Tiedeman is a noted and widely published career theorist.
4. Savickas, in press.
5. Bloch and Richmond, 1997, 1998.
6. See Chapter 2 for clarification of our work together.
7. Fonda, 284.
8. Shriver, in Kantrowitz, *Newsweek*, 70.
9. Franklin, in Kantrowitz, *Newsweek*, 58.
10. The basilica of Saint Anne de Beaupré is widely known to be a place of healing.
11. *The Annals* are still published by the Redemptorist priests at the shrine.
12. Gleick.
13. Aaron, 38–39.

BIBLIOGRAPHY

Aaron, David. *Seeing God: Ten Life-Changing Lessons of the Kaballah*. New York: Tarcher, 2001.
Bloch, Deborah P., and Lee Richmond. *Connections between Spirit and Work*. Palo Alto, CA: Davies-Black, 1997.
Bloch, Deborah P., and Lee Richmond. *Soulwork: Finding the Work You Love, Loving the Work You Have*. Palo Alto, CA: Davies-Black, 1998.
Eanes, Beverly E., Lee Richmond, and Jean Link. *What Brings You to Life: Awakening Women's Spiritual Essence*. Mahwah, NJ: Paulist Press, 2001.
Fonda, Jane. *My Life So Far*. New York: Random House, 2005.
Gleick, James. *Chaos: Making a New Science*. New York: Penguin Books, 1988.
Kantrowitz, B. "In All Their Glory." *Newsweek*. October 15, 2007, 47–79. http://www.newsweek.com/id/42526.
Savickas, Mark L. "Becoming a Constructivist." *Career Development Quarterly*, 2008.

Chapter 20

Voicing My Own Gospel: Stories of Spirituality from Young Women

Guerda Nicolas
Angela M. DeSilva
Maria Coutinho
Kimberly Prater

Spirituality plays an important role in the lives of people of all ages and ethnic backgrounds. However, individual and personal experiences of spirituality are rarely the focus of discussion, and there is even less information about the spiritual experiences of young women. We wrote this chapter to give voice to young women's individual spirituality by providing a description of our personal experiences with spirituality as well as those of a diverse group of young women.

OUR OWN REFLECTIONS ON SPIRITUALITY

Who Are We?

In addition to being students, teachers, researchers, and clinicians, we are each spiritual women. We are diverse with respect to age (twenty-two, twenty-six, thirty-one, and forty years old, with an average age of about thirty years) and ethnicity (White American, Italian American, Cape Verdean, and Haitian). We have had different life experiences that have shaped our views of life and ourselves.

Our Spiritual Experiences

We each embrace our spirituality and use it as a source of strength in our daily lives. Collectively, we view spirituality, or spiritual

connection, as an individual experience, one that is difficult to explain
yet powerful in shaping who we are. We believe that spirituality is
something that people can experience in conjunction with or separate
from religion. For us, it is predominantly defined by a feeling, connection, and belief in something higher than ourselves. Despite some similarities in how we view spirituality, we each use it differently in our
daily lives. The following are our reflections on spirituality in our lives.

Raised as a Roman Catholic, I went to church with my family mainly on
major holidays. Sometimes, when my mom became inspired, we would
attend services on Sunday mornings. Church for me was more a familial
duty than a religious one. I went as an act of faith and devotion to my
mother, not to Catholicism. It was not until I was twenty years old, when
my boyfriend Ryan lost his long and difficult battle with cancer, that I
really had to think about and even question what was supposed to be
my religiosity. Throughout the process of mourning Ryan, I never found
a source of strength or comfort in my religion (which to me entails practicing [for example, attending church] from a particular and structured
faith) as so many people (including my mother) said I would. However,
shortly after Ryan had been buried, I experienced an overwhelming sense
of peace and comfort. Yes, the sadness and the longing were still there,
but somehow I felt that everything was going to be OK. The desperation
and hopelessness were gone because I suddenly felt a very deep sense of
connection with Ryan—with the spirit of Ryan. I knew he was in a better
place where he would watch over me (and everyone he loved) and help
me to do good in the world. This was the first time in my life that I ever
felt a sense of *spirituality*—a sense of connection with people and things
beyond my life on earth. Today, my spirituality (which largely manifests
itself as a feeling of connection to Ryan and God) gives me the strength I
need to help myself and others cope with pain, suffering, and injustice in
the world. Religion and spirituality are very different to me. It is my spirituality, not my religiosity, which helps me to understand the world and
to feel a degree of peace and completeness in times of despair (White
woman and student).

Religion has always been an integral part of my life. Not only because
I am from a culture where we always respond to greetings such as
"How are you?" with *"Bien, grâce à Dieu"* (fine, thank the lord), but as a
Haitian family, we strongly believed that God is the almighty and creator
of all things and that trusting in him was necessary for survival. Our
beliefs were tested when, at the age of two, I was with my grandmother
in the kitchen and she accidentally dropped a pot of soup on me that
resulted in first- and second-degree burns all over my body. Despite the
doctors' negative prognosis, I live to tell this story today. My family
strongly believes that their faith in God healed me and prepared me for
my journey in life. Upon reflection, it is worth noting that although I was
actively involved in the church, it was not until my twenties that I began
to have a deeper understanding and sense of spirituality in my life. In
my late teens, I began questioning everything connected to my religion,

but despite the many criticisms I had about my religion, my faith and belief in a higher power never swayed. This is not to say that my spiritual self has not been challenged. I have had incidents of near-death experiences, extreme poverty, and adjustment to changes that have forced me to evaluate my own beliefs and my connection to God. Nevertheless, I knew and continue to believe that there is a force greater than myself that has accompanied me on my various journeys of life. Although I may not always want to trust in that higher power, I have come to realize and accept that I am not alone and that sometimes I may have to relinquish control of my position. For me, spirituality is that link to something higher than myself, which I view as a continual process. I have had several incidents in my life where I have reached a level of peace and clarity through my connections with God which has shaped my life experiences profoundly. These "spiritual" moments help me to let go of negative times and to relish the happy ones (Haitian American woman, mother, and professor).

I first became aware of spirituality as different from religion in my early teens. Through friends I became involved with a youth group. It was a Catholic youth group, but it was not connected to my church. Its mission was to help its members lead a more spiritual life, bringing spirituality and God to daily life. Having grown up Catholic, this was a different experience; spirituality did not end at the church door. I began to understand the contrasts between religiosity and spirituality. Religiosity was going to Mass each week and praying every night; however, spirituality was about recognizing that God is all around and honoring His presence. With the example of our young-adult group leaders, living a spiritual life became a significant experience for me. My involvement with the church has fluctuated through the years, but my sense of spirituality and connection with God has remained strong. My sense of spirituality impacts many aspects of my life, from relationships, to work, to parenting, to self-care. I continue to strive to lead a life that brings conscious awareness of my connection to God and His presence all around me (Cape Verdean American, mother, and student).

I was raised in a family where religion and spirituality were viewed as individual choices rather than a family tradition. While both of my parents are extremely religious, I was never baptized because they wanted the choice to be mine. Growing up, I went to church each Sunday. However, I was eager to go not so much for devotion to my faith, but because I saw it as a social occasion. Every Sunday I was able to wear my nicest dresses, put on my tights and black patent-leather shoes, and socialize with my friends. When I reached middle school, my soccer team I played on Sunday mornings. Hence, going to church ceased in favor of cleats and mud. It was not until I went to college that I began thinking about my spirituality and religion. For the first time, I began to distinguish between the two. I feel as though spirituality is a personal, internal feeling that is often hard to verbalize, and while religion may include more social participation. I came to this conclusion because, for the first time, I truly felt the sense that someone or something was looking over me; I was connected to an intangible entity. I attended college

3,000 miles from home in a city to which I had never been. Initially I was scared, but as I realized that I could make it on my own, I also felt an inner confidence and peace. Being aware of my inner strength is how I define myself and how I am aware of my spirituality (White woman and student).

As you can see, when we each reflected on our own spirituality, we came up with different answers to the same questions. Our spirituality has been shaped by people and experiences that have had varying impacts on our lives. How are factors such as ethnicity, gender, and work connected to our sense of spirituality?

THE INTERSECTION OF ETHNICITY, GENDER, AND WORK WITH OUR SPIRITUALITY

Although we are all women, we are diverse with respect to ethnicity, age, and work experiences. After reflecting on our understanding and experiences of spirituality, we engaged in a discourse about the intersections between our sense of spirituality and our ethnicity, gender, and work. Through this conversation we noted some striking differences and similarities in our views.

Ethnicity

Looking at our responses, we saw that race and culture were mentioned by only one. The author who discussed culture and spirituality in her response highlighted the inability to separate her cultural background from her sense and understanding of spirituality. She believes that there is an explicit connection between her cultural background and her exposure to religion, understanding of spirituality, and the roles that spirituality and religion play in her life. In addition, she noted that her spirituality helped her deal with the oppression and discrimination that she faces daily as a person of color. Specifically, she shared about her experience of racism in a restaurant. The author relied on her spirituality to forgive and ultimately offer assistance to the person who had made racist remarks to her that day. She attributes her ability to forgive individuals and let go of negative events in her life to her spiritual self that reminds her that she is connected to all things in the universe.

Such an explicit connection between one's ethnicity and spirituality was not so evident for all of us. For example, one of the authors commented that she was raised to not think about her ethnicity. As a result, she does not believe her sense of spirituality developed as part of her identity as a White, Italian, and Portuguese woman. Rather, she thinks that she created her own personal sense of spirituality from certain life events that she does not think were directly connected to her religious or cultural background. Even today, as she has become more aware of her ethnicity, she struggles to find clear intersections between her ethnic background and her spirituality. Rather, she continues to view her spirituality as a very personal and individual part of who she is, irrespective of her ethnic identity. At the end of our conversation, however, she did question whether she would begin to find links between her ethnicity and spirituality as she continues to develop her ethnic identity. She also wondered how her sense of spirituality might have been different had it developed in the context of a stronger ethnic identity.

Gender

Because all in the group are women (and consequently do not have other genders to which to compare our experiences), we found it difficult to examine whether our gender has an influence on our sense of spirituality. What was clear from our conversations was that being women was a major component of our identities, and that this is connected to all that we are and all that we do. Overall, we felt that our spiritual practices help us deal with the many demands placed on us as women. For example, one of the authors, who is a mother, discussed the challenges and benefits of being a mother and using her spirituality to approach the various demands placed on her. Specifically, she highlighted how her spiritual practices allow her to: 1) understand the importance and privilege of being a mother; 2) understand the need to let go of negative experiences; 3) accentuate the positive aspects of her children and her qualities as a mother; and 4) enjoy all of the stages of her kids' development. Another author discussed the important role her spirituality plays in her relationships. In particular, she believes that her spirituality allows her to support and nurture people. For example, she uses her spirituality to provide a sense of comfort and connection to people when they experience negative or difficult life events.

Work

Unlike gender, the intersection between our spiritual selves and our work was more evident. Unanimously, we feel that our sense of spirituality and our spiritual practices shape how we approach the various demands encountered in our jobs. Specifically, we all feel that our spirituality allows us to develop genuine and meaningful relationships with some of our colleagues, approach demands and conflicts in a calm manner, and develop an attitude of "not sweating the small stuff" in dealing with the systemic politics and dynamics that are often associated with the work environment. Additionally, we agree that our spirituality provides us with an important source of strength and support in our work with distressed and disenfranchised people. Overall, the authors discussed the intersection of spirituality and work positively, but one raised the challenges of being spiritual in her professional life. Specifically, she noted that her spiritual perspective (for example, focusing on the larger picture and importance of life and making the time that she has as meaningful as she can) often impacts the way that she responds to various meetings and tasks at her job. She believes that coworkers who have different values and philosophies about life approach meetings and tasks differently than she does, which at times leads her to feeling frustrated. Clearly we cannot separate who we are and what we do from our spiritual selves. There is an interconnection between our identity in terms of ethnicity, gender, work, and our spirituality. Although it may not be obvious to us all of the time (for example, most of us had not explicitly thought about the ways spirituality intersects with various parts of our lives prior to this conversation), our spirituality assists us greatly in dealing with the many demands that we face daily. The conversations that we just summarized played an important role in how we think about spirituality. In particular, they highlighted the involvedness (for example, similarities, differences, and intersections) of the spiritual experiences of women for us and ultimately confirmed our belief that we need to begin to give voice to the individual spiritual experiences of women.

DESCRIPTION OF YOUNG WOMEN'S REFLECTIONS OF SPIRITUALITY

Who Are These Young Women?

To begin to give voice to young women's individual spiritual experiences, we spoke with twenty young women. They were, on average, twenty-two years old. The youngest woman we spoke with was eighteen, the oldest thirty. The women were ethnically diverse. We spoke with twenty women, twelve White, four Black, one Latina, one biracial, one Cape Verdean, and one Korean. The women were also religiously diverse. Eleven identified as Catholic, one as Baptist, one as Presbyterian, one as Presbyterian and Episcopalian, and two as Jewish. Two did not specify a religious affiliation, and two said they were currently not practicing a religion, but one was raised Methodist and the other Catholic. All of the women identified as students (either undergraduate college students or graduate students) and each said she was a spiritual woman.

What Did We Ask Them?

In order to understand the individual spiritual experiences of these young women, we spoke with them about the following dimensions of their spirituality: 1) what spirituality means to them and whether they make distinctions between religion and spirituality; 2) who in their lives have similar views of spirituality; and 3) how spirituality impacts their education, physical health, mental health, and relationships. If one of the topics was not relevant to a woman's spiritual experience, we simply moved the conversation forward to the next topic. It is important to note that, although we reflected on the intersections between our ethnicity, gender, work, and spirituality, we did not initiate discussions with the young women around these areas. And, interestingly, the women did not independently remark on them. We believe, however, that if we had specifically asked the women about these areas, they would have shared a number of experiences with us. Or perhaps if we had provided them with the space to engage in a discourse with one another (as we had), they would have eventually begun to discuss more of the intricacies and intersections of their spirituality.

WHAT DID THEY TELL US?

What Spirituality Means to Them

The young women who we spoke with had very individual experiences of spirituality. About two-thirds of them told us that they believe spirituality and religion are different. They generally believe that spirituality is a personal/individual experience or feeling that entails a sense of connection, love, and happiness, primarily with themselves and God. The following are some of the specific things that the women told us when we met with them: "Spirituality is when you feel connected and feel loved no matter what you do. You don't need to follow the rules for God to love you," "[Spirituality is] loving yourself as God wants you to," "[Spirituality is about] how you feel, a one-on-one [connection with God] without religion," "[Spirituality is] a way of being," and "[Spirituality includes] going beyond [religion], and includes praying, meditating, and thinking about how to bring the teachings of my religion into my daily life. Spirituality represents my personal relationship with God."

On the other hand, the young women identified religion as more of a communal and organized experience that includes certain belief systems, behaviors, traditions, customs, and rules that need to be followed. For instance, some said that religion is "rules in order to become close to God," "a belief system, customs, and traditions," "an outward expression of my faith in God, and it is directly linked to church, attending services, and being involved in events at my church." It was also said that "religion is more like a community [than spirituality]." As you can see from this summary of our conversations with these young women, many of them differentiate between religion and spirituality and have their own personal understandings of spirituality.

Who in Their Lives Has Similar Spiritual Views?

After we spoke with the young women about what spirituality means to them, we initiated conversations about the people in their lives who hold similar spiritual views. Many believed that their views of spirituality are similar to family members' views (that is, parents and grandparents). For example, two made the following comments about similarities between their spiritual views and their parents' views: "[My] spiritual identity has mostly been influenced by my mother," and "My parents have similar perceptions of spirituality as I do. They believe in living and creating your own spiritual life, more so than following a particular religion, and living your life according to those beliefs. Like me, they believe in following your heart and doing what you believe in." Some of the women also commented that their spiritual views are similar to those of their grandparents. For example, one woman said, "My grandparents and I believe in God and use prayer to help us through life."

Despite the fact that an overwhelming majority of the young women felt that their spiritual beliefs were similar to their family members', a few thought they were quite different. For instance, regarding similarity to their parents, one woman noted, "We think differently in terms of outlooks—in terms of definitions and understandings of spirituality." With respect to similarity with grandparents, one woman said, "My grandparents are even more strict and traditional than I am. They have more traditional views of spirituality and religion." Another commented, "My grandparents have more traditional views of spirituality and religion than I do."

Some of the young women felt that their spiritual beliefs were similar to their friends' beliefs. For example, they commented that "My friends are like me spiritually" and "My friends and I believe in a higher power and that higher power is what guides us through life." Another woman remarked, "I have similar worldviews and ideas about spirituality as my friends but different religious beliefs." Importantly, however, equally as many women told us that their spiritual beliefs are different from those of their friends. One woman told us, "[My spiritual beliefs are] different from my friends' beliefs; I am more spiritual than they are." Another said, "I tend to be less spiritual than most of my friends." Some were not able to comment on this portion of the conversation because they do not talk about spirituality with their friends (for example, "I don't talk about spirituality much with my friends," and "It's not something we often discuss."). Again, you can further see from this portion of our conversations that although there are some general trends in terms of similarity of spiritual beliefs, there are important individual differences that should not be lost in the process of trying to understand the spiritual experiences of these young women.

How Spirituality Impacts Their Lives

An important part of the conversation that we had with the young women included a discussion about the ways that spirituality has impacted their lives. Education, relationships, mental health, and physical health are some of the major areas that they discussed with us. Most thought that their spirituality has had an impact on their relationships and their mental health. They spoke about how their spirituality helps them select their friends and manage their relationships. One woman commented, "Being spiritual provided me this sense of guidelines and what I want in a relationship. It is a guideline for me to follow." The women also reported that, "I pray for my relationships," and "Spirituality impacts my choice of friends and a like-minded support system is a consequence." Additionally, the women explained that their spirituality impacts their perceptions of themselves and others, their level of happiness, and their ability to think about things optimistically. For example, one young woman described to us her experience with spirituality and her mental well-being: "A while ago I became depressed because I didn't have friends. The only thing that kept me from killing myself was my belief [in God]." Other women commented that spirituality influences "how I view myself and people around me so it has an impact on my happiness" and "why I think as I do—more optimistic, positive." They described spirituality as providing an important sense of support when they are feeling down or are depressed.

Fewer of the young women, but still more than half, told us that spirituality impacts their education and physical health. Those who felt that spirituality plays a role in their education reported that it impacts the choices they make about schools they attend and also shapes their attitudes toward school. For example, one woman reported that, because of her spirituality, she "chose to go to a Catholic college and be with similar people." Another said, "[spirituality] has helped guide my decisions about education." Other women remarked, "I engage in prayer before tests," and that spirituality is a "positive influence toward learning." The women who believe there is a connection between their spirituality and their physical health told us that their spirituality influences them to take care of themselves. Specifically, one woman said, "I try to take care of myself, as I feel that is part of being connected with God." Another noted, "I don't drink, don't smoke. I take care of myself. Being here is a gift from God. I don't need anything to change that." We believe that these comments underscore the importance of capturing individual experiences of spirituality. You can see that each woman uses spirituality in her daily life. However, the specific way in which she does so varies according to the individual. These are the types of personal events that often get lost when people write and talk about spirituality as a universal experience.

REFLECTIONS ON OUR CONVERSATIONS

There is a depth and complexity to spirituality that, we believe, cannot be understood unless you really listen to someone. Speaking with the young women was enlightening and deeply moving for us. We found that there are similarities and differences in the spiritual experiences of the young women. They each think about and use their spirituality in unique and personal ways that cannot be fully understood if they are considered only within the context of themes and theories.

Like us, the women who we spoke to believe that spirituality is an individual matter—an experience that impacts and intersects with different facets of their lives. The way each woman experiences her spirituality is different. Scholars in fields ranging from religion and theology to psychology have worked to define spirituality.[1] In light of the different spiritual experiences described in this chapter, we believe that spirituality also needs to be considered on an individual level, and not simply in terms of collective definitions.

Unfortunately, there is rarely time for young people to talk about their spirituality on a personal level. As women who depend on our spirituality to make it through each day, we are committed to providing forums where women can express their spirituality freely and openly. We are also committed to offering venues where women can read about the spiritual lives of other women, free from themes and generalizations and rich with personal and individual experiences. Our work with the young women is one example of the ways that we seek to accomplish our objectives. As far as we can tell, it has provided evidence for the importance of further explorations into spirituality on a personal level.

Overall, based on our spiritual experiences and those shared with us by the young women, we have concluded that spirituality is truly an individual and unique experience. Therefore, we believe that the best way to develop a strong sense of what spirituality is and how it manifests in women is to continually explore and share our spirituality with other women. We believe that discourse among spiritual women is essential in promoting spiritual development and knowledge about women's spirituality.

NOTE

1. For a more in depth discussion on divergent meanings of spirituality refer to the sources listed in the bibliography.

BIBLIOGRAPHY

Journal Articles

Gall, Terry Lynn, Claire Charbonneau, Neil H. Clarke, Karen Grant, Joseph Anjali, and Lisa Shouldice. "Understanding the Nature and Role of

Spirituality in Relation to Coping and Health: A Conceptual Framework." *Canadian Psychology* 46 (2005): 88–104.

Guillory, Joyce, A., Richard Sowell, Linda Moneyham, and Brenda Seals. "An Exploration of the Meaning and Use of Spirituality among Women with HIV/AIDS." *Alternative Therapies in Health and Medicine* 3 (5) (1997): 55–60.

Hassed, Craig, S. "Depression: Dispirited or Spiritually Deprived." *Medical Journal of Australia* 173 (10) (2000): 153–157.

Hill, Peter C., Kenneth Pargament II, Ralph W. Hood, Michael E. McCullough, James P. Swyers, David B. Larson, and Brian J. Zinnbauer. "Conceptualizing Religion and Spirituality: Points of Commonality, Points of Departure." *Journal for the Theory of Social Behaviour* 30 (1) (2000): 51–77.

King, Pamela E., and Chris J. Boyatzis. "Exploring Adolescent Spiritual and Religious Development: Current and Future Theoretical and Empirical Perspectives." *Applied Developmental Science* 8 (1) (2004): 2–6.

Lauver, Diane R. "Commonalities in Women's Spirituality and Women's Health." *Advanced Nursing Scientist* 22 (3) (2000): 76–88.

McSherry, Wilfred. "Education Issues Surrounding the Teaching of Spirituality." *Nursing Standard* 14 (42) (2000): 40–43.

Oldnall, Andrew. "A Critical Analysis of Nursing: Meeting the Spiritual Needs of Patients." *Journal of Advanced Nursing* 23 (1) (1996): 138–144.

Rayburn, Carole A. "Religion, Spirituality, and Health." *The American Psychologist* 59 (2004): 52–53.

Zinnbauer, Brian J., Kenneth, I. Pargament, and Allie B. Scott. "The Emerging Meanings of Religiousness and Spirituality: Problems and Prospects." *Journal of Personality* 67 (6) (1999): 889–919.

Books

Cornah, Deborah. *The Impact of Spirituality on Mental Health: A Literature Review.* London: Mental Health Foundation, 2006.

Rayburn, Carole A., and Lee Richmond. "Women, Whither Goest Thou? To Chart New Courses in Religiousness and Spirituality and to Defend Ourselves!" In *Charting a New Course for Feminist Psychology.* Collins, L. H., M. R. Dunlap, and J. C. Chrisler, eds. Westport, CT: Praeger, 2002, 167–189.

PART V

Conclusions

Conclusions

A WomanSoul Quest

Carole A. Rayburn
Lillian Comas-Díaz

I am the woman dancing the world alive.... I am the birthing woman kneel-ing by the river ... I am a God(dess) of a thousand names....
        —excerpt from "The Womanly Song of God" by Catherine de Vinck

Women are the shapers of the soul. Their nurturing, healing, creative, and compassionate abilities promote transformation. Women's rela-tional natures ignite changes in the soul at both individual and collec-tive levels. *WomanSoul* presented a tapestry of female spirituality. Eileen Eppig beautifully described the history of women's relationship with the divine, showing the transformative powers of spirituality on women and how it brings harmony and healing to them and indeed to all creation. Darlene Prestbo and Hazel Staats-Westover showed how the women's movement revitalized longing for psycho-spirituality that celebrated, nurtured, and elevated the ancient wisdom, power, ritual, and, honor of the Great Mother or Goddess. As such, they related the renewal, vibrant energy, and healing of the Princeton Daughters of Gaia. Carole Rayburn was fortunate enough to attend one of these ses-sions and can wholeheartedly vouch for the affirmative, healing, and transformative power of such an accepting and loving group of spirit-ual women.

Female development engages the spirit into reparative, redemptive, and liberating elements. According to Carol P. Christ,[1] women embark on a spiritual quest wherein they "dive deep and surface." Therefore, the process of surfacing entails the development of a deeper connec-tion. Likewise, we identify the WomanSoul development as the deep-ening of connections in the process of becoming whole. Consequently,

WomanSoul spiritual developmental stages include awakening, remembering, initiation, liberation, and wholeness. This development mirrors what Lillian Comas-Díaz[2] called the womanist path. In other words, she argued that the spiritual development of women of color or the womanist path is contextualized in the following stages: 1) rejecting oppression; 2) embracing sacredness; 3) engaging in collective healing; 4) developing solidarity for all oppressed people; and 5) fostering re/evolution. Similarly, WomanSoul spiritual progress is influenced by internal and external events such as developmental milestones, female biological markers (menarche, pregnancy, and menopause), loss, trauma, and others. Lisa Miller's sharing of her uplifting, soulful, healing work with children and their families using her own spiritual awareness psychotherapy demonstrates the transformative and spiritually interactive role that children have with the universe and its lessons. Aphrodite Clamar wrote about the spirituality in senior women who use the positive force in their later lives to connect to the universe to find meaning in the otherwise frightening and mundane, choosing to accept and effectively deal with the hand that they are dealt to reach and maintain a healthy balance of spirituality, autonomy, and religious beliefs. Mary Anne Siderits sensitively pointed out the prejudice and misunderstanding to which agnostic women are often subjected in their search for the spiritual and a sacred space in their lives. The milestones leading to a spiritual life were well described by Jane Simon, whose many religious, philosophical, and spiritual life experiences brought her to a healing place and proved to be stepping stones to a fuller life. Lee Richmond, who has also experienced many religious and spiritual orientations, has been able to use these in her career work to benefit herself, her clients, and her students.

The first spiritual stage of WomanSoul entails an awakening. A mystical experience and/or a transcendental life event usually triggers a spiritual awakening. Several of the contributors to this anthology referred to their spiritual awakening as a turning point in their lives. To illustrate, Guerda Nicolas and her colleagues reminded us that women could be in touch with their spirituality from an early age. Lisa Miller connected the development of her spiritual awareness to parenting her children and to helping other children and their families. Janet Pfunder identified her annihilating relationship with her mother as the impetus for her path into Sufism. Marcella Bakur Weiner stated that she did not find Kabbalah, but Kabballah found her. Lillian Comas-Díaz asserted that the Black Madonna guided her into her sacred sites. Through their awakening, women examine their subordination and thus name their conditions. As they awaken, women become conscious of their reality. For instance, Rose L. Weahkee identified her American Indian spirituality as a process of critical conscientization. Renate Wewerka, an Austrian-born Buddhist, found herself through Buddhism and has been able to derive much sense of acceptance and strength and to use these lessons and insights in healing her psychotherapy patients.

The second stage of WomanSoul development entails a cultural remembering of spiritual traditions. Such remembrance is similar to becoming centered while deepening one's roots. For instance, Oliva Espin studied the lives of female saints to use her cultural resources and exercise her will to live in the spirit. Hence, women's personal spirituality emerges during the remembering phase through a process of identification with a personal spirituality. The third WomanSoul stage embodies initiation. Here women affirm their spiritual nature as defined by themselves. Several of our contributors' stories highlight this moment in their life. For example, Lillian Comas-Díaz discussed her initiation into the Black Madonna during a visit to the goddess Kali's temple in India. Nonetheless, the initiation stage could yield diverse outcomes. To illustrate, out of her quest, Mary Anne Siderits developed an agnostic spirituality. Jane Pfunder articulated an individualized spirituality. Aphrodite Clamar presented her eclectic view of spirituality, integrating Greek Orthodoxy and Reform Judaism.

Women become empowered in their search for wholeness. When they critically analyze the conditions that subordinate them, they begin to challenge their external and internalized oppression. In particular, women of color experience multiple types of oppression and often resort to their spirituality for resilience. To illustrate, Rose L. Weahkee stated that American Indian spirituality has been a source of nurturing support against cultural genocide. The female qualities of spirituality— intuition, nurturing, and healing—constitute antidotes against the masculine images of God. As Pratyusha Tummala-Narra indicated, the issue of power is critical to understand women's spirituality. Therefore, when women reconcile their powerless/powerful duality, they become liberated. Women learn what price they pay for being both religious and feminist.[3] Carole A. Rayburn, a psychologist who sensed a calling to the male-dominated ministry—though a life-long religious and spiritual feminist—was shocked to see so much patriarchal discrimination and disenfranchisement of women as she attended seminary. There, the very scriptural terms for "testament" and "testimony" derived from "testicles," and the ritual of testing how trustworthy one man was to another was by having him swear honorable treatment and no harm by the placement of his hand in the groin and thus next to the testicles of the other man. Further, she discovered that "seminary" and "seminal" both derived from "semen" or "seedbed."[4] She realized that no matter how well she did in seminary, she would not get a ministerial position reserved only for men, nor would any woman, particularly one who had fought for ethnic minority rights. Rayburn first sought justice through her church and then finally took the case to the U.S. Supreme Court. She was declared a minister by the Supreme Court in its efforts to block its having to decide between gender and racial discrimination and freedom of religion.

Liberation is the fourth WomanSoul spiritual stage. Female liberation is the process of owning power and sharing it with others. Liberation can take the form of questioning how religious and spiritual practices oppress women. In assessing African American women's spirituality, Beverly Greene discussed how these traditions perpetuate the status quo by promoting internalized sexism, racism, heterosexism, and other types of oppression. On the other hand, she discussed how her spiritual value of social justice became an inspiration in her life and in her psychotherapy work. Along these lines, WomanSoul instills a passionate spirituality to fight oppression. It helps women to liberate themselves. As they become compassionate illuminata, women attempt to emancipate others. For example, Asuncion Miteria Austria presented how Filipinos' belief in a female divinity—the Virgin Mary—helped to liberate their country.

The final stage in the WomanSoul development is wholeness. In this stage women deeply connect with everything. As an illustration, Pratyusha Tummala-Narra discussed how her growing up in India, where Hindu, Christian, and Muslim faiths cohabit, helped her to identify the commonalities across diverse spiritual practices. Likewise, Rose L. Weahkee articulated how American Indian spirituality aims to infuse holism, particularly through its emphasis on female qualities. Further, Mary Banks Gregerson compared the relationship between spirituality and psychology and named the goal of achieving oneness as common to both disciplines. Further, Kathleen Reedy, a scientist who studies the effects of extreme temperatures on the human body, described her sense of oneness or connectedness with the universe and what it was before, is now, and most likely will be in the future. The spiritual oneness, characteristic of the stage of wholeness, is facilitated by women's receptivity to others and their ability to create new life. In this spiritual state, women do more than identifying with the divinity; they internalize, embody, and merge with sacredness.

NOTES

1. Christ, *Diving Deep and Surfacing: Women Writers on Spiritual Quest*, 1980.

2. Comas-Díaz, "Spirita: Reclaiming Womanist Sacredness into Feminism," 2008.

3. Rayburn, Natale, and Linzer, "Feminism and Religion: What Price Holding Membership in Both Camps?," 1982.

4. Rayburn, "Some Reflections of a Female Seminarian: Woman, Whither Goest Thou?," 1981.

BIBLIOGRAPHY

Christ, Carol, P. *Diving Deep and Surfacing: Women Writers on Spiritual Quest*, Boston: Beacon Press, 1980.

Comas-Díaz, Lillian. "Spirita: Reclaiming Womanist Sacredness into Feminism," *Psychology of Women Quarterly*, 2008, 32 (1), 13–20.

Rayburn, Carole A. "Some Reflections of a Female Seminarian: Woman, Whither Goest Thou?" *Journal of Pastoral Counseling* 16 (2) (1981): 61–65.

Rayburn, Carole, Samuel M. Natale, and Judith Linzer. "Feminism and Religion: What Price Holding Membership in Both Camps?" *Counseling and Values* 26 (3) (1982): 154–164.

Index

About the Contributors

Asuncion Miteria Austria is a licensed psychologist, Professor of Psychology, Chair and Director of Clinical Training of the Graduate Program in Clinical Psychology, an innovative program that she developed for working professionals at Cardinal Stritch University. A fellow of the American Psychological Association (APA), she has served on the APA's governance boards including the Board of Educational Affairs, Policy and Planning Board, Chair of the Committee on Ethnic Minority Affairs, and currently is a member of the Council of Representatives. She also served as President of the APA's Division of Clinical Psychology's Sections on the Clinical Psychology of Ethnic Minorities and the Clinical Psychology of Women. She serves as the Lead Consultant to the American Psychological Association/National Institute of General Medical Science (APA/NIGMS) Project. She has numerous awards for humanitarian service, mentoring, education, and outstanding contributions to the clinical psychology of women. She was also awarded the 2006 Distinguished Leadership for Women in Psychology, 2007 Distinguished Elder/Senior Psychologist, and the 2007 Teaching Excellence and Campus Leadership Award from Cardinal Stritch University.

Aphrodite Clamar is a seasoned senior executive in local, national, and international public relations and advertising. She has a background in economics and psychology, and executive experience in developing and managing political/election campaigns. Founder and former president of Richard Cohen Associates, a Manhattan-based publicity firm, with an advertising affiliate, she has been involved in presidential, senatorial, state, and local politics. A fellow of the American Association for the Advancement of Science and an active member of the American

Psychological Association, she has published extensively in the general and professional media.

Lillian Comas-Díaz is the executive director of the Transcultural Mental Health Institute, a clinical professor at George Washington University's Department of Psychiatry and Behavioral Sciences, and a private practitioner in Washington, DC The former director of the APA's Office of Ethnic Minority Affairs, she was a faculty member at Yale University's Department of Psychiatry, where she also directed the Hispanic Clinic. She received the APA's Distinguished Contribution to Psychology in the Public Interest, the American Psychological Foundation's Rosalee G. Weiss Award for Contributions in Professional Psychology, and the Distinguished Leadership for Women in Psychology Award. The senior editor of two textbooks—*Clinical Guidelines in Cross-Cultural Mental Health* and *Women of Color: Integrating Ethnic and Gender Identities in Psychotherapy*, she is the founding editor-in-chief of the APA's Division on Ethnic Minority Affairs' official journal, *Cultural Diversity and Ethnic Minority Psychology*. She serves as an associate editor for the APA's *American Psychologist*.

Maria Coutinho has a master's degree in mental health counseling from Boston College. She is in the doctoral program at Boston College, in developmental, educational, and counseling psychology. She does research in work status and mental health among immigrant groups.

Angela M. DeSilva received her master's degree from Boston College, in mental health counseling. In the Boston College doctoral program, she is working in developmental, educational, and counseling psychology. Her research interests include social supports and mental health counseling among immigrant groups, and spirituality and belief in God among adolescents and young adults.

Eileen Eppig, SSND, has a doctorate in religious studies from the Catholic University of America and a master's in theology degree from Fordham University. She teaches at the College of Notre Dame of Maryland in the Department of Religious Studies, serves as a spiritual director, and speaks on spirituality, theology, and scripture.

Oliva M. Espín is professor emerita of women's studies at San Diego State University and at Alliant International University (California School of Professional Psychology-San Diego). In her long-standing work as a psychotherapist, teacher, and consultant, she has specialized in psychology of Latinas, immigrant and refugee women, and women's sexuality across cultures. A pioneer in practice and theory of feminist therapy with women from different cultures, she has taught at McGill,

Tufts, and Boston universities, and at the Universidad de Costa Rica. A native of Cuba, she has received an APA Award for distinguished professional contributions to public service for groundbreaking work to expand knowledge on gender issues and international and cultural factors. She also received the Distinguished Career Award from the Association for Women in Psychology. Coeditor of *Refugee Women and Their Mental Health: Shattered Lives*, she authored *Latina Healers: Lives of Power and Tradition* and *Latina Realities: Essays on Healing, Migration, and Sexuality* (an anthology of her collective writings on feminist theory and practice over a twenty-year period) and *Women Crossing Boundaries: A Psychology of Immigration and Transformations of Sexuality*. Her most recent interest has been the study of women saints from feminist and psychological perspectives.

Beverly Greene received a doctorate from Adelphi University, worked in public mental health for ten years, and then joined the faculty of St. John's University and became a professor of psychology. A practicing psychologist in New York City, she is a fellow of the APA's Division 9, 12, 29, 35, 42, 44, and 45, a diplomate in clinical psychology on the American Board of Professional Psychology, and a fellow of the Academy of Clinical Psychology. Recipient of nine national awards for publications deemed outstanding contributions to the psychological literature, she has focused on women of color, lesbians, African Americans, the interactions of race, gender, sexual orientation, and other identities in relation to development and the psychotherapy process. Recipient of a variety of leadership awards largely from the APA, she is completing the book *Phenomenal Women: Psychological Vulnerability and Resilience in High-Achieving Black Women*.

Mary Banks Gregerson (nee Jasnoski) was born in a Catholic convent in the central United States. Baptized Catholic, she was raised Methodist. As a teen she gave her life to Christ, and the journey since has been both comforting and challenging. She studied Eastern religions in her free time during college and went to graduate school in psychology (she received a BA in women's studies, psychology, speech and drama; and an MA and PhD in clinical psychology—all from the University of Kansas. She was the first undergraduate U.S. women's studies major at the University of Kansas. As a postdoctoral psychoneuroimmunology fellow, she returned to Christianity via the Reverend Peter Gomes at Harvard Memorial Church and then in the Episcopal Church. In her church she participates in the liturgy as a chalice bearer and crucifer. This year her call has been to move with her husband to the Midwest near her extended family with fourteen great-nephews and nieces, and where she participates in the life of a Catholic university while working on staff at a community mental health center serving the military and their families, including the prison guard corps. She provided training for the fall 2007 class of From the Inside Out peer counselors at the Emily Taylor Women's Resource Center at the University of Kansas. Challenged to write this chapter, she thinks that it "outs" her from the spiritual closet to many of her psychology colleagues.

Lisa Miller is a spiritually oriented psychologist, with clinical and research interests in spiritual development, thriving, and wellness in youth and family. She has published numerous scholarly articles on these topics and lectures widely on research and policy related to spirituality in youth and family. An associate professor of psychology and education in the clinical psychology program at Teachers College, Columbia University, she currently serves as president of the Division on the Psychology of Religion (Division 36) of the APA.

Guerda Nicolas is a licensed clinical psychologist and full-time professor at Boston College, in the Lynch School of Education, Department of Counseling, Developmental and Educational Psychology. She has been researching spirituality in the lives of adolescents, social support networks of blacks, improving academic performance of ethnic minority high school youths, and clinical adaptation of mental health intervention for ethnic minority adolescents, with special focus on Haitian adolescents.

Janet Pfunder has been a therapist in private practice for thirty years, and began the Sufi work in 1973. She teaches focusing, Sufi, and dream groups. She studied experimental dream work with Montague Ullman, Jungian Alchemy with Nathan Schwartz-Salant, psychoanalysis with Michael Eigen, and gender therapy with Jessica Benjamin. She is certified by Eugene Gendlin's Focusing Institute and is a supervisor for the Relational Focusing Oriented Psychotherapy (RFOP) programs by Lynn Preston in New York and Cape Town, South Africa. Her book chapter, "Sufi Meditations on Psychotherapy" was published in *Psychotherapy and Religion: Many Paths, One Journey* in 2005. A painter, her most recent one-woman art show was at Harvard, as an alumna. Some of her paintings can be seen at http://www.janetpfunderpaintings.com/.

Kimberly Prater is a doctoral student in the clinical psychology program at Fordham University. Her primary research interests include social supports among adolescents and ethnic minority groups.

Darlene Prestbo has a bachelor's degree in theater from Northwestern University and as master's of social work from the University of Illinois. She is a licensed clinical social worker with more than years in private practice. A writer and lecturer on inspiration and emotional health, she participates in theater performance, artistic photography, and gardening.

Carole A. Rayburn is a clinical, consulting, and research psychologist. A past president of the APA's Division on the Psychology of Religion, the Division of Clinical Psychology's Section on the Psychology of Women, the Maryland Psychological Association, and currently president of the Montgomery County (Maryland) National Organization of Women, she chaired the Maryland Association of Measurement and Evaluation, a division of the Maryland Association of Counseling and Development. Receiving several mentoring and research awards, including those from the American Association of University Women, the Washington, DC, and the Maryland Psychological Associations, and the APA Division on Psychology of Religion and Clinical Psychology's Section on the Clinical Psychology of Women. She is an APA fellow of the Divisions of General Psychology, Clinical Psychology, Consulting Psychology, Psychotherapy, State Psychological Affairs, Psychology of Women, Psychology of Religion, Family Psychology, Media Psychology, and International Psychology. She chairs the fellows committee of APA's Division on Clinical Psychology. She developed psychological inventories on attitudes toward children (for early childhood workers), religiousness, the creative personality, and intuition. With others, she developed inventories on clergy stress, state-trait morality, spirituality, agentic and communal life choices, body awareness and intimacy comfort, leadership, mentoring, attitudes toward the supreme and work, peacefulness, well-being, traumatic experiences and health, and proposed and developed the new theory and field of theobiology (the interface of theology, religiousness, and spirituality with the biology and other sciences). Having taught at Strayer College, Johns Hopkins University, and Loyola College in Maryland, she has also served as a coeditor of the Focus on Women Series (Springer Publishing), the special issue on theobiology of the *American Behavioral Scientist*, and is on the editorial board of *Nova Science International Journal of Ethics*. She regards herself as both spiritual and religious and as a practicing feminist.

Kathleen Reedy is recently retired from the Health and Human Services Department of the federal government. At the Food and Drug Administration, she has been a project director in the Drug Review Division, the Business Process Office, and the Advisory Committee System, coordinating three advisory committees. At Naval Medical Research Institute, she began the research in human adaptation to cold climate, which she continued in Antarctica with two National Science Foundation Grants. She is a registered dental hygienist, worked in school systems in New York, county and state health departments in

Michigan, and in private practice. She earned a second undergraduate degree and a master's degree in exercise physiology, and she was Fitness Director of the YMCA system in West Virginia. She earned her master's degree in health care administration while working for the federal government. She has five sons, four who are physicians and one who is a law enforcement officer, and nine grandchildren.

Lee Richmond is a professor of education at Loyola College in Maryland, a Maryland-licensed psychologist, and a past president of the American Counseling Association and the National Career Development Association. She has coauthored inventories on clergy stress, religiousness, spirituality, morality, the relationship between the supreme and work, life choices, body awareness and intimacy, peacefulness, leadership, traumatic experiences and health, and well-being, and has coproposed and codeveloped a new theory and field, theobiology.

Mary Anne Siderits is a clinical psychologist, full-time faculty member in the Department of Psychology at Marquette University, and adjunct clinical professor at the Wisconsin School of Professional Psychology. She teaches courses in the psychology of gender, psychology of religion, developmental psychology, and professional ethics. Having served as and officer in municipal and state psychological associations and in various divisions of the APA, she has also served on the national board of representatives of the American Association of University Professors. A founding member of the group that launched the women's studies program at Marquette, she was the first female chair of Marquette's Committee on Faculty.

Jane Simon, MD, began her career as a pathologist and forensic pathologist, returning after board certification in these specialties for a residency in adult, child, and adolescent psychiatry. In private practice and serving as medical director of the Blanton Peale Counseling Center for more than twenty years, she is a published poet and an author of professional papers on subjects as diverse as love addiction to the mind of the familial murderer. She serves on the editorial board of the *Journal of Religion and Health* and the *Journal of the American Academy of Psychoanalysis*.

The **Reverend Hazel Staats-Westover**, a graduate of Northwestern University and Chicago Theological Seminary, was ordained in the United Church of Christ, and serves as United Church of Christ (UCC) and American Baptist Churches (AMB) chaplain at Princeton University. Cofounder of three women's centers, she cotaught the first course on women and religion at Chicago Theological Seminary and New Brunswick Seminary, as well as the postgraduate women studies program of Boston Theological Institute through Harvard Divinity School.

Pratyusha Tummala-Narra is a supervising psychologist at the University of Michigan Psychological Clinic, and in private practice in Farmington Hills, Michigan. She is also a teaching associate in psychiatry at the Cambridge Health Alliance/Harvard Medical School. She is the founder and former director of the Asian Mental Health Clinic at the Cambridge Health Alliance in Cambridge, Massachusetts.

Marcella Bakur Weiner, a fellow of the APA, recently received a doctorate in metaphysics/theology. A former senior research scientist for New York State Department of Mental Hygiene and an adjunct professor at Columbia University's Department of Psychology, she is currently president of the advisory council of Mapleton-Midwood Community Center, a community outreach center in Brooklyn, New York. Author of twenty-three books and seventy-five articles, she recently published *Psychotherapy and Religion: Many Paths, One Journey* and *Aging Parents, Aging Children: How To Stay Alive and Survive*. She practices and resides in Brooklyn with her husband, Wilhelm.

Rose L. Weahkee is a member of the Navajo nation. She received her bachelor's degree in psychology with a minor in alcohol and drug studies from Loyola Marymount University in Los Angeles, and her doctorate in clinical psychology with an emphasis on multicultural community clinical issues from the California School of Professional Psychology in Los Angeles. She is a licensed psychologist and the administrative clinical director for United American Indian Involvement, Inc.'s Robert Sundance Family Wellness Center, a mental health and substance abuse treatment program for American Indians in California.

Renate Wewerka received her doctorate in psychology from the University of Vienna, Austria. After coming to the United States, she held positions in several medical organizations and Johns Hopkins University. After working for almost twenty years in clinical psychology, she is now a forensic psychologist in New Mexico. Experienced in group and individual psychotherapy with various in- and outpatient populations, as well as conducting training programs for health professionals and students, she utilizes methods such as psychodrama and hypnosis in her work. She attempts to maintain a mindfulness about her Buddhist teachings.

ecclesia
anomie
proselytize